英汉翻译简明教程

庄绎传 编著

A Short Course in English-Chinese Translation

外语教学与研究出版社
FOREIGN LANGUAGE TEACHING AND RESEARCH PRESS
北京 BEIJING

图书在版编目（CIP）数据

英汉翻译简明教程 / 庄绎传编著. — 北京：外语教学与研究出版社，2002（2025.7 重印）
ISBN 978-7-5600-2666-4

Ⅰ. 英… Ⅱ. 庄… Ⅲ. 英语-翻译-教材 Ⅳ. H315.9

中国版本图书馆 CIP 数据核字（2002）第 012193 号

出 版 人　王　芳
责任编辑　张锦平
出版发行　外语教学与研究出版社
社　　址　北京市西三环北路 19 号（100089）
网　　址　https://www.fltrp.com
印　　刷　北京铭传印刷有限公司
开　　本　850×1168　1/32
印　　张　11.125
版　　次　2002 年 3 月第 1 版　2025 年 7 月第 40 次印刷
书　　号　ISBN 978-7-5600-2666-4
定　　价　14.90 元

如有图书采购需求，图书内容或印刷装订等问题、侵权、盗版书籍等线索，请拨打以下电话或关注官方服务号：
客服电话：400 898 7008
官方服务号：微信搜索并关注公众号"外研社官方服务号"
外研社购书网址：https://fltrp.tmall.com

物料号：126660001

编者的话

2001年秋，北京外国语大学推出英语翻译资格证书考试。《英汉翻译简明教程》就是应邀专为配合这一考试而编写的。

本书的结构　本书有两大部分："课文"和"英汉语言对比"。课文部分共分10个单元，涉及故事、历史、地理、经济、文化、文学（一）、文学（二）、科普、法律、演讲等10个方面。每个单元包括一课英译汉，一课汉译英。每课之内有对照阅读和练习，并附有提示和解说。提示和解说中，有些条前面标有星号（★），这些条对于理解或翻译有普遍意义，请读者特别注意。此外每课还有一个专栏，介绍有关翻译的理论和知识。

翻译的实践性　要作好翻译，必须进行大量的实践，亲自动手，取得第一手的经验。但是只靠自己的实践是不够的，还必须借助于别人的经验。因此，每课都有一篇对照阅读，先看别人怎样译，在遣词造句、文章风格等方面得到启发，然后再去做练习。练习的答案都在书里，但最好不要先看答案。要自己先做，然后再与答案对照，这样收获更大。

语言对比　翻译实践要想得到好的效果，必须对英汉两种语言进行对比研究，找出各自的特点，这样就知道同样的意思，用汉语应当怎么说，用英语应当怎么说，而不至于在翻译时过分受原文的影响。考虑到读者一般英译汉的能力较强，汉译英的能力较弱，本书第二部分语言对比中配有10个汉译英的单句练习。

英译汉与汉译英　本书兼顾英译汉与汉译英。既然本书着眼于英汉语言对比，两者兼顾正好为这种对比研究提供了方便。每篇英译汉教材都可以说是一篇汉译英的范文。希望读者在研究英译汉原文的时候，无论是整篇，还是一个单句，都不要只求弄懂原文，而要细心观察，看外国人是怎样使用英语的，怎样表达才是地道的英语。这样做对于提高自己的英语水平、做好汉译英是很有好处的。

翻译理论 我国自公元 1 世纪开始翻译佛经以来，外国自古希腊以来，许多名家根据实践经验对翻译发表了不少真知灼见，他们的治学精神更是译界之楷模。本书作了简单的介绍，希望读者借以扩大视野，加深对翻译的认识，从理论的高度观察和处理实践中遇到的具体问题。

本书是以编者 1998 年为全国高等教育自学考试编写的《英汉翻译教程》和《英汉翻译教程自学辅导》为基础改编而成。这次改编压缩了英译汉部分，突出了汉译英部分。按原书体例，凡借用的现成译文均冠以"译文"二字，编者自己提供的译文均冠以"参考译文"。如果读者想切实提高翻译水平，而且有较充裕的时间，我还是希望他们去学那套内容充实的自考教材。如果读者想在参加"英语翻译资格证书考试"之前，短时间内熟悉一下有关问题，练练笔，《英汉翻译简明教程》就是最合适的参考书了。考试分初级、中级、高级三个层次，就笔译而言，主要是翻译不同难度的东西，其翻译之道是相通的。因此无论报考哪个等级的资格证书，都可以从本书得到益处。

本书引用了多位译界前辈和同行的论述和成果，已在书中一一加以说明，特在此向他们一并表示衷心的感谢。

由于时间紧迫，不妥之处在所难免，请读者和译界同行批评指正。

庄绎传

2002 年 1 月

于北京外国语大学

CONTENTS

Part I Texts

Unit 1 Stories

Lesson 1 (E—C) ·· 3
    Bilingual Reading: The Quest
    译学点滴：翻译的标准
    Exercise 1: Bill Morrow's Birthday Party
    Key to Exercise 1: 比尔·莫罗的寿宴
Lesson 2 (C—E) ·· 14
    Bilingual Reading: 孟轲悔过
    译学点滴：汉译英的基本功
    Exercise 2: 我为乘客服务
    Key to Exercise 2: How I Serve the Passengers

Unit 2 History

Lesson 3 (E—C) ·· 23
    Bilingual Reading: England Before the Industrial
                    Revolution
    译学点滴：把握全篇而后译
    Exercise 3: The Industrial Revolution
    Key to Exercise 3: 工业革命
Lesson 4 (C—E) ·· 34
    Bilingual Reading: 五四运动
    译学点滴："Readability"

　　　　　Exercise 4：北京的第一个"五一"节
　　　　　Key to Exercise 4：First May Day in Beijing

Unit 3　Geography
Lesson 5　（E—C） ·· 44
　　　　　Bilingual Reading：Journey Up the Nile
　　　　　　　　　　　（Excerpt 1）
　　　　　译学点滴：研究句子结构的差异
　　　　　Exercise 5：Journey Up the Nile (Excerpt 2)
　　　　　Key to Exercise 5：沿尼罗河而上（摘录 2）
Lesson 6　（C—E） ·· 58
　　　　　Bilingual Reading：北海公园
　　　　　译学点滴：提高文字水平无止境
　　　　　Exercise 6：天坛公园
　　　　　Key to Exercise 6：The Temple of Heaven

Unit 4　Economy
Lesson 7　（E—C） ·· 66
　　　　　Bilingual Reading：A Global Economy
　　　　　译学点滴：用知识武装自己
　　　　　Exercise 7：New Opportunities in China's Economic
　　　　　　　　　　Cooporation with Other Countries
　　　　　　　　　（An Excerpt）
　　　　　Key to Exercise 7：中国对外经济合作的新机会
　　　　　　　　　　　（摘录）
Lesson 8　（C—E） ·· 78
　　　　　Bilingual Reading：中国能够依靠自己的力量实
　　　　　　　　　　　现粮食基本自给（摘录）
　　　　　译学点滴：严谨的学风
　　　　　Exercise 8：新中国解决了人民的吃饭问题

Key to Exercise 8: New China Has Solved the
　　　　　　　　Problem of Feeding Its People

Unit 5　Culture
Lesson 9　(E—C) ·················· 87
　　　Bilingual Reading: How to Grow Old
　　　翻译理论简介：佛经翻译
　　　Exercise 9: How to Grow Old (Continued)
　　　Key to Exercise 9: 怎样才能活得老（续）
Lesson 10　(C—E) ·················· 101
　　　Bilingual Reading: 旧梦重温
　　　翻译理论简介：严复与"信、达、雅"
　　　Exercise 10: 旧梦重温（续）
　　　Key to Exercise 10: Going Through Old
　　　　　　　　　　　　Dreams (Continued)

Unit 6　Literature (1)
Lesson 11　(E—C) ·················· 111
　　　Bilingual Reading: Tess of the D'Urbervilles
　　　　　　　　　　　(An Excerpt)
　　　翻译理论简介：林纾
　　　Exercise 11: Ella Lorena
　　　Key to Exercise 11: 爱拉·洛雷纳
Lesson 12　(C—E) ·················· 122
　　　Bilingual Reading: 祝福（摘录1）
　　　翻译理论简介：鲁迅与瞿秋白
　　　Exercise 12: 祝福（摘录2）
　　　Key to Exercise 12: The New Year's Sacrifice
　　　　　　　　　　　　(Excerpt 2)

Unit 7　Literature（2）

Lesson 13　（E—C） ················· 131
　　　　Bilingual Reading：East of Eden（An Excerpt）
　　　　翻译理论简介：郭沫若与茅盾
　　　　Exercise 13：The Sound of Music（An Excerpt）
　　　　Key to Exercise 13：音乐之声（摘录）
Lesson 14　（C—E） ················· 143
　　　　Bilingual Reading：找点活
　　　　翻译理论简介：直译与意译
　　　　Exercise 14：找点活（续）
　　　　Key to Exercise 14：Looking for Work
　　　　　　　　（Continued）

Unit 8　Popular Science

Lesson 15　（E—C） ················· 155
　　　　Bilingual Reading：Oil（Excerpt 1）
　　　　翻译理论简介：傅雷
　　　　Exercise 15：Oil（Excerpt 2）
　　　　Key to Exercise 15：油（摘录2）
Lesson 16　（C—E） ················· 171
　　　　Bilingual Reading：海洋可持续发展战略
　　　　翻译理论简介：关于风格
　　　　Exercise 16：中国海洋事业的发展　前言
　　　　Key to Exercise 16：The Development of China's
　　　　　　　　Marine Programs　Foreward

Unit 9　Law

Lesson 17　（E—C） ················· 182
　　　　Bilingual Reading：Environmental Law
　　　　　　（Excerpt 1）

　　　　　翻译理论简介：王佐良
　　　　　Exercise 17：Environmental Law (Excerpt 2)
　　　　　Key to Exercise 17：环境保护法（摘录 2）
Lesson 18　(C—E) ·· 197
　　　　　Bilingual Reading：中华人民共和国中外合资经
　　　　　　　　　　　　　营企业法
　　　　　翻译理论选读：Tytler's Three Principles
　　　　　Exercise 18：中华人民共和国中外合资经营企
　　　　　　　　　　 业法（续）
　　　　　Key to Exercise 18：Law of the People's Republic
　　　　　　　　　　　　　of China on Chinese-Foreign
　　　　　　　　　　　　　Equity Joint Ventures
　　　　　　　　　　　　　(Continued)

Unit 10　Speeches

Lesson 19　(E—C) ·· 213
　　　　　Bilingual Reading：Speech by President Nixon of
　　　　　　　　　　　　　the United Sates at Welcoming
　　　　　　　　　　　　　Banquet
　　　　　翻译理论选读：A New Concept of Translation
　　　　　Exercise 19：Speech by Former U.S. President
　　　　　　　　　　　Carter at Welcoming Banquet
　　　　　Key to Exercise 19：美国前总统卡特在欢迎宴会
　　　　　　　　　　　　　上的讲话
Lesson 20　(C—E) ·· 227
　　　　　Bilingual Reading：增进相互了解　加强友好合作
　　　　　　　　　　　　　——江泽民主席在美国哈佛大
　　　　　　　　　　　　　学的演讲（摘录 1）
　　　　　翻译理论选读：Guard Against Chinglish
　　　　　Exercise 20：增进相互了解　加强友好合作

vii

——江泽民主席在美国哈佛大学的演讲
（摘录 2）
Key to Exercise 20: Enhance Mutual Understanding and Build Stronger Ties of Friendship and Cooperation ——Address by President Jiang Zemin at Harvard University of the United States (Excerpt 2)

Part II English and Chinese Compared

1. 实称、代称与重复 ……………………………… 245
   （1）代词 …………………………………………… 245
       Drill 1
   （2）名词的重复与代称 …………………………… 251
   （3）其他词语的代称 ……………………………… 254
       Drill 2

2. 搭配 …………………………………………………… 258
   （1）主谓搭配——主语 …………………………… 258
       Drill 3
   （2）主谓搭配——动词 …………………………… 262
       Drill 4
   （3）形容词与副词 ………………………………… 267
       Drill 5
   （4）增词与减词 …………………………………… 273
       Drill 6

3. 并列与主从 …………………………………………… 280

    （1）并列——并列 ································ 280
        Drill 7
    （2）从句 ·· 283
        Drill 8
    （3）分词短语 ···································· 288
        Drill 9
    （4）介词短语 ···································· 292
        Drill 10

4．断句与并句 ·· 297

Appendices

    翻译重在实践 ····································· 305
    我怎样学翻译 ····································· 307
    也谈中式英语 ····································· 311
    怎样培养外事翻译
        ——两点体会与一点困惑 ················· 321
    翻译中的创造性
        ——学习《邓小平文选》英译本的一点体会 ······ 328
    北外翻译资格证书考试简介 ························ 339

Part I Texts

Unit 1　Stories

Lesson 1　(E—C)

Bilingual Reading（对照阅读）

The Quest[1]

Taking the train, the two friends arrived in Berlin in late October 1922, and went directly[2] to the address of Chou En-lai. Would this man receive them as fellow countrymen, or would he treat them with cold suspicion and question them cautiously about their past careers as militarists? Chu Teh remembered his age. He was thirty-six, his youth had passed like a screaming eagle, leaving him old and disillusioned.

When Chou En-lai's door opened they saw a slender man of more than average height with gleaming eyes and a face so striking that it bordered on the beautiful. Yet it was a manly face, serious and intelligent, and Chu judged him to be in his middle twenties[3].

Chou was a quiet and thoughtful man, even a little shy as he welcomed his visitors, urged them to be seated and to tell how he could help them.

Ignoring the chair offered him, Chu Teh stood squarely before this youth more than ten years his junior[4] and in a level voice told him who he was, what he had done in the past, how he had fled from Yunnan, talked with Sun Yat-sen, been repulsed by Chen Tu-hsiu in Shanghai, and had come to Europe to find a new way of life for himself and a new revolutionary road for China. He wanted to join the Chinese Communist Party group in Berlin, he would study and work hard, he would do anything he was asked to do but[5] return to his old life, which had turned to ashes beneath his feet.

As he talked Chou En-lai stood facing him, his head a little to one side as was his habit[6], listening intently until the story was told, and then questioning him.

When both visitors had told their stories, Chou smiled a little, said he would help them find rooms,[7] and arrange for them[8] to join the Berlin Communist group as candidates until their application had been sent to China and an answer received[9]. When the reply came a few months later they were enrolled as full members, but Chu's membership was kept a secret from outsiders.

(from Agnes Smedley, *The Great Road*)

提示：

第一单元：故事。这里所选的文章写的都是真人真事。有的选自传记，有的选自自传，有的是作者谈自己的经历。无论是以第一人称谈自己，还是以第三人称记述别人的事迹，其共同点是叙事，文笔细腻生动，所以统称之为故事。

关于第 1 课的对照阅读（BR1），请注意以下各点。

1. 本文作者史沫特莱（Agnes Smedley, 1890—1950）是一位美国女作家、新闻记者。1928 年以《法兰克福日报》特派记者身份来中国，在上海参加中国进步文化运动。抗日战争爆发后，前往延安，在山西前线做过战地救护工作。本文摘自她所著的记述朱德生平的《伟大的道路》。

★ 2. directly = at once

3. in his twenties 可译作 "二十多岁"。in his middle twenties 汉语就没有相对应的说法了，只好译作 "二十五六岁"。请注意 in the twenties 是 "二十年代"，不要混为一谈。

4. more than ten years his junior 是 this youth 的同位语。

★ 5. but = except

★ 6. as was his habit, 此处 as 后面可以省略主语 it, 意思相当于 which was his habit, 或 and that was his habit。

7．请注意：help 后面的动词不定式不加 to。

8．请注意：arrange for them to..., 而不能说 arrange them to...。

9．an answer received 是一个省略句，完整的说法应该是 an answer had been received。

译文：

探 索

他们两个人坐火车于一九二二年十月到达柏林，[1]立即去周恩来的住处。这个人会不会像同胞手足一样接待他们呢？会不会疑虑重重，[2]详细询问他们在军阀时代的经历呢？朱德想起自己的年龄，他已三十六岁，青春像一路鸣叫的鹰，早已一闪而逝，[3]留给他的是衰老和幻灭。[4]

周恩来的房门打开时，他们看到的是一个身材瘦长、比普通人略高一点的人，两眼闪着光辉，面貌很引人注意，称得上清秀。[5]可是，那是个男子汉的面庞，严肃而聪颖，朱德看他大概是二十五六岁的年龄。

周恩来举止优雅，待人体贴，在招呼他们坐下，询问有何见教[6]的时候，甚至还有些腼腆。

朱德顾不得拉过来的椅子，端端正正地站在这个比他年轻十岁[7]的青年面前，用平稳的语调，说明自己的身份[8]和经历[9]：他怎样逃出云南，怎样会见孙中山，怎样在上海被陈独秀拒绝，怎样为了寻求自己的新的生活方式和中国的新的革命道路而来到欧洲。他要求加入中国共产党在柏林的党组织，他一定会努力学习和工作，只要不再回到旧的生活里去——它已经在他的脚底下化为尘埃了——派他做什么工作都行。[10]

他娓娓而谈，[11]周恩来就站在他面前，习惯地侧着头，一直听到朱德把话说完，才提出问题。

两位来客把经历说完后，周恩来微笑着说，他可以帮他们找到住的地方，替他们办理加入党在柏林的支部的手续，在入党申请书寄往中国而尚未批准之前,[12]暂作候补党员。过了几个月,回信来了,两人都被吸收为正式党员,但朱德的党籍对外界保持秘密。[13]

(选自梅念译《伟大的道路》)

解说:

★1. 原文主语前面先用一个分词短语,这在英语书面语里是一种常见的结构。译成汉语就不一定保持这样的结构,硬译为"乘着火车,他们两个人……"。还是先出主语,译作"他们两个人坐火车……"较顺。

2. 前半句里的 as fellow countrymen 和后半句里的 with cold suspicion 形成对照。所以译文在"同胞"后面加了"手足",和"疑虑重重"相对照。

3. 原文 his youth has passed like a screaming eagle 是一个生动的比喻。汉语里有"青春一去不复返"之类的话,但是过于平淡。此处保留了原文的生动形象。

4. "留给他的是衰老和幻灭",这句译文虽然有些外国味,还是可以的。但是请注意,leave 一词在这里并不是"留下什么东西"的意思,而是相当于 cause to be,意思是"使……处于(某种状态)"。所以,如果换一个译法,就可以说"使他衰老,使他感到失望"。

★5. 原文 a slender man 后面有一连串的介词短语作定语。英语在描写一个人的容貌的时候,经常使用这种结构。汉语往往使用一连串的短句,此处就是这样处理的。

6. 在英语里,如果有人来找,被找的人往往说 What can I do for you? 或者说 Can I help you? 意思相当于汉语里的"你有什么事?"。所以此处 urged them ... to tell how he could help them 译作"询问有何见教"。

7. 原文 more than ten years his junior, 应译作"比他年轻十几岁"。

8. told him who he was 译作"说明自己的身份"是恰当的。不必紧跟原文,译作"说明自己是谁"。汉译英时,也不一定把"身份"译作 capacity,可以根据上下文,译作 who he was, who I am 等等。

9. what he had done in the past 在结构上与前面的 who he was 和后面的 how he had fled from Yunnan ... 是并列的,因此它不是概括后面提到的几件事,而是指逃出云南以前做过的事。译文恐应改为:"说明自己的身份,说明过去做过些什么事情,怎样逃出云南……"

10. 这一句似可改为:"……他一定会努力学习,努力工作,派他做什么工作都行,只要不再回到旧的生活里去,旧的生活已经在他的脚下化为尘埃了。"

★ 11. 这句话原文里的 As he talked,和下面一句话里的 when both visitors had told their stories,许多人愿意把这种从句译作"当……的时候"。其实汉语往往不这样说。第一句译作"他娓娓而谈",和后半句是并列的。第二句译作"两位来客把经历说完后",这个说法也是比较自然的。

12. until 往往译作"直到"。前面一句话里的 until the story was told 就译作"一直听到……"。但这一句里的 until their application had been sent to China and an answer received 比较长,译作"直到……"放在句末不顺,所以译作"在……之前",插在句子中间了。

★ 13. 原文最后两段里,有四处用了被动语态。第一处 until the story was told,译文没有用被动式,而是根据上下文,以"朱德"为主语,译成了主动句。第二处 until their application had been sent to China ...,译作"在入党申请书寄往中国……"申请书自己不能寄,显然是被寄的,但是不用"被"字,这叫做主动的形式具有被动的含义。第三处 they were enrolled as full members 译作"两人都被吸收为正式党员"。原文的被动语态译成了被动式,用了"被"字。最后一处 Chu's membership was kept a secret from outsiders，译作"朱德的党籍对外界保持秘密"，也是主动形式被动含义之一例。

―――― 译学点滴 ――――

翻译的标准

开始做翻译时，首先想到的一个问题大概就是：翻译的标准是什么？怎样才算好的译文？

这个问题，无论是在中国，还是在外国，都已经讨论了许多年。我们暂且不做深入的理论上的探讨。不过既然要作翻译，总得有个标准。我们还是根据自己的实际情况确定一个标准，来作为我们的奋斗目标吧。

对我们初学翻译的人来说，我想可以提出两条要求：（一）忠实；（二）通顺。"忠实"主要是指内容。翻译是在理解了别人用某种语言表达的意思之后，把同样的意思用另外一种语言表达出来。也就是说，译者的任务是表达别人的意思，而不是自己进行创作。因此，就要力求准确地表达原作者的意思。"通顺"指的是语言。如果原文是通顺易懂的，那么译文也要尽量做到通顺，易懂。也许有人会问，只提这样两个要求，标准是否定得太低了呢？我以为不然。真正做到上述两条，也并不是很容易的。

外国人用外国话说外国事，我们不是很容易理解透彻的。也许还有许多生词，需要现查词典。有时所有的生词都查出来了，还是不懂。勉强弄懂了，又怎样翻呢？还是问题。如果做汉译英，要把中国事物用英语写出来，让外国人看懂，做到拼法正确，句子平稳，合乎英语的用法，也不是轻而易举的事。在一定的阶段上，在一定的时间内，能做的事是有限的。如果我们的译文真能做到既忠实又通顺，也就可以说基本上达到了要求。

Exercise 1

将下列短文译成汉语：

Bill Morrow's[1] Birthday Party

Several times on his trips to China, which he made as a guest of the Chinese Government, Bill's[2] birthday occurred while he was in Beijing. On these occasions he was given a dinner in his honour[3] and Premier Zhou Enlai would[4] attend. He remembered the first occasion:

At the hotel I always finished the meal with icecream and the girls there would laugh because I liked it so much.

Zhou Enlai was at my birthday party[5] and at the end he got up, went over to the counter and got an icecream and he put it down in front of me—this is the Prime Minister[6] you know! He said 'This is for you'. I said 'I didn't know you could speak English'.[7] He laughed and he said 'a little bit' measuring[8] with his finger and thumb. Sometimes when we were alone then he'd speak to me in English.

'This is for you,' Bill Morrow heard on many occasions he would never forget[9]—such as when he was taken in a boat down the Grand Canal and every boat that passed sounded its siren in salutation. Or when he was shown over the great Nanjing bridge, built where the ferries used to[10] carry trains across the Changjiang River. He was given a chair and asked to wait a little as darkness came on, then suddenly the whole bridge was outlined in lights. 'This is for you.' 'You mustn't use all that electricity to please me,' he protested[11], 'all Nanjing will enjoy it too,' he was told.

Zhou Enlai arranged for experts from Beijing University to give Bill Morrow some up-to-date information he wanted. 'I'm just an

old bum at home,' Bill said, 'but here you treat me like a VIP[12].'
'We know what you have done,' said Zhou Enlai.[13]

(from Audrey Johnson, *Fly a Rebel Flag*)

提示:

1. Bill Morrow（1888—1980）澳大利亚工党议员，20世纪50年代积极参加和平运动，为改善中澳关系做了大量的工作。

★ 2. Bill 是 William 的昵称。类似的例子有：Bob 是 Robert 的昵称。Jack 是 John 的昵称。

3. in his honour = for him/to show respect for him

4. would 表示过去经常发生的动作。

5. 我们看到 party，往往首先想到"政党"。我们用 the Party 专指中国共产党。但在这里它的意思是"一次聚会"。所以 birthday party 就是"生日宴会"。

★ 6. 作者在这里称周总理为 Prime Minister，这是借用外国的说法。澳大利亚总理、英国首相都称做 Prime Minister，我国的总理，我们译作 Premier。

7. 注意这句话的时态。在这种场合，中国学生喜欢用现在时，说 I don't know you can speak English. 这是不对的，因为你说这句话的时候已经知道了。所以要说 I didn't know ...

8. measure 一词在这里用得很妙。它的本意是"量/衡量"，在这里的意思是伸出食指和拇指，两个指头靠得很近，表示数量很少。

9. he would never forget 是一个定语从句，修饰 many occasions。

10. used to 是一个成语，表示过去经常做某事。

11. protest 一词往往首先使我们联想到汉语里的"抗议"。其实它有时只表示 raise an objection/say something against。例如：The children protested loudly when they were told to go to bed early.

12．VIP是very important person的缩写，是社交场合常用的说法。机场等地的贵宾室常以此为标志。

13．本文中Zhou Enlai是根据汉语拼音方案拼写的，这就是现在国内出版物通用的拼法。BR1中出现的Chou En-lai是旧的拼法，现已不用，但仍见于20世纪60年代以前的出版物。

Key to Exercise 1

参考译文：

比尔·莫罗的寿宴

比尔[1]作为中国政府的客人访问中国，好几次都赶上在北京过生日。这时候，主人总要为他举行宴会，[2]周恩来总理也出席。他还记得第一次生日宴会的情景：[3]

我在饭店吃饭，最后总是吃冰激凌。[4]我吃得津津有味，惹得那些女服务员发笑。[5]这次生日宴会，周恩来在场。快到结束的时候，他站起来，走到柜台前，要了一杯冰激凌，放在我面前——别忘了，他可是总理呀！他对我说："这是为您准备的。"[6]我说："没想到您会说英语呀。"他笑了起来，接着说：[7]"一点点。"一面说着，一面用食指和拇指比画着。后来有时候我们单独在一起，他就跟我说英语。

"这是为您准备的。"这句话，比尔·莫罗在许多难忘的场合听到过——比如在他乘船沿大运河南下的时候，[8]从旁边驶过的每一条船都拉响汽笛，表示敬意。再比如参观南京长江大桥；[9]在修这座桥以前，要靠渡船在这里运送火车过江。参观大桥的时候，天快黑了，人家给了他一把椅子，请他坐下等一会儿。[10]忽然电灯全亮了，照出了整个大桥的轮廓。[11]"这是为您准备的。"他不满地说道："你们不应该费这么多电，就为了让我高兴。"人家对他说："南京人都可以欣赏嘛。"

比尔·莫罗想了解一些新的情况，周恩来就安排北京大学的

11

专家向他作介绍。比尔说:"我在国内不过是个流浪汉,而你们在这里却把我当成一位要人。"周恩来却说:"您做过些什么,我们是知道的。"12

解说:

★ 1. 英语往往先出代词,随后才出实体词。如这句话原文是 Several times on his trips...Bill's birthday...汉语则不然。总是先出实体词,后面用不用代词,就看需要而定了。

★ 2. 英语里的被动语态用得很多,在这篇短文里就用了六次。汉语有被动式,但用得不多。此处的 he was given a dinner in his honour 就译成了主动句。上文提到"比尔作为中国政府的客人",这里自然可以用"主人"二字做主语,译作"主人总要为他举行宴会"。

3. 原文 the first occasion,字面上很笼统,但其含义是具体的。所以译作"第一次生日宴会的情景"。

4. 这句话如照原文结构,需译作"在饭店里,我总是以冰激凌来结束我的一顿饭"。但原文并不是这样文诌诌的,而是相当口语化的。所以译作"我在饭店吃饭,最后总是吃冰激凌"。

★ 5. the girls there 如译作"那里的女孩子",则不甚清楚。实际上指的是在餐厅工作的女服务员。I liked it so much 字面上的意思是"那么喜欢它"。但是他之所以惹得服务员发笑,并不是因为他的这种爱好,而是因为他在吃冰激凌时表现出来的样子。所以译作"我吃得津津有味"。另外,原文有 because 一词,汉语不一定译成"因为",只要把"吃得津津有味"放在前面,那因果关系就清楚了。

6. This is for you 这句话,下面还会出现两次,因此译文必须适合三个不同的场合。原文用了一个动词 be,加一个介词短语。英语介词用得很广,而汉语则往往需用动词来表示,因此这里加了"准备"二字。

7. He laughed and he said...没有译作"他笑着说……",因

为原文是把"笑和说"作为两件事来描写的,这笑声正好表现周总理爽朗的性格。

8．When he was taken in a boat down the Grand Canal 是被动语态。译文用了主动句,仍以"他"为主语。

9．Or when he was shown over the great Nanjing bridge 也是被动语态。译文没有用主语,只用了一个动宾短语。

10．He was given a chair and asked to wait a little 译文也用了主动句,加了"人家"做主语。

11．...suddenly the whole bridge was outlined in lights 译文从原句中找了一个适当的词 lights(电灯)做主语。

12．We know what you have done 这句话很简单,反映了周总理朴实的作风。如译作"我们知道您的贡献",或者"我们知道您的功绩",都显得过于花哨。如译作"我们知道您做过些什么",又显得过于平淡。周总理这句话虽然简单,却很有分量。所以译作"您做过些什么,我们是知道的"。

Lesson 2 （C—E）

Bilingual Reading

孟轲悔过

　　孟子[1]是我国古代一个大学问家。他姓孟名轲。幼时家境贫穷，生活困难。不幸在他三岁的时候，父亲去世了，母子无依无靠，处境更加艰难。怎么办呢？孟母向人借了一架机杼，[2]靠织布维持生计。

　　孟轲慢慢长大了。但他非常贪玩，不爱读书学习。

　　有一天，还不到放学的时候，他悄悄溜出学堂，跑回家来。

　　孟母发现孟轲提前逃学[3]回来，非常生气，她从织布机上站起来，严肃地问儿子：

　　"你又逃学？"

　　孟轲看了看母亲，低下头，说：[4]

　　"念书没意思，我不念了！"

　　孟母一听，气得浑身哆嗦，拿起剪刀，把没有织完的绸子剪断了。[5]母亲的行动惊呆了孟轲，他睁着惊愕的眼睛，不知如何是好。[6]

　　孟母痛心地指着那一根根丝线，语重心长地说：

　　"你看，这绸子是一根根丝线用力气织起来的。人的学问是一点一滴慢慢积累起来的。你不读书，荒废学业，就如同我剪断了这没织成的一匹绸子一样，是件废品。[7]你不读书，怎么能长大成材呢！"[8]

　　孟轲听了母亲的话，看着那剪断了的丝绸和伤心的妈妈，心里难过极了。他觉得母亲的话说得有理，自己确实不对，于是惭愧地说：

　　"请母亲原谅我。我错了，今后坚决改掉毛病，努力读书学习！"

从此之后,孟轲变了。他再也没有逃过学,日夜苦读,钻研各家学说,终于成为我国封建时期的一位大思想家。[9]

(选自《北京日报》)

提示:

1. 孟子:Mencius
2. 机杼:loom
3. 逃学:play truant
4. 这里有三个动词,如何处理?
5. 这一句可考虑断句。
6. 这一句可考虑用分词短语。
7. 这一句内部怎样衔接?
8. 这一句前后两部分怎样衔接?
9. 思想家:thinker

参考译文:

Meng Ke[1] Mends His Ways[2]

Mencius was a great scholar of ancient China. His family name was Meng and his given name was Ke.[3] Born into a poor family, he led a hard life in his early childhood. At the age of three, he lost his father. With no one to support them, mother and son found life still more difficult.[4] What was to be done?[5]

Meng's mother borrowed a loom and[6] began to weave for a living.

As he grew older,[7] Meng Ke still loved to play and hated to study.

One day, he slipped out of school and went home before classes were over.

Finding that Meng Ke was playing truant, the mother was

indignant. She rose from the loom and said to her son in a serious tone, "So you are playing truant again!"[8]

Meng Ke cast a glance at his mother and lowered his head, saying, "I find my lessons dull. I'm going to give up."[9]

Hearing this, his mother shook with anger. She took a pair of scissors and cut through the silk on the loom. Confounded by his mother's action, Meng Ke gazed at her in bewilderment,[10] not knowing what to do.[11]

His mother pointed at the loose silk threads, and said with feeling, "Look! With toil, silk is woven thread by thread, and knowledge is accumulated bit by bit. Your giving up school is just like my cutting this bolt of unfinished silk.[12] Such silk is of no use. And how can you be of use when you grow up if you stop studying?"[13]

Hearing this and looking at the severed silk and his heartbroken mother, Meng Ke was conscience-stricken. He realized that his mother was right and he was wrong. He said shamefacedly,[14] "Please pardon me, mother. I'm wrong. I'm determined to overcome this weakness of mine and work hard at my studies."

From that time on Meng Ke was quite another person. He never played truant again. Instead, he worked day and night, studying the doctrines of the various schools, and finally became one of the great thinkers of feudal China.

解说：

1. Meng Ke 应分开写，不要写成 MengKe。

2. 题目一般用现在时。此处"悔过"还可译作 repents，但不宜译作 regrets，因 regrets 只有后悔之心，而无改过之意。

3. 这两句也可以合并，译作 Meng Ke, generally known as Mencius, was a great scholar of ancient China。

4. 此处原文是一句，而译文是两句。原文中间可以用逗号相连，而在英语里，这样两个句子是不能靠逗号连在一起的。译成两个独立的句子，干净利索。

★5. "怎么办呢?"译作 What to do 或 How to do 都是不对的。这些短语只能构成句子的一部分，如 Tell me what to do，而不能独立成句。

★6. 英语两个并列动词要用 and 之类的连词相连，而不能像汉语那样在中间用逗号。

7. 此处需抓住原文的真正含义。此时孟轲尚未长大成人，故不可译作 Meng Ke gradually grew up。此外，请注意，在这个句子里，英语先出代词 he，后出实体词 Meng Ke，而在汉语里一般是先出实体词，后出代词。

8. 学堂里仍在上课，孟轲逃学，溜了出来。所以母亲说的这句话用现在进行时比较好。

9. 原文是两个短句，中间用逗号。而译文是两个句子，因为在英语里，在这种情况下光用一个逗号是不行的。若在中间用 so 之类的连词把两句连成一句，还不如用两个独立的短句简洁有力。

10. 此处也可译作 gazed at her with wide open eyes，但不能说 with widely open eyes。

11. 请注意这段译文在句首和句末用了现在分词或过去分词，而没有用一连串的谓语动词。

12. 现在的译法是把 your giving up school 和 my cutting... 这两件事情相比。也可以把人与绸子相比，译作 If you give up school, you'll be just like the silk I have cut, which is useless.

★13. 原文前后两部分并无连词相连，而在英语里，只有用了连词 if，才能译成一句。

14. shamefacedly 可以改用 ashamedly，但不能用 shamefully（可耻）。

———— 译学点滴 ————

汉译英的基本功

　　汉译英时，原作是汉语，理解一般不构成很大的问题。虽然有时原文写得不清楚，不易理解，但这种情况不多。因此主要问题就在于译者使用英语的能力了。

　　就使用英语而言，有以下三个方面值得注意：

　　一、拼法正确。怎样拼写，不可忽视。如不小心，很简单的词也会拼错。比如 occasion 一词应是两个 c，一个 s。不小心就会误写成一个 c，两个 s。英语里有许多不规则动词如 teach，let，sit 等等，它们的过去式和过去分词有特殊的形式，而不能加-ed，如果加了-ed 就错了。而 welcome 是规则动词，其过去式是 welcomed，如果仿照 come 那样去变，就不对了。这个问题好比在汉语里写错别字。如果写一篇短文有很多错别字，这篇短文的质量也就可想而知了。

　　二、合乎用法。一个词怎样用，和哪个词连用，很有讲究。一不小心，就会违反用法。例如，Zhou Enlai arranged for experts from Beijing University to give Bill Morrow some up-to-date information he wanted. (Ex.1) 汉语可以说"安排某人做某事"，英语则要说 to arrange for somebody to do something。如果省略 for，就不合用法了。再如 as he welcomed his visitors (BR1)，这样说是可以的。但汉语常说欢迎某人做某事，英语就不能说 welcome somebody to do something，而要说 somebody is welcome to do something，在这里 welcome 就不是动词，而是形容词了。

　　三、句子平稳。也就是说每个句子都是合乎语法的。比如 BR2 里有这么两句："不幸在他三岁的时候，父亲去世了，母子无依无靠，处境更加困难。怎么办呢？"如译作：When he was three years old, his father died, mother and son had no support, life became more difficult. What's to be done? 则不妥。第一句译文虽然看上去很接近原文，但这样把几个短句放在一起，结构松散，

18

缺少应有的联系，不合乎英语的句法。第二句时态不对，这是作者的话，不是对话，不能用现在时。总之，汉译英时必须强烈地意识到自己是在使用英语，要多想想怎样说才合乎英语的说法。

以上三个方面可以说是汉译英的基本功。这三个方面做好了，就可以多考虑怎样译得好一些。如果这三方面还有许多问题，那就要先改正错误，怎么能集中精力研究翻译问题呢？当然，我们仍在学习的过程之中，使用英语，不可能很精确，但是要意识到自己的这一弱点，认真对待，准确性就会提高了。

Exercise 2

将下列短文译成英语：

我为乘客服务[*]

有一次，在拥挤的车厢门口，我听见一位男乘客客客气气地问他前面的一个女乘客："您下车吗？"女乘客没理他。"你下车吗？"他又问了一遍。女乘客还是没理他。"下车吗？"他耐不住了，放大声问，那女乘客依然没反应。"你是聋子，还是哑巴？"他急了，捅[1]了一下那女乘客，也引得车厢里的人都往这里看。女乘客这时也急了，瞪起一双眼睛回手给了男乘客一拳。

见此情景，我猛然想起在60路[2]沿线上有家福利工厂[3]，女乘客可能就是个聋哑人[4]听不见声音。我赶忙向男乘客作了解释，又用纸条写了一句话，举到女乘客的眼前：[5]"对不起！他要下车，他问了您好几声，您是不是没听见？"女乘客点了点头，把道让开了。

从此以后，我就特别注意聋哑人的特征[6]，还从他们那里学会了一些常用的手语。[7]比如，我可以用哑语问他们："朋友，您

---

[*] 题目是编者加的。

好!""您到哪里下车?""您请往里走!""谢谢"等等。这样,不仅我能更好地为他们服务,与他们进行感情交流,[8]也减少了一些他们与其他乘客的误会和纠纷。

(摘自李素丽"我属于乘客")

提示:

1. 捅: poke somebody with something/give someone a slight push

2. 60路: Bus No. 60

3. 福利工厂: welfare factory

4. 聋哑人: deaf mute

5. 此处顺序可有所变化

6. "特征"一词是否一定要译出来?

7. 手语: sign language

8. 此处不一定逐字翻译。

Key to Exercise 2

参考译文:

How I Serve the Passengers
by Li Suli

Once I heard a man[1] politely ask a woman in front of him at the crowded door of the bus, "Are you getting off?"[2] The woman made no response. "Getting off?" he asked again. The woman still made no response. "Getting off, or not?" he shouted, as he was getting impatient, but there was still no response. "Are you deaf, or dumb?" he burst out. Very much irritated, he gave her a slight push, which[3] attracted the attention of other passengers. Also irritated, the woman stared at him and hit back.

At this point,⁴ I suddenly remembered that there was a welfare factory on the route of Bus No. 60 and that the woman might be a deaf mute from there. I told the man what I was thinking⁵ and then I wrote on a slip of paper: "Excuse me, but he wants to get off. He's asked you several times, but you didn't seem to hear him. Right?" When I showed it to the woman,⁶ she nodded and made way for him.

Since then I have paid special attention to those who look like deaf mutes.⁷ I have learned from them some sign language with which I can say such things as "Hello, how are you?"⁸ "Where are you going?" "Please move on!" "Thanks!" In this way, I can render them better service and be friends with them⁹ and also reduce their misunderstandings and conflicts¹⁰ with other passengers.

解说:

1. "男乘客"译作 a man，"女乘客"译作 a woman 就够了。passenger 一词不必出现。

2. "下车"译作 get off 就够了，不必说 get off the bus。

3. which 指前半句说的这件事。

★ 4. at this point 是一个比较自然的说法，不要用 situation 之类的词。

5. explain 是及物动词，需要有直接宾语，但此处没有宾语，因此"向男乘客作了解释"译作 I told the man what I was thinking。

6. 这半句原在引语前面，现在移后。这样，前面一句引语紧接 I wrote on a slip of paper；后面一句 she nodded... 紧接 when I show it to the woman，比较紧凑。

★ 7. "特征"如译作 features 或 characteristics，都显得用词太大。其实这句话的意思不过是认出聋哑人，特别给以照顾，因此译作 those who look like deaf mutes。

8. "朋友，您好！"译作"Hello, how are you?"比较自然。

9. 原文"与他们进行感情交流"，不宜照字面直译，因此译作 be friends with them。

10. "纠纷"译作 conflicts，不宜译作 quarrels 或 disputes，因为聋哑人不能说话。

Unit 2　History

Lesson 3　(E—C)

Bilingual Reading

England Before the Industrial Revolution[1]

　　The country[2] was a place where men worked from dawn to dark, and the labourer[3] lived not in the sun, but in poverty and darkness. What aids there were to lighten labour[4] were immemorial, like the mill, which was already ancient in Chaucer's[5] time. The Industrial Revolution began with such machines; the millwrights were the engineers of the coming age. James Brindley of Staffordshire started his self-made career in 1733 by working at mill wheels, at the age of seventeen, having been born poor in a village[6].

　　Brindley's improvements were practical: to sharpen and step up the performance of the water wheel as a machine. It was the first multi-purpose machine for the new industries. Brindley worked, for example, to improve the grinding of flints, which were used in the rising pottery industry.

　　Yet there was a bigger movement in the air[7] by 1750. Water had become the engineers' element[8], and men like Brindley were possessed[9] by it. Water was gushing and fanning out all over the countryside. It was not simply a source of power, it was a new wave of movement.[10] James Brindley was a pioneer in the art of building canals or, as it was then called, 'navigation'.

　　Brindley had begun on his own account, out of interest, to survey the waterways that he travelled as he went about his engineering projects for mills and mines. The Duke of Bridgewater then got him to build a canal to carry coal from the Duke's pits at Worsley to the

23

rising town of Manchester ... Brindley went on to connect Manchester with Liverpool in an even bolder manner, and in all[11] laid out almost four hundred miles of canals in a network all over England.

Two things are outstanding in the creation of the English system of canals, and[12] they characterise all the Industrial Revolution. One is that the men who made the revolution were practical men. Like Brindley, they often had little education, and in fact school education as it then was[13] could only dull[14] an inventive mind. The grammar schools[15] legally could only teach the classical subjects for which they had been founded. The universities also (there were only two, at Oxford and Cambridge)[16] took little interest in modern or scientific studies; and they were closed to those who did not conform to the Church of England.

The other outstanding feature is that the new inventions were for everyday[17] use. The canals were arteries of communication: They were not made to carry pleasure boats, but barges. And the barges were not made to carry luxuries, but pots and pans and bales of cloth, boxes of ribbon, and all the common things that people buy by the pennyworth. These things had been manufactured in villages which were growing into towns now, away from London; it was a country-wide trade.

(from J. Bronowski, *The Ascent of Man*)

提示：

第二单元：历史。这里所选的文章，目的是介绍历史情况，说明事实，并阐发其意义。所用的语言比较文雅，概括性强，不作过细的描写。

关于第3课的对照阅读（BR3），请注意以下各点。

1. 本文作者雅各布·布洛诺夫斯基（Jacob Bronowski，1908—1974）是英国著名学者，出生于波兰。他编写的《人类的发展》(*The Ascent of Man*,1973)是一套共 13 部长约二十小时的电视系列片,从天文、数学、物理、化学、生物、遗传、建筑、工艺等各方面说明了人类在科学技术上的进步。本文和练习3 均选自该书第 8 章。

2. 本文说的是英国工业革命前的情况。The country 指的是英国农村。

3. 单数名词加定冠词表示泛指,此处泛指劳动者。

4. what aids there were to lighten labour = the aids that had been invented to lighten labour,这是全句的主语。

5. Chaucer:乔叟(1340?—1400),英国诗人,著有《坎特伯雷故事集》。

★ 6. having been born poor in a village 表示原因,说明他为什么 17 岁就开始干活。

★ 7. in the air = much talked about

8. the engineers' element = the right thing for engineers

9. possessed = strongly influenced

★ 10. 英语各分句之间一般要有连词相连。但是这一句包含两个一正一反的短句,是可以不用连词的。

11. in all = altogether

12. 注意,这个 and 是必要的。

13. as it then was = as it was at that time,是一个定语从句,修饰 school education。

14. dull (*vt.*) = make ... dull

15. grammar school 指英国的中等学校,过去以拉丁语等为主课。

16. Oxford:牛津,Cambridge:剑桥。牛津大学和剑桥大学是英国最著名的两所大学。

17. 注意,everyday 用作形容词时要写成一个词。

译文：

工业革命前的英国

在农村，人们从早到晚都得干活，劳动者并不是沐浴在阳光下，而是生活在贫困和黑暗之中，那些帮助减轻劳动的机械[1]都不知从哪个年代起就有了。比如磨坊，在乔叟的时代就已经是古老的了。而工业革命[2]就是从这些机械开始的。修造磨坊的匠人就是开创新时代的工程师。斯塔福郡的詹姆斯·布林德雷，出身于一个贫苦的农村家庭；一七三三年，他十七岁，就着手改良磨坊的车轮，从而开始了他那自我奋斗的生涯。[3]

布林德雷所作的改良是很实际的：[4]改善并加强水车的机械功能。这是为新工业提供的第一部多功能机器。例如，布林德雷努力改进燧石的碾磨过程，燧石是新兴的陶瓷工业有用的材料。

然而，到了一七五〇年，一场更大的运动已经在酝酿之中。水成了工程师们大显身手的对象，像布林德雷这样的人对它都着了迷。水在农村到处涌流漫溢。它不仅是一种能源，而且带来了一场新的运动。布林德雷是开凿运河的先驱者，当时人们把开凿运河叫作 navigation。[5]

布林德雷在为他的磨坊和矿井建筑工程到处奔走的时候，出于自愿和兴趣，对沿途经过的河道进行了勘察。[6]于是布里奇瓦特公爵就让他开一条运河，以便把煤从公爵在乌斯利拥有的矿井运往新兴城市曼彻斯特……布林德雷还更加大胆地用运河把曼彻斯特同利物浦联结起来，修凿了总长度为四百英里的遍布全英国的运河网。

在修建英国的运河网的过程中，有两点是非常突出的，而这两点也正是整个工业革命的特点。[7]首先，发动这场革命的都是些实干家。同布林德雷一样，他们一般都没有受过什么教育。事实上，当时那种学校教育也只能窒息人的创造性。按规定文法学校只能讲授古典学科，这些学校的办学宗旨本来就是如此。大学

(当时只有两所，一所在牛津，一所在剑桥）对现代的或科学的学科也不怎么感兴趣；这两所大学还把不信奉英国国教的人关在门外。

　　第二个突出的特点是：新发明都是为日常生活服务的。运河是交通的动脉，开运河不是为了走游艇，而是为了通行驳船。而驳船也不是为了运送奢侈品，而是为了运送瓦罐铁锅、成包的棉布、成箱的缎带，以及那些只花个把便士便能买到的各式日用品。这些物品都是在远离伦敦渐渐发展成为城镇的[8]农村制造的。这是一场全国范围的贸易。

（吴千之译）

解说：

　　1. aids 一词，查一下英汉词典，指人，译作"助手"，指东西，译作"辅助物"或"辅助设备"。用在这里都不合适。aid 本是一个笼统的字眼，可以指人，可以指东西，在不同的情况下，可以指不同的东西。在这个上下文里，把它理解为"某种机械"，是适宜的。这就是在具体场合把一个笼统的字眼具体化了。另外，顺便提一下，由于艾滋病简称 AIDS，现在人们在日常口语及文字中较少使用 aids 这个词。

　　2. Industrial Revolution 可以译作"工业革命"，也可以译作"产业革命"。《辞海》和《简明不列颠百科全书》就都是以"产业革命"立条的。

　　★3. 这句话，译文在结构上与原文有很大的不同。原文先说他的事业，再说他具体做了什么，最后说他的年龄和出身。译文则大致上与此相反，先说出身，再说他哪一年做了什么事，最后才说这件事在他一生中的意义。汉语叙事的顺序往往是和事情发生的顺序大体一致的。

　　4. 这一句照字面译，就是"布林德雷的改良是实际的"。但译者在"改良"前面加了"所作的"三字，这就不显得那么呆板。"实际"前面加了一个"很"字，这"很"字并无实义，不过是满足汉语习惯及节奏上的需要。

★5. 原文 building canals，但汉语里常见的搭配是"开凿运河"，如译作"建筑运河"，就不顺了。另外，原文后半句用 it 代替 building canals，译文重复"开凿运河"而不用代词，这样译是比较清楚的。

6. 原文时间状语放在句末，译文时间状语放在句首。

★7. characterise 一词很不好译，汉语没有简洁的对应词。它的意思是"显示出……的特点"，所以后半句译作"而这两点也正是整个工业革命的特点"。此外，译文重复"这两点"，而不用代词"它们"。

8. 定语从句 which were growing into towns now 译成汉语仍为定语，放在中心词之前。这种短的定语从句常常是这样处理的。

---——译学点滴————

把握全篇而后译

翻译一篇文章，不能一上来就看一句译一句，而必须把握全篇。一篇作品是一个有机的整体，一词一句都是整体的一部分。如果只注意词句，不注意整体，还是难免要出错，也就不能忠实于原文了。

BR1 里的 what he had done in the past 究竟应该怎样理解？逃出云南，去上海等等，都是几个月以前的事。in the past 不会是指这些事。但是在此以前，朱德同志参加过同盟会，参加过辛亥革命、云南起义等许多活动。这些活动在 The Great Road 一书中都有详细的记载。只有联系全书来看，才能理解书中出现的这个短语的真正含义。

Ex.2 最后一句有"纠纷"一词。我们一看见"纠纷"，往往首先想到 dispute。这里指的是公共汽车上的纠纷，也许可以译作 quarrel。但这两个词都意味着当事人要说话争辩，而此文通篇讲的是聋哑人的事，想到这一点，就会意识到以上两个词都不合适，而要另找别的词，如 conflict, trouble, 或 difficulties。

下面请再看一段话。这段话说的是一个七八岁的孩子跟着母亲回老家田纳西州去看望外祖母的情况。

I remember being startled when I first saw my grandmother rocking away on her porch. All my life I had heard that she was a great beauty and no one had ever remarked that they meant a half century before. The woman that I met was as wrinkled as a prune and could hardly hear and barely see and always seemed to be thinking of other times. But she could still rock and talk and even make wonderful cakes. She was captivated by automobiles and, even though it was well into the thirties, I don't think she had ever been in one before we came down and took her driving ...

第一句话里的 rocking away 究竟是什么意思呢？有人说，意思是"蹒跚而去"，有人说是"跳摇摆舞"，有人说是"在安乐椅里不停地摇"。其实 rocking away 没有"蹒跚而去"的意思。"跳摇摆舞"也不对。首先，这位外祖母 50 年前是个大美人，这时至少也有 70 岁了。第三句话说她满脸皱纹，听不清，看不明。这样一位老人怎样能跳摇摆舞呢？最后一句话说明当时是 30 年代后期。根据 Brewer's Dictionary of Phrase and Fable, 摇摆舞是 50 年代后期才兴起来的。因此，这段话里有许多地方都证明 rock 的意思不会是"跳摇摆舞"。它的意思是"坐在安乐椅 (rocking chair) 里摇动"，away 的意思是"不断地"。

有的人对翻译很有兴趣，但缺乏耐心。一拿到原文，看也不看，就开始一句句译起来。这个习惯是不好的。拿到原文以后，总要反复琢磨，研究得透一点再动手译。即使这样，有些地方也难免还是要弄错的。

Exercise 3

将下列短文译成汉语:

The Industrial Revolution

The Industrial Revolution is a long train of changes[1] starting about 1760. It is not alone: it forms one of a triad of revolutions, of which the other two were the American Revolution that started in 1775, and the French Revolution that started in 1789.[2] It may seem strange to put into the same packet[3] an industrial revolution and two political revolutions. But the fact is that they were all social revolutions. The Industrial Revolution is simply the English way of making those social changes. I think of it as the English Revolution.[4]

What makes it especially English[5]? Obviously, it began in England. England was already the leading manufacturing nation. But the manufacture was cottage industry, and the Industrial Revolution begins in the villages. The men who make it are craftsmen: the millwright, the watchmaker, the canal builder, the blacksmith. What makes the Industrial Revolution so peculiarly English is that it is rooted in the countryside.

During the first half of the eighteenth century, in the old age of Newton and the decline of the Royal Society,[6] England basked in a last Indian summer[7] of village industry and the overseas trade of merchant adventurers. The summer faded. Trade grew more competitive. By the end of the century the needs of industry were harsher and more pressing. The organisation[8] of work in the cottage was no longer productive enough. Within two generations,[9] roughly between 1760 and 1820, the customary way of running[10] industry changed. Before 1760, it was standard[11] to take work to villagers in their own homes. By 1820, it was standard to bring workers into a factory and have them overseen.¹²

(from J. Bronowski, *The Ascent of Man*)

提示：

1. changes 在这里怎样译？

2. 定语从句 that started in 1775 和 that started in 1789 怎样处理？

3. packet 一词的本意是"包裹"，在这里是一个比喻。

4. I think of it as ... = I regard it as ...

5. especially English，本段最后一句还有 peculiarly English，有时也说 particularly English，意思都相当于 having English characteristics。

6. Royal Society：皇家学会，是英国的一个科学学会。它成立于 1660 年，由著名科学家组成，是一个独立的民间团体。它的任务是促进科学研究，向政府提出建议，并代表英国参与国际上的科学活动。

★ 7. Indian summer = the pleasant final period

8. 抽象名词 organization 如何处理？

9. 英语里，一代人的时间是 30 年，所以 1760 至 1820 年算两代人的时间。

10. run 用作及物动词，在这里是什么意思？

11. standard 在这里是形容词，如何处理？

12. have them overseen 是英语特有的一种结构。字面上的意思是"使他们受到监督"。怎样才能译得更顺一些呢？

<h2 style="text-align:center">Key to Exercise 3</h2>

译文：

<h3 style="text-align:center">工业革命</h3>

工业革命是指从 1760 年¹ 开始的一长串的变革²。它不是孤

立的,而是当时的三大革命之一。³其它两次革命,一次是从 1775 年开始的美国革命,一次是 1789 年开始的法国革命。把一场工业革命同两次政治革命归作一类似乎有点奇怪,但事实上这三次革命都是社会革命,工业革命只是以英国方式来实现那些社会变革罢了。⁴因此我把它看作是英国革命。

为什么这场革命具有英国的特色呢?⁵不言而喻,因为它开始于英国。英国那时已经成为头号的制造业国家。不过当时的制造业只是农家手工业,而工业革命就是在农村开始的。⁶发动这场革命的都是些匠人:修造磨坊的、做钟表的、开运河的、打铁的。这场工业革命的英国特色正在于它扎根在农村。

18 世纪上半叶,也就是牛顿所处的那个旧时代,皇家学会衰落的那个时代,⁷英国沐浴在农村手工业和商人冒险家从事的海外贸易交织的余晖中。余晖消失了。贸易竞争越来越激烈了。到 18 世纪末,工业的需求更加紧张,更加迫切了。以农家为单位组织劳动⁸已经不能生产足够的产品了。⁹大体从 1760 年到 1820 年这两代人的时间里,办工业的传统方式变了。1760 年前的标准方式¹⁰是把活计拿到农民家里去做,到 1820 年,标准方式已经变成把工人雇到工厂里在工头监督之下劳动。

(吴千之译)

解说:

1. 原文是 about 1760。译文若在"1760 年"后面加"前后"二字,则更确切。

2. changes 在这里不能译作"变化",只能译作"变革"。

3. 译文在这里断句,of which 以下另起一句。

4. 这里译文把原文三句话合并为一句,比较紧凑。句末用了助词"罢了",和前面的"只是"相呼应,值得注意。

★ 5. especially English 译作"具有英国特色",是非常恰当的。如照字面译作"特别是英国的",则意思不清楚。

6. 这一句原文包含两个并列的短句,中间用 and 相连。这样的连词，一般可以不译。此处译文用了"而"字。根据《现代汉语词典》，"而"字可以"连接语意相承的成分"，用在这里正与原意相吻合。

7. 牛顿生于1642年，死于1727年。此处 old age 恐不指旧时代，而指牛顿的晚年，可考虑改为"也就是牛顿的晚年，皇家学会衰落的年代"。

★ 8. The organisation of work in the cottage 是一个名词短语，在句子里做主语，其中包含一个抽象名词 organisation。Organisation 来源于动词 organise。这样的抽象名词往往译为动词。所以整个名词短语就译成了动宾结构，"以农家为单位组织劳动"。

★ 9. productive 可以译作"多产的"，但如果后半句话译作"已经不够多产了"，则很别扭。productive 来自动词 produce，所以后半句也译成了动宾结构，"已经不能生产足够的产品了"。

10. standard 在这里是形容词，意思是"合乎标准的"。如果这样译，就要放在后面，全句译为"1760年前，把活计拿到农民家里去做是合乎标准的"。这就不如现在的译法，把 standard 译为"标准方式"了。

Lesson 4 （C—E）

Bilingual Reading

五四运动

第一次世界大战[1]后，帝国主义对中国加紧侵略，北洋军阀政府[2]对外妥协[3]投降[4]，对内残酷压迫人民，给中国带来了深重的民族危机[5]。一九一九年"巴黎和会"[6]上中国外交的失败，激起了中国人民的极大愤慨。五月四日，北京三千多学生在天安门前集会，他们高呼"外争国权，内惩国贼"[7]、"废除二十一条"[8]等口号，举行示威游行[9]。他们要求惩办卖国贼曹汝霖、陆宗舆、章宗祥，并火烧了曹宅，痛打了章宗祥。北洋军阀政府出动军警镇压，捕去学生三十多名。

那时候，各地学生纷纷响应北京学生的反帝爱国斗争。具有初步共产主义思想的知识分子李大钊、毛泽东、周恩来等同志分别在北京、长沙、天津，指导了这个伟大的反帝运动。

六月三日，北京学生组织演讲队，开展大规模的宣传活动，军阀政府对学生的镇压变本加厉[10]，捕去一百七十多人。"六·三"以后，主要是青年学生参加的五四爱国运动，发展成为无产阶级、小资产阶级和民族资产阶级共同参加的全国范围的革命运动。[11]无产阶级成为运动的主力。上海、唐山、长辛店等地工人纷纷罢工[12]示威，中国工人阶级第一次作为觉悟了的独立的政治力量登上政治舞台，显示了它的伟大力量。

在全国人民反帝爱国斗争的压力下，北洋军阀政府被迫释放被捕学生，撤销三个卖国贼的职务，拒绝在对德"和约"上签字，反帝反封建斗争取得了初步胜利。

五四运动是一次彻底的不妥协的反帝反封建的革命运动，它促成了中国工人运动同马克思主义的结合，在思想上和干部上为中国共产党的成立作了准备,是中国新民主主义革命的开端。

(选自《北京日报》)

提示:

★1."第一次世界大战"译作 World War I 或 the First World War 均可。但请注意,前一种译法不要定冠词,后一种译法要定冠词。

2. 北洋军阀政府:the Northern Warlord government

3. 妥协:compromise

4. 投降:capitulation

5. 民族危机:national crisis

6. "巴黎和会":the Paris Peace Conference

7. "外争国权,内惩国贼":Defend our sovereignty, punish the traitors!"这种对仗的句子,切忌生硬地翻译。

8. "废除二十一条":"Abolish the Twenty-One Demands"

9. 示威游行:to demonstrate, to hold a demonstration

10. 变本加厉:to intensify

11. 这一句比较长。"五四爱国运动"和"全国范围的革命运动"各带一个很长的定语。这两个定语可以译成短语,也可以译成从句,放在各自修饰的中心词后面就行了。

12. 罢工:to go on strike。

参考译文:

The May 4th Movement

After World War I, the imperialists stepped up their aggression against China while the Northern Warlord government resorted to compromise and capitulation externally and to ruthless oppression of the people internally, thus landing China in a grave national crisis.[1] China's diplomatic setback at the Paris Peace Conference in 1919 aroused strong indignation among the Chinese people. On May 4, over three thousand Beijing students gathered in front of the Tian An Men, and then held a demonstration, shouting such slogans as "Defend our sovereignty, punish the traitors!", "Abolish the Twenty-one Demands!"[2] They called for punishment to be meted out to the traitors Cao Rulin, Lu Zongyu and Zhang Zongxiang. They set fire to Cao's residence and beat up Zhang.[3] The government[4] called out troops and policemen to suppress the demonstrators[5] and over thirty students were arrested.

Immediately, the students in one part of the country after another rose in support of the anti-imperialist patriotic struggle launched by the students in Beijing. Comrades Li Dazhao, Mao Zedong, Zhou Enlai and other intellectuals who already had some knowledge of communism guided this great movement in Beijing, Changsha, Tianjin respectively.

On June 3, the students of Beijing formed groups of speakers and carried out extensive publicity work.[6] The government intensified its suppression and arrested over 170 students. From this point on, the May 4th patriotic movement, hitherto conducted mainly by the student youth,[7] became a nation-wide revolutionary movement in which the proletariat, the petty bourgeoisie and the national bourgeoisie all took part, with the proletariat as the mainstay. Large numbers of workers[8] in Shanghai, Tangshan, Changxindian and elsewhere went on strike and held demonstrations.[9] For the first time in Chinese history, the working class appeared as an awakened, independent force in the political arena, demonstrating its tremendous strength.[10]

Under the pressure of the nation-wide anti-imperialist patriotic struggle, the Warlord government had to set free the students it had arrested, dismiss the three traitors from office, and withhold its signature from the "Peace Treaty" with Germany. This marked an initial victory for the struggle against imperialism and feudalism.[11]

The May 4th Movement was a thoroughgoing, uncompromising revolutionary movement against imperialism and feudalism.[12] It was instrumental in bringing about the integration of Marxism with China's labour movement, and it paved the way, both in ideology and in the matter of cadres, for the founding of the Chinese Communist Party. It ushered in China's new-democratic revolution.[13]

解说:

★1. 这一句说明帝国主义和北洋军阀的所作所为及其后果,说明后果的部分是用分词短语来翻译的。

★2. 这一句, 集会和示威游行是主要行动, 高呼口号是次要的, 所以译作分词短语 shouting such slogans as... 放在后面。

3. 前半句说明学生的要求, 后半句说明他们的行动, 译文在中间断句。

4. 上文已说清楚, 当时的政府是 the Northern Warlord government, 这一句, 虽然原文重复"北洋军阀政府", 译文也不重复, 只译作 the government 就够了。

★5. 原文"镇压"后面没有宾语, 译文 suppress 是及物动词, 后面要求有宾语, 所以加了 the demonstrators。

6. "宣传活动"译作 publicity 一词就够了, 不必再加 activities。

7. hitherto conducted mainly by the student youth 是一个分词短语, 这样译比较简洁。也可以译作介词短语 mainly with the student youth taking part in it, 或译作从句 which had been conducted mainly by the student youth。

8. "纷纷"本是状语, 但是 one after another 或 in succession 之类的短语用在这里都不合适, 所以译成 large numbers of, 和 workers 结合起来, 意思是一样的。

9. 前半句说的是上海等地的工人，后半句说的是中国工人阶级，译文在中间断句。

10. "显示了它的伟大力量"是中国工人积极登上政治舞台产生的结果。它的主语也是"中国工人阶级"，所以译作分词短语 demonstrating...

11. 这一句，原文前半句说军阀政府被迫做了三件事，后半句说"反帝反封建斗争取得了初步胜利"，分作两句译，比较清楚。

12. 定语太多，所以"反帝反封建"没有译作 anti-imperialist and anti-feudal，而译作 against imperialism and feudalism。

13. 最后一段，原文是一句，译文根据内容分成了三句。

――――译学点滴――――

"Readability"

记得好几年以前，有一次，一位老翻译家交给我一篇短文，让我译成中文。这篇短文译好以后是准备请人在纪念苏格兰诗人彭斯的晚会上朗诵的。他对我说："我只提出一个字的要求：Readability！"

就先说说 readability 这个词怎样译吧。译作"可读性"好不好？如果这样译，那么这个译文所缺少的正是 readability。我觉得这个词可以译作"读起来上口"。若嫌啰嗦，也可以只用一个字："顺"。

其实，也不一定是只有拿到纪念会上去朗诵的译文才要求 readable，这个要求应适用于一切译文。

BR1 的译文，在这一方面，是相当不错的。其中有这样一句:... they saw a slender man of more than average height with gleaming eyes and a face so striking that it bordered on the beautiful. 译文是："……他们看到的是一个身材瘦长、比普通人略高一点的人，两眼闪着光辉，面貌很引人注意，称得上清秀。"分析一下句子的结构，就可以看出，原文里的几个定语在译文里有的仍是定语，有的则变成相当独立的短句了。如果保持原来的定语，就要译成"……他们看到的是一个比普通人略高一点、两眼闪着光辉、面貌很引人注意、称得上清秀、身材瘦长的人。"这样会把读者累得上气不接下气，就不能说是 readable 了。

BR3 里有这样一段话：The other outstanding feature is that the new inventions were for everyday use. The canals were arteries of communication: they were not made to carry pleasure boats, but barges. And the barges were not made to carry luxuries, but pots and pans and bales of cloth, boxes of ribbon, and all the common things that people buy by the pennyworth. 译文是："第二个突出的特点是：新发明都是为日常生活服务的。运河是交通的动脉，开运河不是为了走游艇，而是为了通行驳船。而驳船也不是为了运送奢侈品，而是为了运送瓦罐铁锅、成包的棉布、成箱的缎带，以及那些只花个把便士便能买到的各式日用品。"这段译文是忠实的，也是通顺的，很像是创作，而没有译作的痕迹。

初做翻译，有人会觉得，为了忠实，译文的词句越接近原文越好，有时甚至把句子弄得非常别扭。其实这是没有必要的，这样译就过于机械了。所谓翻译，是翻译意思，而不是翻译词句。只要抓住了意思，译文在词句上可以有一定的灵活性。

做了一些翻译工作之后，有人会觉得有了经验，或者自以为驾驭语言的能力很强，便撇开原文，任意发挥起来；或者删去原文里重要的词语，或者塞进原文没有的东西。这样译就过于自由了。这也是不可取的。

总之，译文在内容上要忠实于原文，在语言上要 readable，这样的译文才是好的译文。

Exercise 4

将下列短文译成英语：

北京的第一个"五一"节

"五一"国际劳动节，是1889年在第二国际成立大会[1]上确定的。1919年，中国工人阶级作为独立的政治力量，开始登上历史舞台。1920年我国许多城市就展开了庆祝"五一"节的活动，北京也是其中的一个，这也是北京第一次庆祝"五一"国际劳动节。[2]

这年五月，北京出版的进步刊物[3]《新青年》、《新社会》以及《北京大学学生周刊》[4]等都出版了专号。[5]《新青年》上刊登了李大钊同志的《"五一"运动史》，介绍了"五一"节产生的经过和各国工人阶级为争取八小时工作制[6]的斗争史。[7]此外，还有全国十七省市工人状况的调查报道等。

"五一"这天，北京大学五百多名校工和学生举行庆祝大会，李大钊同志在会上讲了话；[8]同时，何孟雄等同志乘两辆汽车，车上悬挂红旗和"劳工神圣"、"'五一'节万岁"的横标，游行示威；[9]以邓中夏同志为首的北大平民教育[10]演讲团也出动，沿途讲演和散发传单。[11]邓中夏同志当天还赶到长辛店铁路工厂向工人群众宣传，并参加他们的活动。北洋军阀政府出动大批武装军警，荷枪实弹，如临大敌，还逮捕了一些同学，但在群众斗争的压力下，不得不释放了。[12]

(选自《北京日报》)

提示：

1. 第二国际成立大会：the congress marking the founding of the Second International

2. 这一句比较长，怎样才能安排得主次分明？可否考虑断句？在何处断句？

3. 进步刊物: progressive magazines
4. 周刊: weekly
5. 专号: special issues
6. 八小时工作制: the eight-hour day
7. 这个句子中间怎样衔接?
8. 这两个短句怎样衔接?
9. 这一句词序要作较大的变动。
10. 平民教育: popular education
11. 传单: leaflets
12. 这一句可考虑断句。

Key to Exercise 4

参考译文:

First May Day in Beijing

In 1889, May lst was designated May Day, International Labour Day, at the congress marking the founding of the Second International. In 1919, the Chinese working class began to appear as an independent political force in the historical arena.[1] And in 1920, it[2] held May Day celebrations in many cities in China,[3] Beijing being one of them.[4] This was the first time May Day was celebrated in Beijing.

In May of that year, progressive magazines in Beijing[5] such as *New Youth*, *New Society* and *Beijing University Students' Weekly* put out special issues. *New Youth* carried Comrade Li Dazhao's article, "A History of the May 1st Movement", in which he[6] gave an account of the birth of May Day and the struggle of the working class in different countries for[7] the eight-hour day. It also carried reports on investigations into the conditions of workers in 17 provinces and municipalities.

On May 1, over 500 workers and students of Beijing University held a rally to mark[8] this day, and Comrade Li Dazhao addressed the meeting. He Mengxiong and other comrades demonstrated through the streets in two trucks decorated with red flags and streamers on which were written the words "Labour Is Sacred!" and "Long Live May Day!" With Comrade Deng Zhongxia in the lead, the university's[9] team for popular education set out to make speeches and distribute leaflets. That same day, comrade Deng went to the Changxindian Railway Factory to do publicity work among the workers and to take part in their activities. Alarmed at all this, the Northern Warlord government dispatched large numbers of troops and police, armed as if they were about to encounter a formidable enemy.[10] They arrested a number of students but, under pressure from the masses, had to set them[11] free.

解说：

1．"舞台"用作比喻，多用 arena，而不用 stage。

2．译文不以"城市"为主语，而以 it 为主语。it 代表前面一句提到的 the Chinese working class。

★3．"我国"多译作 China。

4．此处原文是并列分句，译文用了独立结构，以显出层次。

5．"北京出版的"译作 in Beijing 就够了，不必说 published in Beijing。

6．译文以 he 作主语，和后面的 gave an account of...搭配，比较顺。

★7．for the eight-hour day 就够了，"争取"可以不译。

8．"庆祝"译作 mark，不一定译作 celebrate。

9．"北大"译作 the university 就够了，因上文提到过 Beijing University。

10. 译文在这里断句，句子比较好安排。

★ 11. 虽然原文是"不得不释放了"，译文里这个 them 是不可省的。

Unit 3　Geography

Lesson 5　(E—C)

Bilingual Reading

Journey Up the Nile
(Excerpt 1)
by Robert Caputo

Egypt, wrote the Greek historian Hecataeus,[1] is the gift of the Nile. No other country is so dependent on a single lifeline. Egypt's very[2] soil was born in the Nile's annual flood; with the flood came the life-giving mud[3] that made Egypt the granary of the ancient world. And as rain fell in the Ethiopian highlands and the snows melted in the Mountains of the Moon, the river was everlastingly renewed.

"This is the best place on earth," said Ahmed, an Egyptian fellah, or farmer,[4] I encountered in the Nile Delta, that[5] incredibly fertile 8,500-square-mile triangle between Cairo and the Mediterranean coast. The delta and the narrow Nile Valley to the south make up only 3 percent of Egypt's land but are home to 96 percent of her[6] population. Here nearly 48 million people live in an area only slightly larger than Maryland. The rest of Egypt is desert.

"Truly Allah has blessed us," Ahmed exclaimed piously. "Soil, water, sun—we can grow anything!"

In the gathering dusk Ahmed and his five companions had invited me to join them. Their galabias[7] and turbans stained by the sweat and dirt of a long day's work,[8] they sat in front of a wayside shop, enjoying three of the best things in life along the Nile—tea, conversation, and the water pipe. At the edge of a nearby canal[9], donkeys laden with freshly harvested alfalfa waited for their masters to lead them home, braying a fretful counterpoint to the steady thud of an irrigation pump.

All this suggested ancient harmonies. Yet the Nile has been changed by modern man in ways not yet fully understood. In 1971 engineers and workers completed the Aswan High Dam, nearly 600 miles upriver from Cairo toward the Sudanese frontier. It is the greatest public work to be undertaken in Egypt since the Pyramids. The devastating floods and droughts that imposed a recurrent tax of suffering on the fellahin[10] no longer occur. Egyptian agriculture has been transformed, and industry is benefiting[11] from power generated by the dam.

But there have been negative effects also. Standing on a sandy beach at the mouth of the Rosetta branch of the Nile, I was puzzled by what seemed a ghost town[12]—a sad vista of crumbling buildings, smashed windows, and broken wires dangling from utility poles. One house teetered drunkenly, half in, half out of the sea.

"Last summer, people stayed in those rooms—this was a summer resort," said a voice behind me. The speaker was a young Egyptian named Muhammad, member of a team from Alexandria that had come to this abandoned village to study coastal erosion. "Now the sea is moving in," Muhammad said. He pointed to a lighthouse perched[13] on a tiny island a couple of[14] miles offshore: "That lighthouse used to be on land. About six years ago it became an island. Day by day the sea is eating the land—the dam has stopped[15] the sediment of the Nile from replenishing the shoreline."

As we chatted, a brightly painted sardine boat dropped anchor. The captain[16] came ashore and joined our conversation. "Before they started the High Dam 25 years ago," he said, "the Nile mud had a lot of food in it, and so the sardines gathered near the mouth of the river to feed. Now there is no mud, and no food for the fish—they've left us."

"If all this can happen in 25 years, what will happen after 50 years, or 100 or 200?" asked Muhammad.

(from *National Geographic*)

提示：

第三单元：地理。这里所选的文章，目的是说明地理情况，顺便介绍当地的社会生活，并议论有关的热点问题。第 5 课是一篇考察尼罗河的纪实，谈到沿途看到的景色和与当地人交谈的情况，因此语言生动，描写细腻。第 6 课是导游书里对旅游景点的介绍，语言也比较正式。可见同类文章针对不同的场合，其风格也会是大不相同的。

关于第 5 课的对照阅读（BR5），请注意以下各点。

1. 这个插入语怎样处理？

★ 2. very 在这里不是副词，而是形容词，用来加强语气。

3. 这是一个倒装句，等于 the life-giving mud came with the flood。这里之所以用倒装句，是因为 mud 后面还有一个定语从句。

★ 4. 此处的 or 表示换一种说法，即用后面的 farmer 解释前面的 fellah，说明这两个词的意思是一样的。通常译为"或称"、"即"等。

5. that 在这里不是连词，而是指示代词，指 triangle。从 that 到句末，这个词组是 the Nile Delta 的同位语。

6. 用代词来指一个国家时，传统的用法是用 she（或 her）。现在 it（或 its）也用得很多。

7. galabia: a long, loose cotton gown reaching to the ankles, worn in Arabic countries, esp. by peasants

8. Their galabias and turbans stained by... 是一个独立结构。

9．canal 在这里是什么意思？

10．fellahin 是上面提到的 fellah（farmer）的复数形式。

11．benefit 表示"受惠"时，是不及物动词，后面跟 from。

12．ghost town: the remains of a deserted town, permanently abandoned esp. for economic reasons

13．perched 不是动词过去时，而是过去分词。它引导的分词短语修饰 lighthouse。它的意思是"置于"或"位于"，一般用来指位于高处或危险处的建筑物，例如：a hut perched at the edge of the cliff 悬崖边上的小屋。

14．a couple of 是口语里常用的一个短语，不一定指两个，可以泛指两三个。

15．stop 在这里是及物动词，意思相当于 prevent。

16．captain 在这里是什么意思？

参考译文：

沿尼罗河而上
（摘录1）
罗伯特·卡普托

希腊历史学家赫卡泰奥斯写道：埃及是尼罗河送来的礼物。[1] 任何别的国家都不像埃及这样依赖着唯一的一条生命线。就连埃及的土地也是尼罗河每年泛滥而带来的[2]。河水泛滥带来了泥沙，万物得以生长，[3] 埃及就这样成了古代世界的粮仓。埃塞俄比亚高原上的雨水，和月亮山上融化的积雪，为尼罗河提供了无穷无尽的水源[4]。

"这是世界上最好的地方，"阿赫迈德对我说。他是我在尼罗河三角洲遇见的一位农民（当地人管农民叫"夫埃拉"）。从开罗到地中海之间这块八千五百平方英里的三角地带，土地异常肥沃。[5] 三角洲和南边狭窄的尼罗河河谷只占埃及土地的百分之三，却有百分之九十六的人口住在这里[6]。将近四千八百万人生活的这块地方只比美国马里兰州[7]略大一点。埃及其余的地方全是沙漠。

"真主可真是保佑我们哪，"阿赫迈德虔诚地说道。"我们有土地，有水，有阳光——种什么都行啊！"[8]

天色渐渐暗了下来，阿赫迈德和五个一起干活的人早就约我去和他们玩儿。他们干了一天活儿，袍子和头巾上又是汗，又是土。[9]这时候，他们坐在路旁一家商店门口，享受尼罗河沿岸人们生活里的三件最大的乐事——喝茶、聊天、抽水烟[10]。在附近一条水渠旁，驴子背上驮着刚割的苜蓿，等着主人牵它们回家去，一面发出一阵阵急促的叫声，和浇地的水泵不断发出的突突声交织在一起。

这一切使人感到[11]古代的和谐气氛。然而现代的人却使尼罗河发生了变化，不过就连他们自己也不完全了解尼罗河究竟发生了什么变化。[12]1971年，技术人员和工人建成了阿斯旺高坝。这座水坝在从开罗沿尼罗河向苏丹边境走去将近六百英里远的地方。这是埃及自从修建金字塔以来进行的一项最大的公共工程。过去给农民带来灾难的水旱灾害，现在不再发生了。埃及的农业得到了改造[13]，工业也用上了水坝发出的电力。[14]

但是也有不良的后果。洛塞塔河是尼罗河入海处的一个支流，我站在河口的沙滩上看到一个小镇，感到迷惑不解。[15]这仿佛是一个被人遗弃了的小镇，一片萧索景象，房子濒于倒塌，窗户破碎，断了的电线挂在电线杆子上。有一所房子好像喝醉了的人一样摇摇晃晃，一半泡在海里，一半在陆地上。

"去年夏天，那所房子还有人住过。这是一个避暑胜地。"在我身后有人这样说道。说话的是一位埃及青年，名叫穆罕默德，他是一个考察队的队员，是专门从亚历山大港到这个荒芜的村庄来考察沿海地区水土流失的情况的。[16]"海水越来越往里边来，"穆罕默德说道。他指着座落在离海岸二三英里的小岛上的一座灯塔说："那座灯塔本来是在陆地上的。大约六年前，那地方变成了一个小岛。海水一天天冲刷陆地——水坝已经使得尼罗河的泥沙无法沉积下来加固海岸了。

我们正在聊着，只见一条颜色鲜艳的捕捞沙丁鱼的船抛了锚。船长上了岸，凑过来和我们说话。他说："二十五年前修建高坝之前，尼罗河的泥沙里面有很多可吃的东西，所以沙丁鱼就聚集在河口找食吃。现在泥沙没有了，鱼没有可吃的了，也就不来了。"

"如果说二十五年就发生这么多变化，五十年、一百年、二百年之后又会怎么样呢？"穆罕默德问道。

（摘译自《全国地理杂志》）

解说：

1. 译文在这里不便使用插入语，所以把"希腊历史学家赫卡泰奥斯"作为全句的主语。

★2. was born 是一个形象性的说法，译文无法保存原文里的形象，所以译作"带来"。

3. life-giving mud 等于 mud that gives life，所以译作"万物得以生长"。

4. 字面上的意思是"尼罗河不断得到更新"，这样说有些别扭。所以根据上下文，译作"为尼罗河提供了无穷无尽的水源"。

★5. 原文 that incredibly fertile 8,500-square-mile triangle between Cairo and the Mediterranean coast 是 the Nile Delta 的同位语。在译文里"三角洲"一词不是出现在句子末尾，而是在句子中间。同位语不好安排，所以独立成句。

★6. are home to...若译作"是……的家"则不顺。所以把名词改为动词，译作"……住在这里"。

★7. 本文发表在美国杂志上，所以用美国的一个州来作比较。中国读者不见得知道马里兰州在哪里，所以前面加了"美国"二字。

8. 这是埃及农民说的话，所以译文比较口语化。

9. 原文用的是独立结构，译文单独成句。第二句用"这时候"开始,照顾前后的联系。

10. 原文用了三个名词,表示两件东西,一件事情,非常简洁。汉语如保持这种结构则不顺,所以都改成了动词。

11. suggest 在这里的意思相当于 to imply, to show indirectly,所以译作"使人感到"。

12. in ways not yet fully understood 原是一个状语,但若译作"使尼罗河以尚不完全了解的方式发生了变化",则很别扭,意思也不清楚。所以译作一个分句,仍放在后面。

13. 原文是被动语态,译文不一定用"被"字,所以译作"得到了改造"。

14. 照字面译就是"工业正从水坝发出的电力得到好处"。这里所谓"得到好处",指的就是能够用上电力。直接译作"工业也用上了水坝发出的电力",意思更清楚。

★15. 原文 standing 后面有一个很长的状语,译文用了一个分句,放在前面,先处理,句子比较好安排。

16. 原文 member of a team... 是一个同位语,译文也用了一个分句。

————译学点滴————

研究句子结构的差异

初做翻译,译文的句子结构往往受原文的影响很深。有的译者做汉译英,认为只要把汉语的词换成英语就行了,句子结构可以大体上和原文一样。做英译汉时,也如法炮制。这样的译文自然不会很通顺。其实汉语有汉语的结构,英语有英语的结构。有时也有相同之处,但不同之处要多得多。下面请看几个例子。

例1. It may seem strange to put into the same packet an industrial revolution and two political revolutions. But the fact is that they were all social revolutions. (Ex.3)

把一场工业革命同两次政治革命归作一类似乎有点奇怪,但事实上这三次革命都是社会革命。

例2. 第一次世界大战后，帝国主义对中国加紧侵略，北洋军阀政府对外妥协投降，对内残酷压迫人民……北洋军阀政府出动军警镇压，捕去学生三十多名。(BR4)

After World War I, the imperialists stepped up their aggression against China while the Northern Warlord government resorted to compromise and capitulation externally and to ruthless oppression of the people internally... The government called out troops and policemen to suppress the movement and over thirty students were arrested.

这两个例子，例1原文是两句话，译文合成了一句。原文第二句用代词 they 指第一句中提到的 revolutions。译文却是一句，也没有用代词，而用了实词"这三次革命"。例2原文重复北洋军阀政府，译文却没有重复，而用了一个替代的说法。

例3. What makes it especially English? (Ex.3)
为什么这场革命具有英国的特色呢？

例4. The delta and the narrow Nile Valley to the south make up only 3 percent of Egypt's land but are home to 96 percent of her population. (BR5)
三角洲和南边狭窄的尼罗河河谷只占埃及土地的百分之三，却有百分之九十六的人口住在这里。

这两个例子，例3原文的主语是 what, it 指上文提到的 revolution。如按原文的主谓结构来译，就成了"什么使它……"这就很别扭。因此译文以"这场革命"为主语，不但换了主语，而且没用代词，用的是实词。例4原文后半句谓语是 are home to...，译文却改为"却有……住在这里"，也是考虑到和主语搭配的问题。

例5. Several times on his trip to China, which he made as a guest of the Chinese Government, Bill's birthday occurred while he was in Beijing. (Ex.1)

比尔作为中国政府的客人访问中国,好几次都赶上在北京过生日。

例6. Zhou Enlai arranged for experts from Beijing University to give Bill Morrow some up-to-date information he wanted. (Ex.1)

比尔·莫罗想了解一些新的情况,周恩来就安排北京大学的专家向他作介绍。

这两个例子,原文都是主从复合句,各有一个定语从句。例5的译文是一个主语,带两个并列的谓语。例6的译文是用了两个并列的分句。

少数几个例子很难说明什么问题,但例子多了,就可以看出英汉两种语言有以下三大特点。

第一,英语不喜欢重复,如果在一句话里或相连的几句话里需要重复某个词语,则用代词来代替,或以其他手段来避免重复。汉语不怕重复,连续使用某个词语是常见的事。汉语也用代词,但不如英语用得多。所以汉译英时要注意避免重复,多用代称;不但名词有代称,动词、形容词乃至短语,也都有替代的办法。英译汉时则要少用代称,多用实词。

第二,英汉两种语言的主谓搭配,在大多数情况下是相通的。英语里一个主谓搭配,译成汉语后可以保持原来的搭配。但有时却不行,汉译英时也是一样。一般说来,汉语的主谓关系没有英语那么密切。英语对于主语能否做后面的动作考虑较多。因此,译文以什么作主语,或以什么作谓语,是一个经常需要斟酌的问题。说起搭配,也不限于主谓搭配。动词和宾语,定语,状语等也往往有个搭配问题。

第三,英语大量使用定语从句、分词短语、介词短语等,汉语则没有这么多表达方式。因此英语句子里主从关系很多,体现出不同的层次。汉语则多用并列谓语或并列分句,因此汉语句子里并列关系居多,层次不甚明显。

如果记住这三条,并在实践中很好地加以运用,译文的质量就可以有很大的提高。

Exercise 5

将下列短文译成汉语：

Journey Up the Nile
(Excerpt 2)

Tombs and temples of ancient Egypt follow[1] the Nile well into Sudan. Driving southward from Cairo into the valley[2], I entered a landscape that owed little to the present era[3]. For the next 1,800 miles the thin blue ribbon of the Nile, flowing slowly north, unwound[4] over brown soil and green fields, some only a few yards wide, others as broad as an Iowa cornfield. At the edge of the fields, rising in dramatic[5] hills or stretching flat to the horizon, lay the brown barren deserts.[6]

I had the illusion that I was driving through one immensely long, narrow farm. The villages and towns were usually perched on the edge, so as not to waste arable soil and because there was a need, before the High Dam tamed the Nile, to live beyond the reach of the annual floods. The road followed the course of the Nile, now passing through the fields, now drawing a black line separating them[7] from the desert.[8]

At El Awamia, just south of Luxor, I watched farmers harvest sugarcane. A village elder, Amin Ibrahim, invited me into his house and gave me a cheerier view of the effects of the Aswan High Dam than I had heard before. "Before[9] the dam we were obsessed with the flood—would it be too high or too low?" said Amin. "Like all the generations of my family back to the pharaohs, I used to plant my crops and never know if I would harvest. Now there is no fear;

we know there will be water, and how much there will be. And we can get three crops a year instead of one. There is electricity in our houses and to run pumps, so we do not have to work the shaduf[10]. We used to go to the house of a rich man to hear the radio. Now, since we grow crops all year, we buy our own radios and even televisions."

Judiciously,[11] Amin conceded that there was another, less happy,[12] side to the story: "The land is poorer, because the mud that used to come with the Nile flood has stopped. We must use fertilizers that cost a lot of money. Even so,[13] the crops are less."

He led me through fields near his house. The ground was encrusted[14] with salt. "The flood does not carry away the salt as before,"[15] Amin explained. The annual flood of the Nile used to deposit as much as 20 million tons of silt on the fields along the river. As the flood receded, the water draining through the soil leached out the salts and carried them off to the Mediterranean. It was a natural system of replenishment and cleansing.

Today this treasury of silt is trapped behind the dam, and there is no effective drainage system.

(from National Geographic)

提示：

1. follow 怎样译，句子才比较顺？

2. the valley 指 the Nile Valley。

★ 3. owe...to... 是一个成语。owed little to the present era 意思相当于 there was hardly anything that showed the influence of the present era。

4. unwound 是谓语动词，过去时，其原形是 unwind，意思是"伸展"。

★ 5. dramatic = striking 引人注目的

6．这是一个倒装句，主语是 the brown barren deserts。

7．them 指 the fields。

★ 8．now...now... 意思是"有时……有时……"。

9．before 在这里指时间，而不是指地点。

10．shaduf：桔槔，water bucket suspended on a weighted rod, used in Egypt and other Eastern countries for raising water, esp. for irrigation.

11．judiciously = wisely; with good judgment

12．less happy = less favourable

★ 13．so 在这里代替前面一句话所说的内容。Even so 相当于 Even when we use fertilizers。

14．encrusted = covered

15．这一句，字面上的意思是"洪水不再像以前那样带走盐分了"。究竟是什么意思？

Key to Exercise 5

参考译文：

沿尼罗河而上
（摘录 2）

尼罗河沿岸直到苏丹境内很远的地方，到处可以见到古埃及的坟墓和寺庙。[1] 我从开罗驱车南行，[2] 进入尼罗河河谷，这里的景色还没有受到多少现代的影响。从这里再往前一千八百英里，尼罗河像一条细细的蓝色丝带，缓缓流向北方，[3] 沿途穿过棕色的土地和绿色的田野，这田地窄的不过几码，宽的则赶得上美国依阿华州的玉米地。田地外边是寸草不生的棕色沙漠，有的地方突然隆起像是小山，有的地方则平平地伸向地平线。[4]

我感到仿佛是[5]在开车穿过一个狭窄而极长的农场。大小村镇一般都处于田地的边上，这是为了不浪费耕地，同时也是因为在高坝控制尼罗河以前，有必要住得远一点，以躲避每年发生的洪水。[6]公路是顺着尼罗河修筑的，有时穿过庄稼地，有时像是划的一条黑线，这边是庄稼，那边是沙漠。[7]

在卢克苏尔以南不远的阿瓦米亚村，我曾看着农民收割甘蔗。村里一位长者，名叫阿明·易卜拉欣，请我到他家去做客，向我介绍了阿斯旺高坝的影响。他的话比我以前听到的更为乐观一些。[8]他说："还没修坝的时候，我们老惦记着洪水，——今年的洪水会太大呢，还是会太小呢？我过去种庄稼，从来不知道能不能收。我的祖辈以至古代的法老也都是这样。[9]现在不用害怕了，我们知道一定会有水，也知道会有多少水。我们不是收一季，而是收三季了。家里用上了电，还用电开水泵，不需要再用吊桶提水了。过去我们到富人家里去听收音机。现在我们一年到头种庄稼了，就自己买收音机了，甚至还买电视机呢。"

不过阿明也看得很清楚，[10]他承认这件事还有另外一面，不那么好的一面。他说："土地更差了，因为过去尼罗河一泛滥就带来泥沙，可现在没有了。我们不得不用化肥，而化肥是很贵的。即便这样，庄稼还是不如以前打得多。"

他带我在他家附近的庄稼地里走了走。只见地面上结了一层盐。"现在不像从前了，河水不泛滥，盐分就冲不走了。"[11]阿明对我解释说。过去每年尼罗河泛滥，可以给沿岸的农田留下细沙两千万吨。河水退去的时候，就把土壤里的盐分冲走，冲到地中海里去。那是自然形成的一个补充土壤和清除盐分的体系。现在宝贵的泥沙被水坝拦住了，却没有除盐的有效办法。

（摘译自《全国地理杂志》）

解说：

★ 1. 这一句里的动词 follow 很不好译。它在原文里是一个形象性的说法。译文无法保留原文的形象，所以译作"到处可以见到……"。

2. 此处不宜译作"驱车南下"。在中国，说"南下"、"北上"是很顺的。但尼罗河自南往北流,而作者是逆流而上。因此译作"驱车南行",以避免方向上的冲突。

3. 此处不宜译作"向北流去",因为作者此时是从开罗向南展望尼罗河的景象。

4. 首先要弄清楚,rising…和stretching…这两个分词短语形容deserts,而不形容fields,因此译文把它们放在"棕色沙漠"后面处理。

5. illusion的本意是"错觉",或"幻觉"。但这两个词用在这里都不合适,所以译作"我感到仿佛是……"。

6. 这一句,注意句子内部的衔接。前半句加了"这是"二字,因为如不加这两个字,就要把"为了不浪费耕地"提前,句子不好安排。后半句,如照原文译作"有必要住在每年的洪水到达的以外的地方"则有些别扭。所以译作"……住得远一点,以躲避……"。如译作"需要住在每年洪水冲不到的地方"也是可以的。

★7. 与其照原文译作"把庄稼和沙漠分开",不如译作"这边是庄稼,那边是沙漠"。

★8. cheerier…than I had heard before分出来单独处理,句子比较好安排。

9. 这一句也可译作"我过去和我的祖辈以至古代的法老一样,种庄稼,从来不知道能不能收"。但不如现在的译法简洁。

★10. 把一个副词放在句首,现在是一种常见的用法。hopefully(常常译作"我希望……"),ideally(常常译作"理想的情况是……"),都有这种用法。judicious的意思是"明智",或"有见识"。所以judiciously译作"看得很清楚"。

11. 这一句,不要译作"洪水不像以前那样冲走盐分了"。高坝修好以后,河水不再泛滥,也就无所谓洪水了。

Lesson 6 （C—E）

Bilingual Reading

北海公园

北海公园原是辽、金、元、明、清历代封建帝王的"御花园"[1]。总面积共有 68.2 公顷。公园的中心——琼岛，周长 1,913 米，高 32.8 米，是 1179 年（金代）用挖海的泥土堆成的。岛上白塔[2]建于 1651 年，塔高 35.9 米。

琼岛东北部有"琼岛春阴"碑，为 1751 年建立，附近风光秀丽，过去是燕京[3]八景之一。海北岸有"五龙亭"，建于 1602 年，是封建皇帝钓鱼和看焰火的地方；"九龙壁"，建于 1756 年，全壁用五彩琉璃瓦[4]砌成，两面各有蟠龙九条，姿态生动，反映了我国劳动人民的创造才能；"铁影壁"，[5]是元代文物。[6]

提示：

1. 御花园：the imperial garden
2. 白塔：the White Dagoba
3. 燕京：北京市的别称，可译作 Beijing
4. 琉璃瓦：glazed tiles
5. 影壁：screen
6. 本篇有许多并列的短句和并列谓语，翻译时如何处理才合乎英语的说法？

参考译文：

Bei Hai Park

Bei Hai (North Lake) Park, covering an area of 68.2 hectares,[1] was the imperial garden in the Liao, Jin, Yuan, Ming and Qing

Dynasties. The centre of the park is Qiong Island, 32.8 metres high and 1,913 metres in circumference.[2] It was made in 1179 (in the Jin Dynasty) with the earth that came from the digging of the lake. The White Dagoba built on it in 1651 is as high as 35.9 metres.

There is a stone tablet erected in 1751 in the northeast of Qiong Island, with "Qiong Dao Chun Yin" (Spring Shade on the Qiong Island) written by Emperor Qian Long (1736—1796A. D.)[3] engraved on it. This area, noted[4] for its beautiful scenery, was counted as one of the eight outstanding views of Beijing.

On the north shore of the lake are[5] the Five-Dragon Pavilions, built in 1602,[6] where the emperors enjoyed fishing and watched fireworks. Not far to the northeast[7] stands the Nine-Dragon Screen, put up in 1756, which is made of colourful glazed tiles. With nine lively dragons on each side, it has proved the creativeness of the working people of China. Near there is the Iron Screen, which is a relic of the Yuan Dynasty.

解说：

★1. 原文关于公园的面积单写一句。这样的内容在英语里是不单独成句的，所以译成了分词短语 covering an area of...

★2. 汉语"周长"在前，"高"在后。译文把 high 放在前面，把 in circumference 放在后面。把长的词语放在后面，节奏比较好，句子压得住。

3. written by Emperor Qian Long (1736—1796A.D.) 是译者所加，这样可以引起读者的兴趣。

4. noted 在这里不是过去分词，而是形容词，相当于 well-known。

5. 这句话，原文的动词是"有"，译文却不能用 have，而要用 are，这是因为译文用的是倒装句，主语是 the Five-Dragon Pavilions，而 on the north shore of the lake 是地点状语。

★ 6. built in 1602 和下面一句里的 put up in 1756 都是分词短语，而没有像原文那样用并列成分。

7. Not far to the northeast 和下一句里的 Near there 也都是译者所加，借以说明景物的相对位置，免得孤立地介绍景物，显得单调。

附录：

Bei Hai Park

...Bei Hai Lake surrounds Qiong Hua Island which is 5,166 ft. (1,912m.) in circumference. On the Island you will find many pavilions and multi-storied buildings with colorful glazed tiles. It is on this Island that the lovely Fang Shan Restaurant can be found. Occupying the whole center of the Island is the White Dagoba built in 1651 A.D. on the ruins of the original palace 119 ft. (35.9m.) high. If one climbs to the top of the hill on which it stands and gazes out, the scenery near and far spreads itself out and it is a spectacular view.

On the northern shore of Bei Hai is the Pavilion of the Five Dragons. Constructed in 1602 A.D. and jutting out over the water, their reflections resemble five clusters of new flowers blooming on the water's surface. Here you will also find the famous Nine Dragon Screen. This Screen, or wall, is 87 ft. (26.5m.) long and over 15 ft. (4.6m.) high. On both sides there are nine dragons chasing a pearl amid the waves. The wall is made entirely of colorful glazed tiles and one gets the feeling that each of the dragons is about to break forth from the wall.

(from *The Official Guidebook of China*)

―――― 译学点滴 ――――

提高文字水平无止境

常常有人对我说：这段英文我看懂了，只是翻不出来，或者说，只是翻不好。为什么外国文字能看懂，用自己的语言反倒说不出呢？这说明我们使用汉语的能力还有待于提高。要提高，就要看别人是怎样使用汉语的。可以看长篇巨著，也可以看报刊短文。编者就很喜欢看报纸上的小文章。

吕叔湘在《光明日报》发表过一篇文章，题目是"新的和旧的语文教学"。第一段是这样写的：

旧的教学法只管三件事：识汉字，读汉字读物，写汉字作文。目标单纯，循序渐进，应该收效快，效果好，可是实际并非如此。新的教学法，既要学会读拼音读物，写拼音作文，又要学会读汉字读物，写汉字作文，外带还要学好普通话，学会口头表达，学习的项目比旧的教学法多，可是任务完成得比旧教学法好。这不是很奇怪的吗？

这段话，开门见山，文字简洁，论点清楚。若按我们那种四平八稳的写法，至少一开头要说"旧的语文教学法……"，加"语文"二字。但作者只说"旧的教学法……"，这就和下面的"新的教学法"形成鲜明的对照。其实，题目已经说明本文谈的是语文教学，所以不会引起误解。

冰心在《北京晚报》发表过一篇文章："漫谈赏花和玩猫"。其中有这样一段话：

我最记得的是一只名叫"哈奇"的全黄色的哈巴狗，最机灵了，会逮耗子。它是我弟弟们的好朋友。我的弟弟们到北海划船，它会凫水跟在船后。弟弟们玩够了，骑车回家，它就水淋淋地跟在车后飞跑。惹得一位站在门口看街的老太太，向我弟弟们叫："学生，别让您的狗跑了，看它跑的这一身汗！"

这段文字多么生动活泼、自然流畅，而作者竟是一位86岁高龄的老人。如果不是读了全文,我真会以为这是从四十多年前的《寄小读者》里摘出的一段呢。

以上两位作者写文章时都已年逾古稀,但他们的作品却仍充满活力,大概因为作者的心永远是年轻的。此外,他们勤于写作,永不停笔,也是他们永葆青春的一个原因吧。

读名家的作品,不但能从风格上得到启发,细心的读者还会在遣词造句方面,在探索语言的规律方面,有很大收获。

赖少其写过一篇悼念冯雪峰的文章,题目是:"战斗、友谊与诗"。其中有这样一句:

> 在《霞光》一诗中,既写丁玲同志,又不限于写丁玲同志,而是更为广阔与深沉,主要是写苦难中的祖国、苦难中的人民和母亲。

这句话重复"丁玲同志"、重复"苦难中的",是很自然的,是合乎汉语的表达方式的。但若译成英语,恐怕就要用代词her,miserable 大概也只能出现一次吧。

周良沛写过一篇悼念丁玲的文章,题目是"三月雪"。文章是这样结尾的:

> 我想到噩耗传去,三月春城的雪,都像凝固成了素洁的花,在她的遗像前。

汉语散文一般是把地点状语放在动词之前。把状语放在动词之后,是英语的说法。"在她的遗像前"不但放在了动词后面,而且放在全文的最后。这样,文章最后给读者留下的印象就不是素洁的花,而是丁玲的遗像。这不更能引起人们的哀思吗?

《光明日报》发表过一篇郑义的文章,悼念37岁在西藏以身殉职的女编辑龚巧明,题目是"她走在永恒的路上"。其中有这样一段话:

> 据说龚巧明生前最后的文字是:"这积雪的山路上,每公里都摆着一个坚强的英灵。我是无数后来者中的一个,循着无数的英灵往前走,在这条永恒的路上。"……她的这段充满使命感与忧患意识的文字,不仅是她的墓志铭,也将是

我们大家的墓志铭。

这里有两点值得注意：第一，"在这条永恒的路上"放在动词之后，放在整个这段话的末尾，给人的印象是非常深刻的。郑义的文章不正是以此为中心思想的么？第二，"墓志铭"出现两次，这样的重复在汉语里听起来是很自然的。然而若把这句话译成英语，epitaph 恐怕也只能出现一次。

我们可以说也是走在一条永恒的路上，因为提高文字水平是没有止境的。

Exercise 6

将下列短文译成英语：

天坛公园

天坛[1]是明、清两代皇帝"祭天祈谷"[2]的地方，建于1420年，占地面积273公顷。主要建筑有祈年殿、[3]圜丘、[4]皇穹宇。[5]

祈年殿建于1420年，1545年改建为一座镏金宝顶的三重檐圆殿，[6]1890年重修，[7]1971年又进行了修整。祈年殿是皇帝祈谷的地方，殿高38米（包括6米高石座），直径30米，砖木结构，中间没有横梁。

皇穹宇建于1530年，著名的"回音壁"、[8]"三音石"[9]就在这里。

圜丘建于1530年，是皇帝冬至[10]"祭天"和夏季"祈雨"的地方。圜丘是镶有汉白玉[11]石栏杆的三层石台，站在台面中心说话，声音显得格外宏亮。

提示：

1. 天坛：the Temple of Heaven
2. 祭天祈谷：to worship heaven and pray for good harvest
3. 祈年殿：the Hall of Prayer for Good Harvest

4. 圜丘: the Circular Mound Altar

5. 皇穹宇: the Imperial Vault of Heaven

6. 镏金宝顶的三重檐圆殿: a cone-shaped structure with triple eaves and a gilded ball on the top

7. 据《中国名胜词典》这次重修是因为祈年殿于1889年遭雷击焚毁。

8. 回音壁: the Echo Wall

9. 三音石: the Triple Sound Stones

10. 冬至: the winter solstice

11. 汉白玉: white marble

Key to Exercise 6

参考译文:

The Temple of Heaven

The Temple of Heaven, built in 1420 and covering an area of 273 hectares,[1] was the place where the emperors of the Ming and Qing Dynasties worshiped heaven and prayed for good harvest. It[2] mainly consists of the Hall of Prayer for Good Harvest, the Circular Mound Altar and the Imperial Vault of Heaven.

The Hall of Prayer for Good Harvest, originally built in 1420, was turned into a cone-shaped structure with triple eaves and a gilded ball on the top in 1545. Burnt down in a thunderstorm,[3] it was rebuilt in 1890, and repaired in 1971. Used as a place for the emperors to pray for good harvest, the hall,[4] 38 metres high (including 6 metres of stone terrace) and 30 metres in diametre, is built of wood and brick,[5] with no beam in the centre.

Built in 1530,[6] the Imperial Vault of Heaven contains the famous Echo Wall and the Triple Sound Stones.

The Circular Mound Altar, also[7] built in 1530, was a place for the emperors to worship heaven on the winter solstice and to pray for rain in summer. It is a 3-layer stone terrace decorated with white marble railings. Speaking in the middle of the altar, one's voice will sound particularly loud and clear.

解说：

★ 1. 原文这一部分放在句末，和前面是并列谓语。译文把这一部分译作分词短语，放在主语和谓语之间，这样可以使句子分出层次，突出了天坛的作用。

★ 2. 这一句原文以"主要建筑"为主语，译文以 it 为主语，指前面一句所说的 The Temple of Heaven。这样可以保持前后主语一致。

3. 这是译者根据资料加的。如果不加，直接说 It was rebuilt... 显得突然。

★ 4. 原文重复"祈年殿"，译文用 the hall 就够了。

5. brick 作为建筑材料，可算是物质名词，不用复数。

6. 前面两段都以地名开始，此段以 Built in 1530 开始，使得文字有些变化。

7. 此处的年代和前面一句相同，所以加了 also。

Unit 4   Economy

Lesson 7 (E—C)

Bilingual Reading

A Global Economy

President Clinton realized—as all of us must—that today's economy is global. We live in an era in which information, goods and capital speed around the globe, every hour of every day. Whether we like it[1] or not, all of our fortunes are tied together. We are truly interdependent.

America supports international trade because we believe fundamentally that trade will enrich those nations who embrace[2] its discipline. The great promise[3] of trade is its potential to promote mutual prosperity—and to strengthen the bonds between sovereign nations.

The U.S. and China both demonstrate the potential of trade to improve the lives of our people. You know better than I the great achievements of the Chinese economy over the past two decades. In 1977, the sum total[4] of Chinese imports and exports was less than $15 billion,[5] putting China's share of world trade at 0.6 percent.[6] The most populous country in the world, China ranked a distant 30th among exporting nations. By 1993 China's exports and imports totaled nearly $200 billion. China had become the world's tenth largest exporter.

Since 1978, when China began opening its economy to increased foreign investment and trade, aggregate output has more than doubled. The strongest growth has occurred in the coastal areas near Hong Kong and opposite Taiwan, where foreign investment and modern production methods have spurred production of both domestic and export goods. Per capita[7] GNP[8] has grown at an average rate of 7.6% from 1980—1992.

The numbers are interesting, but how has this affected the people of China? In the last decade,[9] telephone connections rose more than 60%. Electrical production more than doubled to 621 million kilowatt hours. In short, China has improved the economic well being of its people.

The people of the United States also have experienced the benefits of world trade. Since World War II, the U.S. has been the world's largest economy[10] and, in most years, the world's largest exporter.

But the importance of trade in our economy has exploded[11] in the past three decades. In 1970, the value of two way trade was equal to just 13% of the U.S. economy. Last year, that figure, at 28%, was more than twice as high. In just the last seven years, jobs supported by U.S. exports (goods and services) have risen by 4 million, to a total of 11 million. That's almost one out of ten American jobs. Last year U.S. trade equalled $1.8 trillion.

Nor is the importance of trade likely to diminish for either China or the United States. China will continue to depend upon lucrative export markets to earn the foreign exchange it needs to develop and grow. At the same time, China's imports will supply the much needed machinery and technology to fuel[12] its continued development.

For the United States, new commercial opportunities will grow most rapidly in the emerging markets. We estimate that three quarters[13] of new export opportunities over the next twenty years—that's an incredible $1.9 trillion in potential exports—will come in the emerging markets of Asia and Latin America. This means jobs for American workers and a higher standard of living for the

American people.

（Excerpted from "Remarks by Ambassador Kantor at the University of International Business and Economics", 1995）

提示：

　　第四单元：经济。这里所选的文章着重说明经济形势，提出主张和建议，并且列举大量数据以说明问题。第 7 课是演说，所用语言虽然正式，但句子短，结构简单，比较上口。第 8 课选自一篇论述中国粮食问题的文件，语言正式而精练。

　　经济是一个很大的领域。要想作经济方面的翻译工作，必须熟悉大量的术语，而且要力求知晓新的术语。除了熟悉词语本身，还需要知道它们的用法，它们经常与哪些词连用。例如 statistics 一词，可以表示"统计"，也可以表示"统计数字"，因此 a couple of statistics 意思就是"几个统计数字"。

　　此外，经济文章总要涉及许多数字，而数字在英汉两种语言中都有一定的说法，不过有时也用不着翻译，抄上就行了。但数字特别容易出错，而且带来严重后果。要避免出错，只有一个秘诀——仔细核对。和数字有关的动词、介词、形容词、副词也十分重要。因此，原文要看准，译文要确切，不可马虎。比如"增加到"和"增加了"是不能混用的；"是……的几倍"和"增加了几倍"也是不同的。

　　关于第 7 课的对照阅读（BR7），请注意以下各点。

1．此处 it 指后面所说的情况。

2．embrace：to take up or adopt, esp. eagerly or seriously

3．promise：basis for expectation

4．sum total：总数，总额，是一个固定的说法。

★ 5．请注意本文中关于数量及数量变化的各种说法。

6．请注意这一说法，等于 accounting for 0.6 percent of world trade。

7．per capita：人均

8．GNP = gross national product 国民生产总值

9．in the last decade 指从说话的时候起，往前推算10年，即1985至1995年。

10．请注意 economy 的这一用法，此处指国家。

11．explode = to increase very rapidly

12．fuel 作为一个动词，意思是提供燃料。此处是形象性用法，相当于 to support。

13．请注意这一说法。一般不说 three-fourths，而说 three quarters。

译文：

一个全球性的经济

正如每个人必须认识到的那样，克林顿总统认识到当今的经济具有全球性质。我们生活在这样一个时代中，信息、货物和资金每时每刻在世界上流动。不管我们喜欢与否，我们所有的命运[1]都是相连的。我们真的需要相互依靠。

美国支持国际贸易，因为我们确信，贸易会使那些遵守行为准则的国家富裕起来。极其光明的贸易前景是促进相互繁荣和加强主权国家之间联系的潜在力量。

美中两国都显示一种能提高两国人民生活的贸易潜力。你们比我更清楚中国经济在过去20年中所取得的伟大成就。在1977年，中国进出口总额还不到150亿美元[2]，仅占世界贸易总额的0.6%，世界上人口最多的中国在出口国家中排名靠后，仅是第30位。到1993年，中国进出口总额接近2,000亿美元，它已成为第10个最大的出口国。

自从1978年以来，中国经济为日益增加的外国投资和贸易敞开大门，总产量增加了一倍多。[3]最强劲的增长发生在靠近香港和台湾对面的沿海地区。在这个地区，外国投资和现代生产手段的使用促进了国内和出口货物的生产。从1980年至1992年，人

均国民生产总值平均增长率为 7.6%。

看看数字是很有趣的。然而它又是怎样影响中国人的呢？在过去 10 年中，电话用户增加了 60% 以上。电力生产增加了一倍多，达到 6.21 亿千瓦小时。总之，中国提高了人民的生活水平。

美国人民也有得益于国际贸易的经历。自从第二次世界大战以来，美国一直是世界上最大的经济大国。[4]在大多数年代中，它又是世界上最大的出口国。[5]

但在过去 30 年中，我们经济贸易的重要性大大地增加了。在 1970 年，双边贸易[6]的总值占了整个美国经济的 13%。去年上升到 28%，比 1970 年增加了一倍多。[7]就在过去 7 年中，美国的出口（货物和服务）创造的就业机会增加了 400 万个，总数上升到 1,100 万个。这个数字就占美国就业总数的 1/10。[8]去年，美国贸易总额达到了 1.8 万亿美元。

无论是中国还是美国，都不会缩小贸易的重要性。中国会继续依靠获利的出口市场来赚取外汇以发展和增长自己的经济。同时，中国可用进口的机械和技术来加速它继续发展的速度。

对于美国来说，在不断涌现的市场上，新的贸易机会将以最快的速度增加。我们估计过，在未来的 20 年中，新的出口机会中的 3/4，即数量可观的 1.9 万亿美元的潜在出口额，将来自亚洲和拉丁美洲不断出现的市场上。这将意味着为美国工人创造就业机会，使美国人民提高生活水平。

（原文及译文均选自李正中《国际经贸英汉翻译》之附录）

解说：

1. fortune 一词可以理解为"命运"，也可以理解为"财富"。考虑到上一句提到"信息、货物和资金"，此处译作"我们所有的财富"可能更好。或者笼统一点，译作"我们的利益"。

★2. 在数字方面，汉英两种语言在"千"以上便没有相对应的数量单位了。汉语里有"万"和"亿"，在英语里是 ten thousand 和 hundred million；英语里有 million 和 billion，在汉语里则是"百万"

和"十亿"。因此，遇到较大的数字，千万要仔细算一算。此处 15 billion 译作 150 亿是对的，如不小心，是很容易译错的。

★ 3．翻译倍数，也是很容易出错的。double 是个常用的动词，表示翻一番，可译作"增加一倍"，而不是"增加两倍"。

4．economy 的本意是"经济"。此处的意思是"从经济角度看这个国家"，所以译作"经济大国"。

★ 5．exporter 可以指"出口商"、"出口公司"或"出口国"。此处指国家，当然译作"出口国"。

6．two way trade 可能是泛指"进出口贸易"，而不是某两个国家之间的贸易。恐应译作"双向贸易"。

7．was more than twice as high 字面上的意思是：是原来的两倍以上，和上面所说的 more than doubled 是一个意思。可译作"增加了一倍多"，但不能译作"增加了两倍多"。

★ 8．one out of ten 是英语里常见的一种说法,字面上的意思是"每十个里就有一个"。为了行文方便,可以译作"十分之一"。

————译学点滴————

用知识武装自己

第 3 课的对照阅读和练习都是选自雅各布·布洛诺夫斯基所著《人类的发展》一书第 8 章。这两篇短文涉及不少的人物、机构和历史事件。译者如果一无所知，便不能很好地理解原文，也就难以很好地翻译了。

比如文中提到 Newton，大家都知道他是有名的英国物理学家。Chaucer 是谁呢？是什么时代的人呢？知道的人可能就少一些了。James Brindley 和 the Duke of Bridgewater 又是谁？他们在英国历史上起过什么作用？知道的人恐怕就更少了。

再说机构。the Royal Society 是什么机构？谈到大学的时候，说 there were only two, at Oxford and Cambridge，这指的是哪两所大学？Grammar schools 是否只教语法？如果在谈论英国的教育制度时提到 public schools，这种学校是公立的，还是私立的呢？

除了 the Industrial Revolution 以外，文中还提到 the American Revolution that started in 1775 和 the French Revolution that started in 1789，这些革命的具体内容是什么呢？

此外，Manchester 在哪里？Liverpool 在哪里？the Church of England 是不是一所教堂的名字？

这些问题如不解决，便很难说对原文有了透彻的理解。

地理方面的文章，要译好，则需要一定的地理知识。第 5 课介绍尼罗河。尼罗河的一个支流是 the Blue Nile，汉语的定译是"青尼罗河"，如译为"蓝尼罗河"就不对了。此外，尼罗河的流向和我国江河的流向也很不一样，它自南向北流。如不意识到这一点，有些地方的词句就不一定能处理得好。

翻译经济方面的文章，所需要的知识就更广了。近年来用得比较多的两个词，一个是"知识经济"，knowledge-based economy 或 knowledge economy，一个是"世界贸易组织"，the World Trade Organization，简称 the WTO。译者不但要知道这两个词，还要对它们有所了解才好。

总之，翻译工作要求译者具有丰富的知识。而知识是慢慢积累起来的。我们每看一篇材料，译一篇文章，都会从中得到一定的知识。对于进取者来说，知识宝库的大门永远是敞开的。

Exercise 7

将下列短文译成汉语：

New Opportunities in China's Economic Cooperation with Other Countries
(An Excerpt)
by Robert D. Hormats

China is the world's largest developing nation and the US is the world's most developed large nation. Bilateral trade between the two[1] has grown impressively. In the early part of the 1970s, there was virtually no trade. Today, two way trade is something in the order of[2] $ 6 billion and increasing. Increasing amounts of American investment have taken place in China, and Chinese investment in the United States is also beginning. The result, I believe, is that we have built the beginnings of a sound foundation for future commercial and financial ties.[3] China's imports from the US, which amounted to $ 900 million in 1978,[4] rose to nearly $ 3 billion in 1982. Exports rose from $ 300 million to $ 2.3 billion during that period. Total Chinese trade has also risen dramatically,[5] from 1978 to 1983 Chinese exports increased from roughly $ 10 billion to $ 22 billion, while imports increased from $ 10 billion to just over $ 21 billion.

US investments in China in 1983 totalled roughly $ 85 million, there are more than 20 joint ventures[6] between the US and Chinese investors. In addition, over one half billion dollars have been invested by US corporations in offshore oil exploration.

There are reasons to be optimistic and to expect that commercial and financial relationships will grow in the future. But there are also difficulties to be resolved. Let me first address[7] reasons for expecting growth and then discuss the problems.

Reasons for Optimism

China's Strong Economic Performance

After a period of dramatic shifts in economic policy, China has decided on a stable and promising[8] economic course. It is aimed at adjusting the pace of modernisation to[9] China's resource capabilities and its goal of major increases in employment, providing incentives for agricultural and industrial productivity; strengthening light, labour intensive industries, using technology to modernise and promote the technological transformation of existing industries; and removing bottlenecks imposed by energy and transportation constraints.[10]

In many of these areas, particularly agriculture, the results have been very positive. Food production is increasing rapidly. Modernisation of industrial production is occurring throughout the country, and production units are merging to achieve important economies of scale. Economic growth has been roughly 10 per cent although it is faster in heavy industries and slower in some light industries than hoped for. I believe Chinese economic authorities recognise the problem and the next Five-Year Plan will address[11] it effectively.

提示：

1. nation 一词在前面已连续出现两次，所以这里只用 two, 就不重复了。

★2. in the order of 是一个固定词组，用于数量，表示"大约"。从文体上看，这是一个比较文的说法。

3. commercial and financial ties 和下面第 3 段里的 commercial and financial relationships 是同样的意思。

4. 这个定语从句如何处理？

5. dramatically = markedly, impressively

6. joint ventures: 合资企业

7. address 在这里和下面的 discuss 是同样的意思。

8. promising: indicating future success or good results

9. adjust...to...: 调整……使之适合于……

10. 此处 energy 和 transportation 都修饰 constraints。

11. 此处的 address 和注 7 不同，相当于 deal with, 但不是用语言，而是用行动。

Key to Exercise 7

译文：

中国对外经济合作的新机会
（摘录）
罗伯特·霍马茨

中国是世界上最大的发展中国家，而美国是最发达的大国，两国之间的双边贸易已有显著的发展。[1]70年代早期，美中之间实际上无贸易可言。[2]如今，两国双边贸易大约为60亿美元，并且还在增加。美国在中国的投资越来越多，中国在美投资也在进行。我相信，我们已经为今后的贸易与金融关系初步打下了坚实的基础。[3]中国从美国的进口额，1978年为9亿美元，到了1982年增加到近30亿美元。[4]在那个时期，出口额从3亿美元增长到23亿美元。中国的总贸易额也显著增长，从1978年到1983年，中国的出口额从大约100亿美元增加到220亿美元，进口额从100亿美元增长到210多亿美元。

1983年，美国在中国投资大约总计为8,500万美元；有20多个美中合资企业。此外，美国公司对近海石油勘探投资5亿多美元。

我们有理由感到乐观，并预期未来的贸易及经济关系将会发展，但也有困难尚待解决。[5]让我先谈谈可望发展的原因，然后再讨论问题所在。

乐观的理由：
中国在经济上的出色表现[6]

中国的经济改革经过戏剧性的转变后，[7]决定走上稳定而大有前途的道路，[8]它的目的在于：调整现代化的步伐，以适应其资源潜力及其大量增加就业机会的目标，刺激工农业生产率，加强轻工业及劳动密集型工业，利用技术重建及改造现有企业并使之现代化,[9] 以及排除由于能源及交通运输紧张所造成的障碍。

中国在许多领域里,特别是在农业上已经获得良好的效果。粮食迅速增产,[10] 全国都在发展现代化工业生产,生产单位合并构成大规模企业。经济增长率约有 10%,虽然重工业发展速度比希望的要快些,某些轻工业要慢一些。我相信中国经济管理部门已认识到这个问题,在下一个五年计划有效地克服这一问题。

(原文及译文均选自李正中《国际经贸英汉翻译》之附录)

解说:

★ 1. 原文是两句,译文合成一句。原文第一句说明两国的情况,用的是并列句,中间用 and 相连(这个 and 是一定需要的)。然后另起一句,说明两国间的贸易情况。若把两句合在一起,则还需要加连词,光靠逗号是不行的。所以分两句说,干净,利落。汉语则不需要这么多连词,译成一句,显得紧凑。

2. there was virtually no trade 不是绝对没有贸易,而是少得不值一提,就说没有,也是可以的,所以译作"实际上无贸易可言"。

★ 3. I believe 在原文里是插入语,插在主语和谓语之间。这样的插入语,在译文里还是放在句首较顺。此外,have built the beginnings of a sound foundation,若照字面译作"建立了坚实基础的开端"则十分别扭,因此译文不受词类的限制,加了一个副词"初步",译作"初步打下了坚实的基础"。

★ 4. 这一句原文是个复合句,定语从句提一下 1978 年的情况,句子的重点是说明 1982 年的情况。译文则用了并列结构。这种句子一般都是这样处理的。

5. 这里也是原文两句,译文合成了一句。分两句说,论点较为突出。译文合成一句,比较紧凑。

6. 舞台上的 performance 是"表演",工作中的 performance 就是"表现"了。修饰语 strong,若单独处理,很不好译,译文"出色表现"则是一个很好的搭配。此处,把 economic 一词译为

"在经济上的"放在前面,就比按照原文的语序译作"出色的经济表现"通顺多了。

7. dramatic 恐应译作"重大的"。另外,原文说的是 economic policy,而不是 economic reform。因此,这半句恐应译作"中国在对经济政策进行重大调整之后"。

★8. 译文在"决定"后面加了"走上"二字,就比"决定了稳定而大有前途的道路"通顺多了。汉语动词比英语用得多。在适当的地方加一个动词,往往可使译文更加流畅。

9. 原文没有"重建"的意思。这一部分似应译作"利用技术促进现有工业的技术改造并使之现代化"。

10. 原文 Food production is increasing rapidly 单独成句。译文把这个短句与下面一句合在一起。但从上下文看,可能与上面一句合在一起更为适宜。

Lesson 8 （C—E）

Bilingual Reading

中国能够依靠自己的力量实现粮食基本自给
（摘录）

　　立足国内资源，实现粮食基本自给，是中国解决粮食供需问题的基本方针。中国将努力促进国内粮食增产，在正常情况下，粮食自给率不低于95%，净进口量不超过国内消费量的5%。

　　现阶段中国已经实现了粮食基本自给，在未来的发展过程中，中国依靠自己的力量实现粮食基本自给，客观上具备诸多有利因素。根据中国农业自然资源、生产条件、技术水平和其他发展条件，粮食增产潜力很大。

　　——提高现有耕地单位面积产量有潜力。目前，中国同一类型地区粮食单产水平悬殊，高的每公顷7,500—15,000公斤，低的只有3,000—5,000公斤。在播种面积相对稳定的前提下，只要1996—2010年粮食单产年均递增1%，2011—2030年年均递增0.7%，就可以达到预期的粮食总产量目标。这样的速度与过去46年年均递增3.1%相比，是比较低的。即使考虑到土地报酬率递减的因素，也是有条件实现的。目前，中国的粮食单产水平与世界粮食高产国家相比也是比较低的，中国要在短时间内达到粮食高产国家的水平难度较大，但经过努力是完全可以缩小差距。通过改造中低产田、兴修水利、扩大灌溉面积、推广先进适用技术等工程和生物措施，可使每公顷产量提高1,500公斤以上。

　　——开发后备耕地资源有潜力。中国现有宜农荒地3,500万公顷，其中可开垦为耕地的约有1,470万公顷。中国政府将在加强对现有耕地保护的同时，加快宜农荒地的开发和工矿废弃地的复垦，未来几十年计划每年开发复垦30万公顷以上，以弥补同期耕地占用，保持耕地面积长期稳定。通过提高复种指数，使粮食作物播种面积稳定在1.1亿公顷左右。

（摘自《中国的粮食问题》第三部分）

译文：

China Can Basically Achieve Self-Sufficiency in Grain Through Self-Reliance
(An Excerpt)

The basic principle for solving the problem of grain supply and demand in China is to rely on the domestic resources and basically achieve self-sufficiency in grain.[1] China endeavors to increase its grain production so that its self-sufficiency rate of grain under normal conditions will be above 95 percent and the net import rate 5 percent, or even less, of the total consumption quantity.

China has basically achieved self-sufficiency in grain at the present stage, and[2] there are many favorable objective factors for her to maintain such achievement[3] by her own efforts in the course of future development: Natural agricultural resources, production conditions, technical level and some other conditions ensure[4] great potential in this respect.[5]

There is potential for increasing the yield per unit area on the existing cultivated land.[6] At present, the per unit area yield of grain[7] varies widely in the same districts, the highest yield being 7,500 kg to 15,000 kg per hectare, and the lowest 3,000 kg to 5,000 kg.[8] Given a relatively stable sown area,[9] China[10] can achieve its desired total grain output target if the annual average increase rate of per unit area yield is one percent from 1996 to 2010 and 0.7 percent from 2011 to 2030. Compared to[11] the annual average increase rate of 3.1 percent of the per unit area yield in the past 46 years, it is clear that one percent and 0.7 percent are fairly low. So, to achieve the target is totally possible even if the factor of diminishing land returns rate is considered. At present, China's per unit area yield of grain is low compared with countries with high grain yields.[12] It will be difficult for China to reach the level of countries with high grain production in a short period of time, but the gap can certainly be narrowed through earnest efforts. The grain output per hectare can be increased by[13] more than 1,500 kg through the upgrading of medium and low yield land, intensifying water-control projects, enlarging irrigated areas and spreading the use of advanced agrotechnology.[14][15]

There is also potential for exploiting untouched arable land resources. China now has 35 million hectares of wasteland which are suitable for farming.[16] Of this, about 14.7 million hectares can be reclaimed. The Chinese government will make efforts to speed up the reclamation of wasteland suitable for farming as well as land discarded by factories and mines, while measures will be adopted to protect the existing cultivated land.[17] In the next few decades China plans to reclaim more than 300,000 hectares each year to make up for the loss of cultivated land appropriated for non-farming uses and to keep the area of cultivated land constant for a long period of time. The grain-sown area will be stabilized at about 110 million hectares through the increase of the multiple crop index.

(from *Beijing Review*)

解说：

★1. 这个句子，原文的结构是先说具体内容，再说"是……的基本方针"。这样的句子译成英语，一般都是从 The basic principle 说起，顺着说下去。

★2. 这句话比较长，前半句说已经做到的事，后半句说将来要做的事，中间并不需要用连词连接。译成英语，如果仍在一个句子里用两个分句，中间则需用 and 连接。这是一种最简单最常见的连接办法。

★3. 原文前半句说了"实现粮食基本自给"，后半句又重复一遍，这种重复在汉语里是很普遍的，在英语里则不行，如果重复，就显得太啰嗦了。所以译文在后半句用了 to maintain such achievement，以避免重复。

★4. 句中的名词在译文中都有相当确切的对应词，选择的余地很小。但译文用了一个原文里没有而又非常灵活的动词 ensure，把那些名词组织起来，成为一个句子。结构虽与原文不同，意思却是一样的。

★5. 增产粮食的意思，上面说了很多，所以这里译作 in this respect 就够了。

6. 译文以 There is potential 开头，后面多长都不怕，否则就显得头重脚轻了。

★7. "水平"二字没有译出，但意思包含在里面了。译文 the per unit area yield of grain varies widely 是很顺的。产量差别很大，就是水平悬殊。若硬把 level 一词塞进去，反而很别扭。

★8. 这一句原文包含三个短句，貌似并列，但仔细分析起来，可以看出不同的层次。先总地说一下水平悬殊，再具体说高的多少，低的多少。因此译文用一个简单句说明总的情况，接着用了两个并列的独立结构：the highest yield being...和 the lowest...，中间用 and 相连。这样分出层次的译法是符合英语的表达方式的。

★9. 请注意 given 的这种用法。given 在这里不是过去分词，而是介词，相当于 taking something into account，表示考虑到某种情况，或具备了某些条件，因此"前提"二字的意思就包含在里面，不必再单独处理了。

10. 这一句原文是个无主句。根据上下文，也考虑到本文的文体，译文加了 China 作主语。

★11．过去 compare to 和 compare with 有严格的分工，前者用来比较不同的事物（即用作比喻），后者用来比较相同的事物。近年来有一种趋势，两种情况都可以用 compare to。但用作比喻时，仍要说 compare to，而不能说 compare with。

12．译文在这里断句。先说水平比较低，然后另起一句，说明可以缩小差距，这样处理，句子比较利索。

★13．英语表示增加多少数量，要在数量前加 by，因此这里的译文是 can be increased by more than 1,500 kg...

14．原文有"生物措施"，译文显然是漏掉了。

15．这一句的结构是"通过……可使……"，可以说是个无主句。译文没有增加主语，而是把原来的宾语作主语，谓语用被动语态。

16．宜农荒地，译文找不到简短的形容词放在前面，因此译作定语从句 which are suitable for farming，放在 wasteland 后面。这样一来，句子虽然不长，也在这里断了句，这样处理比较利索。

17．在这一句里，"在……的同时"显然不是句子的重点，因此译作 while measures... 放在后面，而把后面要紧的话提到前面来了。

————译学点滴————
严谨的学风

翻译工作是极其细致的文字工作。除了在译初稿时就要尽量照顾到各项细节以外，译完初稿后还要进行修改和核对。译初稿时，注意力往往放在每个句子上，而对句子之间的联系可能照顾不够，修改时便可多注意通篇是否联贯，语气是否通顺。有时这里去掉一个"的"字，那里加上一个"了"字，就会显得通顺多了。如果在译完初稿后，放上几天再来修改，往往会比当时修改效果更好。如果能把译文朗读一下，自己亲耳听一听，对修改译文也是大有好处的。

　　细致的核对也是非常必要的。就连最细心的译者，在译初稿时也难免有所疏漏。即使句子的主要部分都在，也会这里丢掉一个时间状语，那里丢掉一个地点状语，或者少一个副词或形容词。日期、数字更是容易出错，如把 September 译作 12 月，把 December 译作 9 月，把 July 译作 6 月，把 Thursday 译作星期二，把 3,000 译作 300,000，把 12 亿译作 12 billion 等。提到一系列的国家或人名时，很容易丢掉一两个。最好数一数原文里有几个，再数一数译文里有几个，看是否一致。当然，即使数目一致了，也还可能把字写错了，如把"土耳其"写成"土尔其"，把"菲律宾"写成"菲列宾"，把"新西兰"写成"新锡兰"，等等。这些错误一定要避免。

　　在这一方面，我国已故著名考古学家夏鼐为我们做出了榜样。他逝世以后，《光明日报》发表了一系列文章介绍他的事迹。其中提到这样一件事：他在未审完的最后一份译稿里，把原译"英国协会"改为"英国科学促进协会"。他这样改是很有道理的。原译者所依据的原文大概是 British Association，但这只是一个简称。英国人往往喜欢用这个简称。萧伯纳在《十六幅自画像》一书里也用了这个简称。全称应该是 British Association for the Advancement of Science。如果只译作"英国协会"，中国读者会不知道这是个什么组织，改为"英国科学促进协会"就清楚了。

　　在另一篇文章里还提到这样一件事：夏鼐在审阅一本 37 万字的大书时，把全书末尾的一张内容非常详细的表格同文章的有关内容做了核对，结果发现一座汉墓中男女尸体的位置和文字部分不同。此书作者对他的治学精神表示极为佩服。的确，这样严谨的治学精神，我们也应该努力学习。我愿以此与这本翻译教程的读者共勉。

Exercise 8

将下列短文译成英语：

新中国解决了人民的吃饭问题

饥饿始终是半殖民地、[1]半封建[2]的旧中国的一大难题。旧中国的农业发展水平极为低下，有80%的人口长期处于饥饿半饥饿状态，[3]遇有自然灾害，更是饿殍遍地。1949年新中国成立时，全国每公顷粮食产量只有1,035公斤，人均粮食占有量仅为210公斤。

中华人民共和国建立后，政府废除了封建土地所有制，[4]带领人民自力更生，[5]奋发图强，大力发展粮食生产，用占世界7%左右的耕地，养活了占世界22%的人口。1995年与1949年相比，粮食总产量增长了3倍多，年均递增3.1%。目前，中国粮食总产量位居世界第一，人均380公斤左右（含豆类、[6]薯类[7]），达到世界平均水平。人均肉类产量41公斤、水产品21公斤、禽蛋14公斤、水果35公斤、蔬菜198公斤，均超过世界平均水平。据联合国粮农组织[8]统计，在八十年代世界增产的谷物中，中国占31%的份额。中国发展粮食生产所取得的巨大成就，不仅使人民的温饱问题基本解决，生活水平逐步提高，而且为在全球范围内消除饥饿与贫困作出了重大贡献。

(摘自《中国的粮食问题》第一部分)

提示：

1. 半殖民地的：semi-colonial
2. 半封建的：semi-feudal
3. 此处可以断句。
4. 所有制：ownership
5. 自力更生：self-reliance
6. 豆类：legume

7. 薯类: tuber

8. 联合国粮农组织: the UN Food and Agriculture Organization

Key to Exercise 8

译文:

New China Has Solved the Problem of Feeding Its People

The semi-colonial and semi-feudal old China was perennially haunted by the specter of starvation.[1] For long periods of time in the old days 80 percent of the population suffered from starvation or semi-starvation because of the extreme backwardness of agricultural production. Natural disasters nearly always resulted in widespread deaths from starvation.[2] In 1949 when the People's Republic of China was founded, the national grain yield per hectare was only 1,035 kg, and the per capita share of grain was only 210 kg a year.

After the founding of the People's Republic, the feudal ownership of land was abolished. Under the leadership of their government, the Chinese people devoted themselves to developing grain production through self-reliance and hard work. As a result, China is now able to feed 22 percent of the world's population on about 7 percent of the world's cultivated land.[3] Total grain output in 1995 more than quadrupled[4] the 1949 figure, or[5] an average increase of 3.1 percent a year. At present, China ranks first in total grain output in the world, with[6] the per capita share of grain reaching approximately 380 kg (including legume and tuber crops), which is the global average. The per capita production of meat, aquatic products, eggs, fruit and vegetables has reached 41 kg, 21 kg, 14 kg,

35 kg and 198 kg respectively,[7] which are all higher than the world average. Statistics from the UN Food and Agriculture Organization show[8] that China contributed 31 percent of the world's increased grain output in the 1980s. China's significant achievements in developing grain production have not only basically eradicated the problem of people not having enough to eat and wear[9] and gradually raised the living standards of the Chinese people, but also made great contributions to the worldwide efforts to eliminate starvation and poverty.

(from *Beijing Review*)

解说：

★1. 这一句译文用了一个不同的结构。以 old China 为主语，后接被动语态 was haunted by...，表示"为……所困扰"。此处用实义动词比用连系动词更为生动有力。

2. 译文用了一个简单句，通过动词 resulted 把主语 natural disasters 和宾语 widespread deaths 连结起来，显得特别简洁。

3. 这一句原文较长，包括许多内容。译文分为三句，每句有一个中心内容，比较清楚。

4. 原文"增长了三倍多"，也就是相当于原来的四倍多。译文 more than quadrupled 正是此意。

★5. 此处以 or 相连，表示"也就是说"。参看 BR5 提示第 4 条。

★6. 原文前后两个分句中间并无关联词。译文以 with 相连，引出一个介词短语。

7. 此处译文把五种产品集中起来说，把五个数量也集中起来说，是为了避免重复。按照原文的结构，主语应该是 The per capita production of...，即便后面只重复 that of，也会显得很累赘的。

★8. Statistics from... show 是一个常见的说法。"据……"不一定译作 according to...。

9. "温饱问题"还可译作 adequate food and clothing。

Unit 5   Culture

Lesson 9   (E—C)

Bilingual Reading

How to Grow Old

by Bertrand Russell[1]

In spite of the title, this article will really be on[2] how not to grow old, which, at my time of life, is a much more important subject. My first advice would be to choose your ancestors carefully.[3] Although both my parents died young, I have done well in this respect as regards my other ancestors.[4] My maternal grandfather, it is true, was cut off in the flower of his youth at the age of sixty-seven, but my other three grandparents all lived to be over eighty. Of remoter ancestors I can only discover one who did not live to a great age, and he died of a disease which is now rare, namely, having his head cut off. A great-grandmother of mine, who was a friend of Gibbon,[5] lived to the age of ninety-two, and to her last day remained a terror[6] to all her descendants. My maternal grandmother, after having nine children who survived, one who died in infancy, and many miscarriages, as soon as she became a widow devoted herself to women's higher education. She was one of the founders of Girton College, and worked hard at opening the medical profession to women. She used to relate[7] how she met in Italy an elderly gentleman who was looking very sad. She inquired the cause of his melancholy and he said that he had just parted from his two grandchildren. "Good gracious," she exclaimed, "I have seventy-two grandchildren, and if I were sad each time I parted from one of them, I should have a dismal existence!" "Madre snaturale," he replied. But speaking as one of the seventy-two, I prefer her recipe.[8] After the age of eighty she found she had some difficulty in getting to sleep, so she habitually spent the hours from midnight to 3 a.m. in reading popular science. I do not believe that she ever had time to notice that she was growing old. This, I think, is the proper recipe for remaining young. If you have wide and keen interests and activities in which you can still be effective, you will have no reason to think about the merely statistical fact of the number of years you have already lived, still less[9] of the probable brevity of your future.

As regards health, I have nothing useful to say since I have little experience of illness. I eat and drink whatever I like, and sleep when I cannot keep awake. I never do anything whatever on the ground[10] that it is good for health, though in actual fact[11] the things I like doing are mostly wholesome.

Psychologically there are two dangers to be guarded against in old age. One of these is undue absorption in the past. It does not do to live in memories, in regrets for the good old days, or in sadness about friends who are dead. One's thoughts must be directed to the future, and to things about which there is something to be done. This is not always easy; one's own past is a gradually increasing weight.[12] It is easy to think to oneself that one's emotions used to be more vivid than they are, and one's mind more keen. If this is true it should be forgotten, and if it is forgotten it will probably not be true.

The other thing to be avoided is clinging to youth in the hope of sucking vigour from its vitality. When your children are grown up they want to live their own lives, and if you continue to be as interested[13] in them as you were when they were young, you are likely to become a burden to them, unless they are unusually callous. I do not mean that one should be without interest in them, but one's interest should be contemplative and, if possible, philanthropic, but not unduly emotional. Animals become indifferent to their young as soon as their young can look after themselves, but human beings, owing to the length of infancy, find this difficult. (to be continued)

(from *Portraits from Memory and Other Essays*)

提示：

第五单元：文化。这里所选的文章探讨了人生，生与死，以及人与人之间的关系。文章夹叙夹议，语言生动，文情并茂，感人至深。

关于第 9 课的对照阅读（BR9），请注意以下各点。

1. 本文作者罗素（Bertrand Russell, 1872—1970）是"20世纪声誉卓著、影响深远的思想家之一。在其漫长的一生中，完成了四十余部著作，涉及哲学、数学、科学、伦理学、社会学、教育、历史、宗教以及政治等各个方面。"（《简明不列颠百科全书》）在本文中，作者没有板起哲学家的面孔，而是先以诙谐的语调和生动的语言讲述自己家中的一些情况，使人倍感亲切，继而严肃地阐述人生的哲理，令人信服，给人以莫大的启迪。

2. 介词 on 在这里是什么意思，怎样处理？

3. to choose your ancestors carefully, 这当然是不可能的。作者之所以这样说，无非是为了幽默，以创造一种轻松的氛围。

4. my other ancestors 指什么人，怎样处理？

5. 在英国一提 Gibbon, 一般人都会知道指的是谁。在中国，知道的人恐怕就不多了。可以加注。

★ 6. a terror: a terrifying person

★ 7. relate: give an account of/tell, 这个词比较文。

8. recipe: method of achieving something

9. still less... 是一个简略的说法，为了避免重复，意思是 you will have still less reason to think about the merely statistical

fact of the probable brevity of your future。

10. ground: reason/justification

11. in actual fact 意思与 in fact 相同。加 actual 一词，是为了加强语气。

12. weight: burden of responsibility/worry

13. interested 以及下面一句里的 interest 是什么意思，如何处理？

参考译文：

怎样才能活得老
罗　素

　　题目虽然这样写，[1]实际上本文所要谈的却是人怎样才可以不老。对于像我这样年纪的人来说，这个问题[2]就更是重要得多了。我的头一条[3]忠告是，你可得要挑选好你的先人[4]啊。我的父母年纪轻轻就去世了，可是说到祖辈，[5]我还是选得不错。[6]我外祖父固然是在风华正茂之年就弃世了，当时他只有六十七岁，[7]但是我的祖父、祖母和外祖母[8]却都活到了八十以上。再往远一点说，在我的先人之中，我发现只有一位活得不长，他得了一种现在已不多见的病，那就是头让人砍掉了。我的一位曾祖母，和吉本*是朋友，活到了九十二岁，她直到临终都使儿孙望而生畏。我外祖母有九个孩子活了下来，有一个孩子很小就死了，她还流产过多次。丈夫一死，她就致力于女子高等教育。[9]她是戈登学院的创办人之一，曾竭力使医学专业对妇女开放。她常对人说，她在意大利碰到过一位愁容满面的老先生，就问他为什么闷闷不乐，他说两个小孙孙刚刚离开他。"我的天哪！"我外祖母就说，"我的孙子孙女有七十二个，要是每离开一个都要难过，我的生活可就

---

　　* 吉本（Edward Gibbon, 1737—1794）是英国历史学家，著有《罗马帝国之衰亡》(*The Decline and Fall of the Roman Empire*)。——译注

太痛苦了。"听了这话,[10]老先生竟说,"Madre snaturale"。* 但是我作为七十二人中的一员,倒是赞成她的办法的。她过了八十以后,常睡不着觉,所以从午夜到凌晨三点总要读些科普读物。我相信她从来没有工夫[11]去注意自己是不是在日益衰老。我认为,要想永葆青春,这是最好的办法。你要是有广泛的爱好和强烈的兴趣,而且还有能力参加一些活动,你就没有理由去考虑自己已经活了多少岁这样的具体数字,更没有理由去考虑自己的余年大概是很有限的了。[12]

谈到健康问题,我就没有什么可说的了,因为我没怎么生过病。我想吃什么就吃什么,想喝什么就喝什么,[13]眼睛睁不开了就睡觉,从来不为对身体有益而搞什么活动,然而实际上我喜欢做的事大都是有助于增进身体健康的。

从心理方面来说,到了老年,有两种危险倾向需要注意防止。一是过分地怀念过去。[14]老想着过去,总觉得过去怎么好怎么好,或者总是为已故的朋友而忧伤,这是不妥的。[15]一个人应当考虑未来,考虑一些可以有所作为的事情。要做到这一点并非总是很容易的;自己过去的经历就是一个越来越沉重的包袱。[16]人们往往会对自己说,我过去感情多么丰富,思想多么敏锐,现在不行了。[17]如果真是这样的话,那就不要去想它,[18]而如果你不去想它,情形就很可能不是这样了。

另一件需要避免的事就是老想和年轻人呆在一起,希望从青年的活力中汲取力量。孩子们长大之后,就希望独立生活,如果你还像在他们年幼时那样关心他们,你就会成为他们的累赘,除非他们特别麻木不仁。我不是说一个人不应当关心孩子,而是说这种关心主要应该是多为他们着想,可能的话,给他们一些接济,而不应该过分地动感情。[19]动物,一旦它们的后代能够自己照料自己,它们就不管了;但是人,由于抚养子女的时间长,[20]是难以这样做的。(待续)

(译自《记忆中的肖像及其它》)

---

* 这句话是意大利语,意思是:"这个做母亲的真怪呀!"——译注

解说：

1. in spite of 用作介词，后面可以跟名词。在汉语里，"尽管"或"虽然"后面却不能直接用名词，因此译文用了主谓结构。

★2. which 指前面提出的问题，用在这里很方便。译文将一句分两句，汉语也没有类似 which 的词，因此用"这个问题"来概括前面的话。

3. my first advice 若译作"我的第一条忠告"，就显得过于正式，译作"我的头一条忠告"，语气就比较灵活，合乎整个第一段话的风格。

4. 看到 ancestor 一词，往往容易联想到"祖先"，但"祖先"的含义是指年代比较久远的上代，而从下文看，ancestors 在这里要包括父亲，所以译作"先人"。

5. other ancestors 在这里显然不包括父母，所以译作"祖辈"。

★6. 原文前面一句说了 to choose your ancestors carefully，这一句为了避免重复，换了一个说法，I have done well in this respect。汉语不怕重复，而且译文把这一部分调到了句末，因此译作"我还是选得不错的"，而没有译作"我在这一方面还是做得不错的"。

7. 此处若译作"在风华正茂的六十七岁就弃世了"，则显得过于局促，不如分开译较为从容。

★8. 汉语没有一个适当的词能够兼顾祖父、祖母、外祖父、外祖母。所以这里只好把 grandparents 具体化，根据上下文，译为"祖父、祖母和外祖母"。

★9. 原文这一句较长，主语和动词之间有好几个定语、状语从句和短语，译文无法保持这样的结构，将一句分为两句，先说她生过几个孩子，再说她在丈夫死后的生活。

10. 这里加了"听了这话"四个字，这是为了语气上的连贯。

★11. 原文 I do not believe that she ever had time to... 否定词跟第一个动词连用，这是英语的用法。汉语则是否定词与第二个动词连用，因此译作"我相信她从来没有工夫去……"。

12. 原文为了避免重复，用了一个省略的说法。汉语无法省略，只好重复"没有理由去考虑自己……"。

13. I eat and drink whatever I like, 英语把吃喝连在一起说，汉语则不能说"我想吃喝什么就吃喝什么"，而只好分开译作"我想吃什么就吃什么，想喝什么就喝什么"。

★14. undue absorption in the past 是一个名词短语，其中包含一个抽象名词。若照字面译作"对过去的过分怀念"，则不顺。因此译文用了一个动宾结构，译作"过分地怀念过去"。处理抽象名词，这是一个常用的方法。

★15. It does not do to... 英语是先表态，后说明情况，汉语则往往先说明情况，后表态，因此译文最后才说"这是不妥的"。

16. weight 的本意是"重物"或"负担"，汉语"包袱"二字正是此意。

17. 这一句也可照原文的结构译作"我过去感情比现在丰富，思想比现在敏锐"。但考虑到与下文的连接，就不如译作"我过去感情多么丰富，思想多么敏锐，现在不行了"。

★18. it should be forgotten 没有照字面译作"那就应该把它忘掉"，而译作"那就不要去想它"，也是反译之一例。

★19. 原文用了三个形容词：contemplative, philanthropic 和 emotional, 这三个形容词含义比较丰富，汉语很难找到与之相对应的形容词，因此分别译作"多为他们着想"，"给他们一些接济"和"动感情"。

★20. 看到 infancy 一词，往往容易想到婴儿时期。但从上下文看，此处的 infancy 指一个人能独立生活以前的整个时期，对父母来讲，也就是"抚养子女的时间"了。

翻译理论简介

佛经翻译

我国的翻译事业最初是从翻译佛经开始的。东汉时代,天竺人摄摩腾、竺法兰翻译《四十二章经》,这是我国现存佛经中最早的译本。佛经翻译经过晋朝逐渐发展,到了隋唐达到鼎盛时期。南宋以后趋于衰微。

在这漫长的一千年中,出现了不少著名的译师。下面只介绍其中的三个人:释道安、鸠摩罗什和玄奘。

释道安(314—385) 东晋前秦时高僧。在他的监译下译了《四阿含》、《阿毗昙》等。他还对以前的译本作了校录和整理工作。他是主张直译的。译文不增不减只在词序上作些调整。

鸠摩罗什(344—413) 后秦高僧。他和弟子僧肇等译出《摩诃般若波罗蜜经》、《妙法莲华经》、《金刚般若波罗蜜经》等,共74部,384卷,对佛教在中国的发展起了重要的作用。在翻译过程中,他倾向于意译,常对原文加以改动,以适应中国的文体。他的译法虽然灵活,态度却很谨慎。因此他的译文既准确又流畅。

玄奘(602—664) 唐高僧,俗称唐僧。曾游学天竺各地达17年之久。回国后,译出经、论75部,1335卷。他译的经籍不但丰富了祖国的文化,而且为古印度佛教保存了珍贵的典籍。玄奘的译文与鸠摩罗什的译文相比,是倾向于直译的。但是他对自己提出的要求是"既须求真,又须喻俗。"再加上他工作勤恳、认真,他的译文质量是很高的。

综上所述,我国古代著名的佛经译师有的倾向于直译,有的倾向于意译,或者说有的直译成分多一些,有的意译成分多一些。说到这里,想起英国学者剑桥大学乔治·斯坦纳教授说过的一段话:"罗纳德·诺克斯把整个题目归结为两个问题。第一个问题是以何为主:文学性的译文,还是逐字翻译。第二个问题是译者是否有权选择任何文体与词语来表达原文的意思。把翻译理论局限于这样两个问题,而且这两个问题实际上也只是一个问题,未免过于简单化了。但是诺克斯的论点是提得适当的。大约两千年来,关于翻译之性质的看法与争论几乎始终是一样的。"这段话可以说是一个很好的概括吧。

参考书目:

1. 中国科学院文学研究所,《中国文学史》第一册,人民文学出版社,1963年。
2. 罗新璋编《翻译论集》,商务印书馆,1984年。
3. 马祖毅,《中国翻译简史》,中国对外翻译出版公司,1984年。
4. 赵朴初,《佛教常识答问》,中国佛教协会,1983年。
5. 释慧皎,《高僧传》,中华书局,1997年。

Exercise 9

将下列短文译成汉语:

How to Grow Old

(Continued)

by Bertrand Russell

I think that a successful old age is easiest for those who have strong impersonal interests involving appropriate activities. It is in this sphere that long experience is really fruitful, and it is in this sphere that the wisdom born of experience[1] can be exercised without being oppressive[2]. It is no use telling grown-up children not to make mistakes, both because they will not believe you, and because mistakes are an essential part of education. But if you are one of those who are incapable of impersonal interests, you may find that your life will be empty unless you concern yourself with your children and grandchildren. In that case you must realize that while[3] you can still render them material service,[4] such as making them an allowance[5] or knitting them jumpers, you must not expect that they will enjoy your company.[6]

Some old people are oppressed by the fear of death. In the young there is a justification for this feeling. Young men who have reason to fear that they will be killed in battle may justifiably feel bitter in the thought that they have been cheated of the best things[7] that life has to offer. But in an old man who has known[8] human joys and sorrows, and has achieved whatever work it was in him to do, the fear of death is somewhat abject and ignoble. The best way to overcome it—so at least it seems to me[9]—is to make your interests gradually wider and more impersonal, until bit by bit the walls of the ego recede, and your life becomes increasingly merged in the universal life. An individual human existence should be like a river—small[10] at first, narrowly contained within its banks, and rushing passionately past boulders and over waterfalls. Gradually the river grows wider, the banks recede, the waters flow more quietly, and in the end, without any visible break,[11] they become merged in the sea, and painlessly lose their individual being.[12] The man who, in old age, can see his life in this way, will not suffer from the fear of death, since the things he cares for will continue. And if, with the decay of vitality, weariness increases, the thought of rest will be not unwelcome. I should wish to die while still at work, knowing that others will carry on what I can no longer do, and content in the thought that what was possible has been done.

(from *Portraits from Memory and Other Essays*)

提示:

1. the wisdom born of experience: the wisdom that comes from

one's experience

2. oppressive: hard to bear; causing distress

★ 3. while = although

★ 4. render 和 service 常在一起搭配，可以说 render somebody a service，或 render a service to somebody，但这种说法比较正式。

5. allowance: money that is given regularly to someone, especially a child, for them to spend

6. company: being together with...

7. been cheated of the best things: been cheated so that they cannot enjoy the best things

★ 8. know: have personal experience of

9. so at least it seems to me = at least it seems so to me

10. small 的本意是"小"，在这里如何处理？

11. break: interruption in the continuity

12. being: existence

Key to Exercise 9

参考译文：

怎样才能活得老
（续）
罗　素

我认为，如果[1]老年人对于个人以外的事情怀有强烈的兴趣，并参加适当的活动，他们的晚年是最容易过得好的。在这一方面，他们[2]由于阅历深，是能够真正做得卓有成效的，也正是在这一方面，他们从经验中得出的智慧既可以发挥作用，又不致使人感到强加于人。告诫成年子女不要犯错误，那是没有用的，一来[3]他们不听你的，二来犯错误本身也是受教育的一个重要方面。但是如果你这个人对于个人以外的事情不发生兴趣[4]，就会感到生活空虚，要不你就老是惦记着儿孙。在这种情况下，你可要明白，虽然你还可以在物质方面给他们以帮助，比如给他们零用钱，或者为他们织毛衣，但你决不要指望他们会喜欢跟你作伴。

有些老年人因怕死而惶惶不安[5]。年轻人有这种情绪是情有可原的。如果[6]青年人由于某种原因认为自己有可能在战斗中死去，想到生活所能提供的最美好的东西自己都无法享受，觉得受了骗，因而感到痛苦，这是无可指责的[7]。但是对老年人来说，他经历了人生的酸甜苦辣，自己能做的事情都做到了，怕死就未免有些可鄙，有些不光彩了[8]。要克服这种怕死的念头[9]，最好的办法——至少在我看来——就是要逐渐使自己关心更多的事情，关心那些不跟自己直接有关的事情[10]，到后来，个人主义的壁垒就会慢慢消失，个人的生活也就越来越和社会生活融合在一起了。人生应当像条河，开头河身狭窄[11]，夹在两岸之间，河水奔腾咆哮，流过巨石，飞下悬崖。后来河面逐渐展宽，两岸离得越来越远[12]，河水也流得较为平缓，最后流进大海，与海水浑然一体，看不出任何界线[13]。从而结束其单独存在的那一段历程，但毫无痛苦之感[14]。如果[15]一个人到了老年能够这样看待自己的一生，他就不会怕死了，因为他所关心的一切将会继续下去。如果随着精力的衰退，日见倦怠，就会觉得长眠[16]未尝不是一件好事。我就希望工作时死去，知道自己不再能做的事有人会继续做下去，并且怀着满意的心情想到，自己能做的事都已做到了。

（译自《记忆中的肖像及其它》）

解说：

★ 1. 原文 who have... 是一个定语从句，概括地说明某些老年人的情况，并不专指任何人，若译作定语则因太长而显得累赘，因此在前面加了"如果"二字。

2. 原文先以 experience 为主语，又以 wisdom 为主语，后接被动语态，说得比较笼统，不涉及任何人。译文用了"他们"，这样前后呼应，语气比较连贯。

★ 3. both because... and because... 看见 because，往往容易想到"因为"。但"因为"、"所以"之类的词用多了，会使人觉得文字生硬。据《现代汉语词典》，"来"字"用在'一、二、三'等数词后面，列举理由"。因此，这里译作"一来……，二来……"，文字就显得比较灵活些。

★ 4. 原文 incapable of 后面接名词就行了，但汉语没有类似的结构，因此后面用了动宾结构，译作"对于个人以外的事情不发生兴趣"。

5. 这一句原文中的 oppressed 和前面一段里的 oppressive，其基本意思是一样的，都表示"引起烦恼"。不同之处在于 oppressive 是主动的，是使人烦恼，所以译作"使人感到强加于人"。而 are oppressed by 是被动的，是自己感到烦恼，所以译作"惶惶不安"。

6. 原文 who have reason to fear that they will be killed in battle 是个定语从句，译文也用了"如果"二字来引导，理由同注1。

★ 7. 原文 justifiably feel... 这个状语和动词的搭配在英语里是可以的，但在汉语里就不行。如果勉强译作"正当地感到"，"有理由地感到"，或者"无可指责地感到"，都不好。在这种情况下，可以把状语拿出来，单独处理，放在全句末尾，译作"这是无可指责的"。下面还有一句，根据同样的原因，把 painlessly lose... 译为"结束……但毫无痛苦之感"。

★ 8. somewhat abject and ignoble，两个形容词用 and 连接，这是英语中极为普通的一种说法。译成汉语就不一定保留这个结构，而可以分开说，译作"有些可鄙，有些不光彩了"。这样说较为自然，重复"有些"也没关系。

★ 9. 原文 The best way to overcome it，此处 it 指前面一句里的 the fear of death。译成汉语，不可能用代称。译成"这种念头"也不清楚。所以，不怕重复，译作"这种怕死的念头"。

★ 10. wider and more impersonal，又是两个形容词，用 and 相

连。译文参照注8所说的办法，分开处理，所以译作"关心更多的事情，关心那些不跟自己直接有关的事情"。

11. small 怎样译，要看它指的是什么。若指源头，可以说"源头很小"。但从上下文看，small at first 是指河的上游，因此译作"开头河身狭窄"。

12. the banks recede 是描写乘船航行所见景色常用的说法。recede 的本意是"向后退去"，河岸并不能退，因此这种感觉完全是航行时视觉造成的。此处译作"两岸离得越来越远"，也保留了原文的形象。

★ 13. without any visible break 的意思是：在河流入海的地方，很难看出河到哪里为止，海从哪里开始，海与河是难以划分的，所以这个词组译为"看不出任何界线"。此外，这个词组里本来没有动词，译成汉语却成了动宾词组，这也是汉语多用动词之一例。

★ 14. painlessly lose their individnal being 译作"结束其单独存在的那一段历程，但毫无痛苦之感"。副词拿出来，在后面单独处理。参看注7。

15. 这里又用了一个"如果"，情况如注1和注6。

★ 16. 此处 rest 是"死"的一种委婉说法，并不是指"休息"，所以译作"长眠"。

Lesson 10 （C—E）

Bilingual Reading

旧梦重温
冰　心

　　王一地同志从 1957 年就当了中国少年儿童出版社的编辑，我们在多次"儿童文学"的聚会中早就认识了。如今，能为他的这本散文集子作序，我觉得很荣幸。

　　我必须承认，我的时间和精力似乎越来越少了。一地同志送来的他的部分稿子，我不能仔细地欣赏，但我却充分感觉他的文章的魅力。如《海乡风情》写出了他对童年生活的眷恋。《心上的河流》写出了他对于小河流水的深情，这使我忆起我所热爱的无边的大海。

　　他在国内旅游过的地方，除了井冈山以外，都是我没有到过的！如丝绸之路上的阿克苏，青藏公路上的唐古拉、昆仑等，这又使我十分羡慕。这几年来，我因行动不便，整天过着"井蛙"的无聊生活，读了这游记，绚丽生动得如经其境，给了我很大的快乐。

　　他到过的国外地方，我在半个世纪以前就到过了，如伦敦、巴黎、罗马、佛罗伦萨等欧洲城市。虽然时代不同，我想历史古迹总该是依旧吧。如同旧梦重温一般，我回忆起 1936 年在伦敦的 3 个星期，在昼夜看不到日、月、星三光的浓雾之中，参观了大英博物馆、敏纳斯特教堂——访问了一些英国朋友。使我喜欢的就是在这个国家到处都是绿茵茵的，比解放前的北京看去舒服多了。

　　提到巴黎，我永远忘不了我在那里逗留的 100 天。我住在第 7 区以意大利诗人马利亚·希利达命名的一条街的 7 层楼上（我在《关于女人》里写的《我的房东》说的就是我在巴黎那一段生活中的一部分)。因为住处离罗浮宫很近,我就整个上午"泡"在罗浮宫里。蒙娜丽莎的画像是悬挂在一条长案的上面,在两根绿色蜡烛的中间。我常常立在这长案旁边,吃我的简单早餐——一包巧克力糖!吃过早餐,就出来坐在宫门台阶上,欣赏宫门口那一座大花坛,花坛里栽的是红、黄、白、紫四色分明的盛开的郁金香!(待续)

(选自《光明日报》)

参考译文:

Going Through Old Dreams
by Bing Xin

Comrade Wang Yidi became an editor of the China Children Press as early as 1957 and we came to know each other at the meetings[1] held by "Children's Literature". I find it a great honour to be asked to write a preface to this collection of his essays.[2]

I must admit that my time and energy seem to be running short.[3] I was unable to read carefully and enjoy[4] all the articles he had sent me, but I was fully aware of the charm of his writings. In "Episodes in My Homeland near the Sea", he revealed his love for his childhood life.[5] In "A River at Heart", he expressed his deep feelings towards the flowing water of a creek, which reminded me of my own love for the boundless, vast sea.

In China,[6] he has been to many places which I have never visited, with the exception of the Jinggang Mountains.[7] His trips to Aksu[8] on the Silk Road, the Danggula and the Kunlun Mountains on the Qinghai-Tibet Highway and many other places all aroused my envy. In recent years, unable to move about easily, I have been leading a dull life like that of "a frog at the bottom of a well".[9] Reading his travel notes gave me great pleasure because they are so colourful and vivid that I felt I was actually there.[10] Overseas,[11] he has been to places such as London, Paris, Rome and Florence in Europe, which I had visited half a century ago. Times are different, but the historic sites, I presume,[12] must have remained the same. Just like going through old dreams,[13] I remembered the three weeks I had spent in London in 1936. During that time,[14] when the sun, the moon and the stars were hidden behind the thick fog day and night, I visited the British Museum and the Westminster[15] and called on my English friends. What I liked best was the refreshing green which could be seen all over the country. It was much more pleasant to the eye than Beijing before liberation.

  Speaking of Paris, I could never forget the hundred days I had spent there. I lived on the sixth floor of a building in a street named after the Italian poet Maria Hilida in District 7 ("My Landlady"[16] included in my book *About Women* was based on some of my experiences in Paris at the time). As I was very close to the Louvre, I would loiter in the palace[17] the whole morning. The portrait of Mona Lisa was hung above a narrow, long table with two green candles on either side. I would often stand at the table,[18] having my simple breakfast—a bar of chocolate. After that,[19] I would come out and sit on the steps[20] at the entrance of the palace, enjoying the big flower beds near the gate filled with blooming tulips of distinctive red, yellow, white and purple.

解说:

  1. 此处"聚会"译作 meetings。parties 强调娱乐，get-togethers 过于随便，主要是闲聊。用在这里都不合适。"聚会"在这里恐怕主要是商量工作，所以还是 meeting 比较合适。

  2. 这一段，还可以译作: I find it a great honour to be asked to write a preface to this collection of articles by Comrade Wang

Yidi, who became an editor in the China Children Press as early as 1957. I came to know him at the meetings held by "Children's Literature".

3. running short 是一个成语，意思是"所剩不多"。short 在这里是副词。

★4. 原文是"仔细地欣赏"，在译文里，carefully 和 enjoy 不好搭配，所以译作 to read carefully and enjoy...

★5. 这一句和下一句，原文以篇名为主语，下面接"写出了……"，译文不以篇名为主语，而以 he（指作者）为主语，这样比较自然。

6. In China 提至句首，下面 many places 可以与 which 连得更紧一些。

7. 井冈山译作 the Jinggang Mountains，注意要加定冠词。

★8. 注意阿克苏、唐古拉、昆仑等地名的译法。

9. "井蛙"乃是"井底之蛙"的意思，所以译作 a frog at the bottom of a well。

10. 译文在中间断句。在最后一句里，译文先说感受，再解释原因，比较顺。

11. Overseas 放在句首，和前面一段的 In China 相呼应。

12. I presume 放在句中作为插入语，比放在句首作为主句，更为自然。

13. 此处点题，译文应与题目一致。

14. 这句译文断句，比较好安排。但加了 During that time，以保持与上文的联系。

15. the Westminster 是常用的省略说法，全称是 the Westminster Abbey。正式的中文译名是"威斯敏斯特教堂"，在较早的文学作品里有时译作"西敏寺"。

16. 原文《我的房东》本看不出性别。但此文收入《关于女人》一书，估计文中所说的房东是女性，所以译作 landlady，而不译作 landlord。另外，在英语里，篇名用引号，书名用斜体。

★17. 原文"罗浮宫"出现两次，译文为避免重复，第二次提到时译作 the palace。

★18. "长案"第一次出现时译作 a narrow, long table，第二次提到时只译作 the table。

★19. 原文是"吃过早餐"，前面一句刚说过 having my simple breakfast，所以此处只译作 After that。

20. 户外的台阶译作 steps。

————翻译理论简介————

严复与"信、达、雅"

我国近代翻译理论中最有影响的，要算严复提出的"信、达、雅"了。

严复（1853—1921）曾留学英国学习海军。1894年中日战争爆发后，发表文章主张维新变法。他翻译《天演论》，[1]宣传"物竞天择，适者生存"的观点，对当时思想界有很大影响。戊戌变法后，他又翻译了《原富》、[2]《群学肄言》、[3]《法意》、[4]《穆勒名学》[5]等。他是中国第一个系统介绍西方哲学的人。

严复在《天演论·译例言》里首次提出了"信、达、雅"的翻译标准。"信"指的是"忠实"，"达"指的是"流畅"，"雅"指的是"尔雅"。所谓"尔雅"，用严复自己的话来说就是"用汉以前字法、句法"。

用严复提出的标准来衡量他译的《天演论》，可以看出他并不十分重视"信"，他说"译文取明深义，故词句之间，时有所颠倒附益、不斤斤于字比句次"。他还说，这种作法"实非正法"。[6]然而对于"雅"，他是十分重视的。为了把西方的思想介绍给当时的中国知识分子，必须使用他们熟悉的语言。严复是达到了自己的目的的。

一百年来，严复提出的"信、达、雅"在中国翻译界起了很大的作用。人们对"信"和"达"没有什么争论，唯有"雅"字例外。再"用汉以前字法、句法"进行翻译是不行了。因此人们对"雅"字作过各种解释,发过各种议论。纵观各家之言,我认为周煦良教授的解释是比较可取的。

周煦良教授在"翻译三论"一文中说:"我认为应当作为'得体'来理解。得体不仅仅指文笔,而是指文笔基本上必须根据内容来定;文笔必须具有与其内容相适应的风格。"[7]他还说:"信、达、雅三者哪一个最重要?我以为要看内容而定。如果译的是《读者文摘》或旅游见闻,那就要着重达,便是漏译一两句也无关宏旨。如果译的是哲学、社会科学,特别是经典著作,信就应当放在首位。……至于文学翻译,那当然要讲究文笔。"[8]

如果一篇译文在内容上是忠实的,在语言上是通顺的,在风格上是得体的,那的确就是一篇很好的译文了。

---

1. T. H. Huxley, *Evolution and Ethics and Other Essays*.
2. A. Smith, *Inquiry into the Nature and Cause of the Wealth of Nations*.
3. H. Spencer, *Study of Sociology*.
4. C. D. S. Montesquieu, *L'esprit des Lois*.
5. John Stuart Mill, *System of Logic*.
6. 罗新璋编《翻译论集》,商务印书馆,1984年,第136页。
7. 同上,第973页。
8. 同上,第974—975页。

参考书目:

1. 王栻,《严复传》,上海人民出版社,1959年。
2. 严复译,《天演论》,科学出版社,1971年。
3. 马祖毅,《中国翻译简史》,中国对外翻译出版公司,1984年。

4．王佐良，"严复的用心"，《翻译：思考与试笔》，外语教学与研究出版社，1989年。

5．周煦良，"翻译三论"，《翻译论集》，商务印书馆，1984年。

Exercise 10

将下列短文译成英语：

旧梦重温
（续）
冰 心

意大利是我最喜欢的一个欧洲国家。它是用石头建造起来的：石头的宫殿、教堂，石头的斗兽场，[1]石头的雕像，[2]石头的道路，路边也常有喷泉。罗马是建在七山之上的城市，拥有大小500座教堂，我几乎都去过了。最大的是圣彼得、[3]圣玛利亚、圣约翰和圣保罗。梵蒂冈[4]就是在圣彼得教堂附近，是罗马教皇[5]的宫殿，这是一个"国中之国"！我进去看了，只记得门警是瑞士兵士，穿着黄色制服，别的没有印象了。

佛罗伦萨给我留下的，除了美术馆里的雕像和壁画[6]之外，还有一座座府第墙壁上的灯座，每座灯下都有一只拴马的铁环，是聚会或宴客时拴马用的，十分别致![7]

一地同志关于这些地方的描写，由于时代和注意点的不同，使我看到了那些地方的许多其他的侧面，也扩大了我的知识。

信笔写来，竟然差不多都是写我自己的回忆，这就说明了这本散文的魅力。我应该说一地同志这本回忆童年和旅游的散文集子，不但是青少年最好的读物，大人们也应当拿来看看。因为这是一本写情真挚、写景鲜明；[8]流畅、健康、引人向上的散文作品。[9]

1987年2月26日

（选自《光明日报》）

提示：

1. 斗兽场：arena
2. 雕像：statue
3. 圣彼得（教堂）：St Peter's
4. 梵蒂冈：Vatican
5. 教皇：Pope
6. 壁画：mural
7. 别致：unique
8. 鲜明：lucid

★ 9. 在英语里，because 引导的从句一般不能单独成句。

Key to Exercise 10

参考译文：

Going Through Old Dreams
(Continued)

Italy was my favourite country in Europe[1]. Built up with stone, it had stone palaces and churches, stone arenas, stone statues and stone[2] roads dotted with fountains on either side[3]. Rome was located on seven hills with 500 churches, big and small[4], and[5] I visited nearly all of them. The biggest ones were St Peter's, St Maria's, St John's and St Paul's. Not far from St Peter's was the Vatican[6], the palace of the Pope in Rome, constituting a country within a country[7]. I went there to have a look[8]. All I remember now is that the guards at the entrance were Swiss soldiers in[9] yellow uniforms[10].

What remains of Florence in my memory[11] is, apart from the sculptures and murals in the art galleries, the lamps on the walls of the mansions, with an iron ring under each of them, for tying horses at parties and banquets. It was just unique[12].

Owing to the difference in times and perspective, Yidi's description of those places has brought their other aspects to my attention[13] and broadened my knowledge.

Letting my pen take its course, I have written about practically nothing but my own memories and[14] this is proof of the charm of this collection of essays. I must say that Yidi's book about his childhood and his travels is a best choice for young people and should be read by adults as well, because[15] it is sincere in feeling and lucid in description. It is a very readable, healthy and inspiring book[16].

解说：

1. 这一句乃至这一段，说的都是过去的事。所以基本上都是用过去时。

2. 原文里，"石头"一词重复出现五次，是为了强调而有意重复的。因此译文用同样的手法，以取得同样的效果。

3. dotted with...是一个常见的说法，表示"到处可见"的意思。

★ 4. 原文是"大小500座教堂"，译文 big and small 却不能放在前面，而要放在 churches 后面，这是固定的用法。

★ 5. 这一句用 and 连接前后两个分句。

★ 6. 这是一个倒装句。以地点状语开始的句子，往往可以用倒装句。请参看：At the edge of the fields, rising in dramatic hills or stretching flat to the horizon, lay the brown barren deserts. (Ex.5)

7. 这一句原文用了三个"是"作谓语，而译文用了一个简单句，包含一个同位语，一个分词短语。

★ 8. 译文在此处断句。前面一句说的是过去的事，后面一句说的是现在的事，时态也不同，断句比较利索，否则还要设法用连词把两句连在一起。

9. 汉语表示穿着什么衣服，总离不开动词"穿"，但在英语里，用 in 就够了。

★10. 原文最后还有半句话"别的没有印象了"，没有译。汉语说一件事情，往往从正面说了，还要从反面说一说，并不觉得累赘。英语则不然。试把这一句译成 All I remember now is... and I don't remember anything else，是不是显得太啰嗦了？

★11. 原文"佛罗伦萨给我留下的"，联系上面一段最后一句来看，显然是指"给我留下的印象"，因此译文加了 in my memory。此外，请注意，remain 是个不及物动词，不能说 What Florence remains for me...。

12. 这一段原文只有一句话，最后以"十分别致"结束。译文里，the lamps 后面有三个修饰语：on the walls..., with an iron ring... 和 for tying horses...，结构十分谨严。此时若在句末把第二个修饰语中的 an iron ring 再拿出来单独谈一谈，则势必打乱原来的结构。因此，最后四个字单独处理，译作 It was just unique。如果不这样译，也可以把 unique 一词放在句子里，译作 with a unique iron ring...，不过，这样一来语气就减弱了。

★13. 原文"使我看到了……，也扩大了……"译作 has brought...to my attention and broadened... 句子比较平衡。不要一看见"使我……"，就译作 make me...。须知 make me do something 往往有强制的意思，要慎用。

14. 此处用 and 连接两个分句，与注5所说的情况相同。

★15. because 引导的从句，除非紧跟在一个问句后面，否则是不能单独成句的。若一定要单独成句时，可以说 This is because...。此处的译文中，because 把从句与上文连在一起了，这是最为常见的用法。

16. 原文的最后半句话单独译成一个句子，对本文推荐的作品作了概括的评价，作为文章的结尾，也格外显得简洁有力。

Unit 6 Literature (1)

Lesson 11 (E—C)

Bilingual Reading

Tess of the D'Urbervilles
(An Excerpt)

Once the club[1] was in the field, dancing began. Some girls started to dance with each other immediately; others just stood around, talking and looking.

Among this group there were three young brothers. They were too well-dressed to be villagers. The oldest was a vicar. The second was obviously a student. It was more difficult to guess the job of the third brother. Probably he was too young to have started anything yet. These three brothers were on a walking holiday[2] in the Vale of Blackmoor. They leant over the gate by the road, and asked someone about the meaning of the club dance. The two older brothers plainly[3] wanted to move on quickly, but the sight of a group of girls dancing without men seemed to amuse the third. He didn't want to leave in a hurry. So he took off his pack, put it on the grass, and opened the gate.

'What are you going to do, Angel?' asked the oldest.

'I want to go and have a dance with them. Why don't we all go in? Just for a minute or two—it won't take long.'

'No, no. Nonsense!' said the first. 'Dancing in public with a lot of country girls! I'm surprised that you could even think of it. Come along, or[4] it will be dark before[5] we get to Stourcastle. That's the only place we can stay tonight.'

'All right. I'll catch up with you and Cuthbert in five minutes.

Don't stop. I promise that I will,⁶ Felix.'

The two older brothers then left, and the youngest entered the field.

'This is a great shame,'⁷ he said, to two girls near him. 'Where are your men, my dears?'

'They haven't finished work yet,' answered one of the bravest. 'They'll be here soon. Would you dance with us, until they come?'

'Certainly. But what is one man among so many girls?'⁸

'Better than none. It's sad work dancing with one of your own sex. Now, pick and choose.'⁹

The young man looked at the group of girls, and attempted to choose someone. But because they were all so new to him, he didn't know where to start. So he took the nearest. This was not the speaker, as she had hoped; nor was it Tess Durbeyfield. Her noble D'Urberville blood had not yet started to help Tess.

The sound of the church clock suddenly reminded the young man that he ought to leave. As he left the dance, he saw Tess Durbeyfield. She looked at him, and he felt sorry, then, that he had not danced with her. When he had climbed the hill above the field he looked back. He could see the white shapes of the girls dancing on the grass. They all seemed to have forgotten him already.

All of them, except perhaps one. This white shape stood apart by the gate alone. He knew it was the pretty girl with whom he had not danced. Unimportant as the matter was,¹⁰ he felt that she was hurt by this. He wished that he had asked her to dance, and that he knew her name. She was so sweet, so soft-looking in her thin white dress. The young man felt he had acted foolishly. However, there was nothing he could do about it now. He turned and walked away, forgetting the matter.

  (from Thomas Hardy,[11] *Tess of the D'Urbervilles*, Simplified Version, Chapter 1)

提示：

  第六单元：文学（1）。这里所选的作品主要是对话，穿插一点叙述和心理描写。翻译对话要像对话，要能上口。不同的人在不同的场合，说起话来，更有其各自的特点。

  关于第 11 课的对照阅读（BR11），请注意如下几点。

  1. the club: women taking part in the club walk

  2. on a walking holiday = spending their holiday on a walking tour

  3. plainly: obviously

  4. or: otherwise

  5. How will you translate this "before"?

  6. I will = I will catch up with you and Cuthbert in five minutes.

  7. a great shame = a great pity

  8. what is one man among so many girls? = What is the use of one man when there are so many girls?

  ★ 9. pick and choose: an idiom, meaning "to select"

  ★ 10. unimportant as the matter was = although the matter was unimportant

  11. Thomas Hardy（1840—1928）English novelist and poet. His most important novels are: *Far from the Madding Crowd*（1874），*The Return of the Native*（1878），*The Mayor of Casterbridge*（1886），*Tess of the D'Urbervilles*（1891），and *Jude the Obscure*（1896）.

译文：

《德伯家的苔丝》
（摘录）

　　游行会一进场地，跳舞便立即开始。有几个姑娘马上互作舞伴[1]，开始跳起来，有一些只是站在四周，边看边说着话儿。

　　这群人中间，有三个年轻的兄弟。他们衣着讲究，所以不会是村里人。最年长的那个是牧师，第二个显然是学生。要猜出第三个兄弟是干什么的，可就困难多了。也许他年纪还太轻，还未曾开始做什么。这三兄弟正在布莱克摩山谷徒步游历度假。他们靠着路旁的栅门，探身[2]向人打听这游行会跳舞是什么意思。两个哥哥显然想赶快上路，可是那第三个却似乎被这没有男舞伴的姑娘们对舞的情景逗乐了。他不想急着离去。所以他卸下行装，放在草地上，把栅门打开了。

　　"安吉尔，你要干什么？"[3]老大问。

　　"我想去同她们跳一回。我们为什么不都去呢？就跳一两分钟[4]——用不了多少工夫。"

　　"不，不要去。胡闹！"[5]老大说。"在公共场所，与一大群乡下毛丫头跳舞！我真想不到[6]你竟会转到这么一个念头。一道走吧，要不然[7]，我们赶不到[8]斯图堡天就要黑了，那可是我们今晚上唯一能投宿的地方啊。"

　　"好吧。过五分钟[9]我就会赶上你和卡思伯特的。别停下来等我。我保证准赶上你们，费利克斯。"

　　两个哥哥走了，那最小的兄弟便走进场地里。

　　"真是万分可惜，"他对近旁的两个姑娘说。"亲爱的[10]，你们的小伙子[11]都上哪儿去啦？"

　　"他们还没干完活儿[12]哪，"胆子最大的姑娘[13]里有一个答道。"他们马上就会来的。你愿不愿意与我们一起跳，跳到[14]他们来啊？"

　　"当然愿意啦。可是这么多姑娘只有一个男人，又有什么用

114

呢?"

"总比一个都没强。女的跟女的跳[15],可没劲啦。来,挑一个吧。"

那年轻人看着这群姑娘,打算挑一个。但是,这些姑娘他一个也不认识,不知从哪个开始才好。所以他挑了一个离他最近的。他挑中的并不是那个答话的姑娘,那姑娘倒是希望自己中选的;也不是苔丝·德贝菲尔。她那高贵的德伯维尔家血统还没来帮她的忙呢。

一阵教堂钟声使这个年轻人突然想起他该走了。他在退出舞队时看见了苔丝·德贝菲尔。她朝他瞧瞧,他呢,对于没有同她跳舞,心里感到一阵懊丧。当他爬到高出舞场的那座小山时,他还回头张望[16]了一下。他看得到姑娘们的白色身影在草地上舞动着。看来,她们全都把他给忘了。

她们全都把他给忘了,可或许有一个人没忘[17]。这个白色的身影独自离群站在栅门边。他知道这就是他不曾同她跳舞的那个漂亮姑娘。虽说事非重要,但他感觉得到她为此而伤了心。他真希望自己当时请她跳了舞,现在又知道她的芳名,那该有多好[18]。穿着那身薄薄的白衣裳,她是多么可爱,多么温柔哪。那年轻人觉得自己刚才的行为太傻。可是现在他对此已不能做什么了。他转身走去,把这件事丢到了脑后。

(选自周令仪译《德伯家的苔丝》简写本)

解说:

★ 1. with each other 一般译作"互相",但此处修饰的是 dance,若译作"互相跳舞"就不通了。译文灵活处理,译作"互作舞伴,开始跳起来",是很合适的。

2. 乡间路边的小门,一般很低,只有半人高。此处译作"探身向人打听"是适宜的。

★ 3. 从这里开始是一段对话,请注意口语的特点。"你要干什么?"显然比"你要做什么?"更合乎口语的说法。此外,把对方的称呼放在前头，也比较符合汉语的习惯。

★4．在对话里，往往不用完整的句子。Just for a minute or two 只是一个时间状语，译文"就跳一两分钟"，也不是一个完整的句子。甚至还可以译得更短些，去掉动词"跳"字，译作"就一两分钟"，那就与原文更接近了。

5．nonsense 除了表示 meaningless words，还可以表示 foolish ideas 或 foolish behaviour，因此这里没有译作"胡说"，而译作"胡闹"。

★6．I'm surprised 译作"我真想不到"或"我真没想到"都合乎口语的说法，要译作"我感到惊讶"，就显得太文了。

★7．or 往往译作"否则"，这里译作"要不然"，体现了口语的特点。

8．before we get to Stourcastle 字面上的意思是"在我们赶到斯图堡之前"，这里译作"我们赶不到斯图堡……就……"意思是一样的，但文字更加通顺，也合乎口语的说法。所以，不要一看见 before，就先想到"之前"。

★9．in five minutes 不是"五分钟以内"，而是"五分钟之后"。此处译作"过五分钟"是对的。

10．my dear 是口语里常用的说法，尤其是老年人见着年轻人，更喜欢这样称呼他们。"亲爱的"也是一种常见的译法，此处似乎也可以译作"姑娘们"。

11．men 在不同的上下文里，可以有不同的含义。此处译作"小伙子"是适宜的。

★12．看到 work 一词，往往首先想到"工作"。此处 finished work 译作"干完活儿"，是比较自然的。

★13．看到 brave 一词，往往首先想到"勇敢"。其实这里无所谓勇敢不勇敢，只是有的姑娘比较腼腆，不愿与生人搭话，有的则胆子大些，愿意与生人搭话。因此这里将 the bravest 译作"胆子最大的姑娘"。

★14．看到 until 一词，往往首先想到"直到"。此处的译文是

"你愿不愿意与我们一起跳,跳到他们来啊?"重复一个"跳"字是很妙的。如果把"跳到"改成"直到",就不顺了。

15. 原文 It's sad work dancing with one of your own sex,说得比较笼统,大概是为了避免重复,若说得具体一点儿,可能就要说 It's sad work for a girl to dance with another girl。但汉语不怕重复,所以译作"女的跟女的跳,可没劲啦。"

★16. 最后这三段里有许多心里描写。此处原文是 he looked back,他之所以回头,是因为他感到有什么值得留恋的东西,译作"回头张望了一下",正好表达了他这种心情。

17. 这一句原文是个省略句,显然是与前面一段的最后一句密切相连。因此译文重复了前面的话,加上了动词。

★18. 原文 He wished that he had asked... 表示他有一种悔恨的心情,因此译文在句末加了"那该有多好"这几个字。

―――――翻译理论简介―――――

林 纾

林纾(1852—1924)字琴南,光绪举人。他不懂外语,依靠他人口述意思,由他以惊人的速度审词缀句,笔录下来。就这样,在将近三十年的时间里,他用文言文翻译欧美等国小说184种,其中不少是外国名作。例如《巴黎茶花女遗事》[1]《鲁滨孙漂流记》[2]《海外轩渠录》[3]《吟边燕语》[4]《块肉余生述》[5]《贼史》[6]《黑奴吁天录》[7]等。林纾的译作第一次使中国读者接触到这些外国文学作品,引起了他们对外国文学的兴趣,同时也打破了章回小说的旧格式,对中国的文学创作有很大的影响。

林纾为自己的许多译作写了序言,主要是说明译书的背景或对书中内容发些议论,涉及翻译理论和方法的地方极少。

六十年代初,我国著名学者钱钟书先生发表一篇文章,题为"林纾的翻译",对林纾的译文作了很高的评价。他写道:"我自己就是读了他的翻译而增加学习外国语文的兴趣的。""接触了林译，我才知道西洋小说会那么迷人。"[8] "最近，偶尔翻开一本林译小说，出于意外，它居然还没有丧失吸引力。我不但把它看完，并且接二连三，重温了大部分的林译，发现许多都值得重读，尽管漏译误译随处都是。我试找同一个作品的后出的——无疑也是比较'忠实'的——译本来读，譬如孟德斯鸠和迭更司的小说，就觉得宁可读原文。这是一个颇耐玩味的事实。"[9]他还说："林译除迭更司、欧文以外，前期的那几种哈葛德的小说也颇有它们的特色。我这一次发现自己宁可读林纾的译文，不乐意读哈葛德的原文。理由很简单：林纾的中文文笔比哈葛德的英文文笔高明得多。哈葛德的原文很笨重，对话更呆蠢板滞，尤其是冒险小说里的对话，把古代英语和近代语言杂拌一起。……林纾的译笔说不上工致，但大体上比哈葛德的轻快明爽。"[10]

更重要的是钱钟书先生在"林纾的翻译"一文中提出了一条新的标准。他写道："文学翻译的最高标准是'化'。把作品从一国文字转变成另一国文字，既能不因语文习惯的差异而露出生硬牵强的痕迹，又能完全保存原有的风味，那就算得入于'化境'。"[11]这个标准不是轻易可以达到的。钱先生本人也说："彻底和全部的'化'是不可实现的理想。"[12]因此，它只能作为一种努力的目标，而且限于文学作品。非文艺作品的翻译就更不要用这个标准来衡量了。

---

1. Alexandre Dumas, fils, *La dame aux camélias* (1848)
2. Daniel Defoe, *Robinson Crusoe* (1719)
3. Jonathan Swift, *Gulliver's Travels* (1726)
4. Charles Lamb and Mary Lamb, *Tales from Shakespeare* (1807)
5. Charles Dickens, *David Copperfield* (1850)
6. Charles Dickens, *Oliver Twist* (1838)
7. Harriet Beecher Stowe, *Uncle Tom's Cabin* (1852)
8. 罗新璋编《翻译论集》，商务印书馆，1984年，第699页。

9. 同上，第 700—701 页。
10. 同上，第 719—720 页。
11. 同上，第 696 页。
12. 同上，第 698 页。

参考书目：

1. 郑振铎，"林琴南先生"，《翻译论集》，商务印书馆，1984 年。

2. 钱钟书，"林纾的翻译"，同前。

3. 马祖毅，《中国翻译简史》，中国对外翻译出版公司，1984 年。

4. Wang Zuoliang, "*Two Early Translators Reconsidered*", Eastern Horizon, Dec. 1980.

Exercise 11

将下列短文译成汉语：

Ella Lorena[1]

'A new baby[2]! Why, Scarlett, this is a surprise!' he laughed, leaning down to push the blanket away from Ella Lorena's small ugly face.

'Don't be silly,'[3] she said, blushing. 'How are you, Rhett? You've been away a long time.'

'So I have. Let me hold the baby, Scarlett. Oh, I know how to hold babies. I have many strange accomplishments. Well, he certainly looks like Frank. All except the whiskers, but give him time.'

'I hope not. It's a girl.'

'A girl? That's better still. Boys are such nuisances. Don't ever have[4] any more boys, Scarlett.'

It was on the tip of her tongue to reply tartly[5] that she never intended to have any more babies, boys or girls, but she caught herself in time and smiled...

'Did you have a nice trip[6], Rhett? Where did you go this time?'

'Oh—Cuba—New Orleans—other places. Here, Scarlett, take the baby[7]. She is beginning to slobber and I can't get to my handkerchief. She is a fine baby, I'm sure, but she's wetting my shirt bosom.'

(from Margaret Mitchell, *Gone with the Wind*, Chapter 43)

提示:

1. 这个标题是编者加的。这篇短文是书中的男主人公和女主人公的一段对话,其中没有方言土语,没有不规范的说法,语言正规,但又非常上口。翻译时需注意这一特点,并在译文中尽量加以体现。

2. 这里需要一个很好的搭配。

3. 说这句话,是轻微地责怪对方不该说上面那样的话。

4. have: bear or beget (offspring)

5. tartly: sharply

6. 这是欢迎外出归来的人常用的一句话。译文听起来要自然。

7. 这里需要一个恰当的动词与"孩子"搭配。

Key to Exercise 11

参考译文:

爱拉·洛雷纳

"刚生的孩子!哎呀,思嘉,可真没想到哇!"[1]他一边说,一边笑了，同时弯腰掀开毯子，看了看爱拉·洛雷纳难看的小脸。

"看你说的，"[2]思嘉说，脸也红了。"瑞德，你好吧？你离开的时间不短啊。"[3]

"的确是这样。思嘉，让我抱抱孩子吧。唔，我知道怎么抱孩子。我有许多奇怪的才能[4]。他的确很像弗兰克，就是没有胡子，不过到时候会长的。"[5]

"还是别长的好。这是个女孩儿。"

"是个女孩儿？那就更好了。男孩子都讨人嫌。你可别再生男孩儿了，思嘉。"

思嘉本来想回敬他一句[6]，说无论男孩儿女孩儿都不想再生了，可是话到嘴边，她又收住了。她笑了笑……

"这次出去，一切都好吗，瑞德？你这次到了哪里？"

"唔，到了古巴——新奥尔良——还有一些别的地方。哎呀，思嘉，快把孩子接过去吧。她流哈喇子了[7]，我又没法掏手绢儿。我知道，她是个好孩子，不过她把我的前襟弄湿了。"

（选自《飘》第43章）

解说：

★ 1. surprise 若直接译作"惊讶"就比较文，所以从相反的角度来处理，译作"可真没想到哇！"

2. 这是口语里常说的一句话，有轻微责怪的意思。

★ 3. a long time 译作"时间不短"，也是反译之一例。

4. strange accomplishments 也可译作"你意想不到的才能"。

5. but give him time 若译作"但要给他时间"，意思就不清楚了。所以译作"不过到时候会长的"。

6. "回敬他一句"就把 reply tartly 的意思全包括进去了。

7. slobber 也可译作"流口水"，但"流哈喇子"更合乎口语的说法。

Lesson 12 （C—E）

Bilingual Reading

祝福
（摘录 1）
鲁　迅

　　她不是鲁镇人。有一年的冬初，四叔家里要换女工，做中人的卫老婆子带她进来了，头上扎着白头绳，乌裙，蓝夹袄，月白背心，年纪大约二十六七，脸色青黄，但两颊却还是红的。卫老婆子叫她祥林嫂，说是自己母家的邻舍，死了当家人，所以出来做工了。四叔皱了皱眉，四婶已经知道了他的意思，是在讨厌她是一个寡妇。但看她模样还周正，手脚都壮大，又只是顺着眼，不开一句口，很像一个安分耐劳的人，便不管四叔的皱眉，将她留下了。试工期内，她整天的做，似乎闲着就无聊，又有力，简直抵得过一个男子，所以第三天就定局，每月工资五百文。

　　大家都叫她祥林嫂；没问她姓什么，但中人是卫家山人，既说是邻居，那大概也就姓卫了。她不很爱说话，别人问了才回答，答的也不多。直到十几天之后，这才陆续的知道她家里还有严厉的婆婆；一个小叔子，十多岁，能打柴了；她是春天没了丈夫的；他本来也打柴为生，比她小十岁：大家所知道的就只是这一点。

　　日子很快的过去了，她的做工却毫没有懈，食物不论，力气是不惜的。人们都说鲁四老爷家里雇着了女工，实在比勤快的男人还勤快。到年底，扫尘，洗地，杀鸡，宰鹅，彻夜的煮福礼，全是一人担当，竟没有添短工。然而她反满足，口角边渐渐的有了笑影，脸上也白胖了。

（选自《鲁迅全集》第二卷）

译文：

The New Year's Sacrifice
(Excerpt 1)
by Lu Xun

  She was not from Luzhen. Early one winter, when my uncle's family wanted a new maid,[1] Old Mrs. Wei the go-between[2] brought her along.[3] She had a white mourning band round her hair and was wearing a black skirt, blue jacket, and pale green bodice. Her age was about twenty-six, and though her face was sallow her cheeks were red.[4] Old Mrs. Wei introduced her as Xianglin's Wife, a neighbour of her mother's family, who wanted to go out to work now that her husband had died.[5] My uncle frowned at this, and my aunt knew that he disapproved of taking on a widow. She looked just the person for them, though,[6] with her big strong hands and feet; and, judging by her downcast eyes and silence, she was a good worker who would know her place. So my aunt ignored my uncle's frown and kept her.[7] During her trial period she worked from morning till night as if she found[8] resting irksome, and proved strong enough to do the work of a man; so on the third day she was taken on[9] for five hundred cash a month.[10]

  Everybody called her Xianglin's Wife and no one asked her own name, but since she had been introduced by someone from Wei Village as a neighbour, her surname was presumably also Wei.[11] She said little, only answering briefly when asked a question.[12] Thus it took them a dozen days or so to find out bit by bit that she had a strict mother-in-law at home and a brother-in-law of ten or so, old enough to cut wood. Her husband, who had died that spring, had been a woodcutter too, and had been ten years younger than she was.[13] This little was all they could learn.[14]

123

Time passed quickly. She went on working as hard as ever, not caring what she ate, never sparing herself.[15] It was generally agreed that the Lu family's maid actually got through more work than a hard-working man. At the end of the year, she swept and mopped the floors, killed the chickens and geese, and sat up to boil the sacrificial meat,[16] all single-handed, so that they did not need to hire extra help. And she for her part was quite contented. Little by little the trace of a smile[17] appeared at the corners of her mouth, while her face became whiter and plumper.[18]

(Translated by Yang Xianyi and Gladys Yang)

解说：

★1. 时间状语后面跟一个 when 引导的从句，这是英语里常见的说法，值得注意。原文里的并列关系在译文里变成了主从关系，突出了后半句。"四叔"第一次出现时译作 Fourth Uncle，以后译作 my uncle。

2. 原文定语"做中人的"译成了同位语 the go-between。

3. 译文此处断句，下面另起一句描写祥林嫂的穿戴和相貌。

★4. 这一句原文先是一个短句，接着是三个名词短语，接着又是三个短句，译文则分为两句，先说她的穿戴，再说她的容貌，但两句都是主谓完整，连词齐全，这是英文行文所需要的。

★5. 这个 who 引导的定语从句，主要说明"出来做工"，所以把这一部分放在前头，然后再说原因是死了当家人，这和汉语按因果顺序安排句子迥然不同。

6. though = however

7. 这一句和上一句在原文里本是一句，没有主语。译文断为两句，第一句以 she 为主语，第二句以 my aunt 为主语。

★8. 此处加了 she found，保持前后主语一致。

9. 原文"定局"是个笼统的说法，译文则比较具体 she was taken on，这样好与下文衔接。

★ 10. 原文"每月工钱五百文"是一个完整的主谓结构，但英语只要一个介词短语 for five hundred cash a month 就够了。

★ 11. 原文的第二个短句省略的主语应是"大家"。第四个短句省略的主语应是"中人"，第五个短句省略的主语应是"祥林嫂"。英语不喜欢老换主语，要相对集中。因此译文主要突出了 Everybody 和 Xianglin's Wife，而把"中人"放到次要的位置上。

★ 12. 原文这一句虽然很短，却有三个独立的主谓结构，各有自己的主语。英语喜欢主语相对集中，所以译文只以 She 为主语，以 She said little 为主句，其余内容用分词表述。

13. 这一句主要是说明祥林嫂的丈夫生前做什么，多大年纪，因此译文将死去一事放在 who 引导的定语从句里了。在对人物作介绍的时候，经常要用 who 引导从句。

14. 这句话孤立地来看，也可以用动词 to know，全句译作：This little was all that people knew about her。但此处译文用了 could learn，和上文扣得紧一些，说明这就是十几天来人们能够了解到的情况。

★ 15. 原文"力气是不惜的"，译文是 not sparing herself，而没有译作 not sparing her strength，因为 to spare oneself 就是这个意思。

★ 16. 原文"彻夜的煮福礼"译作 sat up to boil the sacrificial meat。英语 to sit up，就是晚上不睡觉的意思，可以做各种事情，不一定是坐在那里。

17. "笑影"还不是明显的笑，只是微微的一点笑意，所以译作 the trace of a smile。

★ 18. fat 指全身发胖，而且略带贬义。此处说脸上显得胖了，译文用了 plumper。

———— 翻译理论简介 ————

鲁迅与瞿秋白

1957年人民文学出版社出版了十卷的《鲁迅全集》，又于

1958年出版了十卷的《鲁迅译文集》。

鲁迅曾在1932年编了一个"鲁迅译著书目"。从1921年至1931年这短短的11年中,鲁迅翻译和校订的作品就有34种之多,这包括苏联、日本、荷兰、匈牙利、美国等国家许多作家的作品。鲁迅的译作约占他全部作品的一半,可见他对翻译工作是何等重视。

鲁迅对翻译工作的态度是极其严肃认真的。他的好友许寿裳说:"那时我和他同住,目睹其在骄阳满室的壁下,伏案工作,手不停挥,真是矻矻孜孜,夜以继日,单是动植物的译名,就使他觉到不少的困难,遍问朋友,花去很多的精力和时间。"[1]他的妻子许广平说:"鲁迅自己对待他的翻译工作,也承认不是那么容易随便处理,而是逐字逐句、一丝不苟地,做一个把别地的异卉奇花移植到中土的辛勤的劳动者。"[2]

在理论方面,鲁迅曾针对当时赵景深的"宁顺而不信"的提法,提出了"宁信而不顺"的主张。[3]鲁迅强调要输入新的表现法,所以现在要容忍"多少的不顺"。[4]关于这个问题,鲁迅和瞿秋白于1931—1932年在他们关于翻译的通信中进行了详细的讨论。瞿秋白认为:"'信'和'顺'不应当对立起来……这里最重要的问题是:要创造新的表现方法,就必须顾到口头上'能够说得出来'的条件。"[5]他还说:"翻译应当把原文的本意,完全正确的介绍给中国读者,使中国读者所得到的概念等于英俄日德法……读者从原文得来的概念,这样的直译,应当用中国人口头上可以讲得出来的白话来写。为着保存原作的精神,并不用着容忍'多少的不顺'。相反的,容忍着'多少的不顺'(就是不用口头上的白话),反而要多少的丧失原作的精神。"[6]

1935年,鲁迅在"'题未定'草"一文中又对翻译作了新的概括。他说:"凡是翻译,必须兼顾着两面,一当然力求其易解,一则保存着原作的丰姿。"[7]也就是说,翻译既要通顺,又要忠实。这不但是必要的,而且也是可能的。

1.《翻译论集》，商务印书馆，1984 年，第 320 页。
2. 同上，第 320 页。
3. 同上，第 275 页。
4. 同上，第 277 页。
5. 同上，第 280—281 页。
6. 同上，第 270 页。
7. 同上，第 301 页。

参考书目：

1. 鲁迅，"鲁迅译著书目"，载于《鲁迅全集》第 4 卷，人民文学出版社，1957 年。
2. "鲁迅和瞿秋白关于翻译的通信"，载于《翻译论集》。
3. 李季，"鲁迅对于翻译工作的贡献"，载于《翻译论集》。
4. 许广平，"鲁迅与翻译"，载于《翻译论集》。

Exercise 12

将下列短文译成英语：

祝　福
（摘录 2）[1]
鲁　迅

"我真傻，真的，"祥林嫂抬起她没有神采的[2]眼睛来，接着说。"我单知道下雪的时候野兽在山墺[3]里没有食吃，会到村里来；我不知道春天也会有。我一清早起来就开了门，拿篮盛了一篮豆，叫我们的阿毛坐在门槛上剥豆去。他是很听话的，[4]我的话句句听；他出去了。我就在屋后劈柴，[5]淘米，米下了锅，要蒸豆。我叫阿毛，没有应，出去一看，只见豆撒得一地，没有我们的阿毛了。他是不到别家去玩的；各处去一问，果然没有。我急了,⁶央人出去寻。直到下半天,寻来寻去寻到山墺里,看见刺柴⁷上挂着一只他的小鞋。大家都说,糟了,怕是遭了狼了。再进去;他果然躺在草窠里,⁸肚里的五脏⁹已经都给吃空了,手上还紧紧的捏着那只小篮呢。¹⁰……"她接着但是¹¹呜咽,说不出成句的话来。

(选自《鲁迅全集》第二卷)

提示:

1. 这一篇是祥林嫂讲的一段话,用的是口语体,翻译时请注意。
2. 没有神采的: lackluster
3. 山墺: gully/hills
4. 听话: to be a good boy
5. 劈柴: to chop wood
6. 急了: to get worried
7. 刺柴: bramble
8. 草窠: the wolf's den
9. 五脏: innards
10. 这一句包含四个短句,怎样译才比较紧凑。
11. 但是 = 只是

Key to Exercise 12

译文:

The New Year's Sacrifice

(Excerpt 2)

by Lu Xun

"I was really too stupid, really..." put in¹ Xianglin's Wife, raising her lacklustre eyes. "All I knew was that when it snowed and wild beasts up in the hills had nothing to eat, they might come to the villages. I didn't[2] know that in spring they might come too. I got up at dawn and opened the door, filled a small basket with beans and told our Amao to sit on the doorstep and shell them[3]. He was such a good boy; he always did as he was told[4], and out he went. Then I went to the back to chop wood and wash the rice, and when the rice was in the pan I wanted to steam the beans. I called Amao, but[5] there was no answer. When[6] I went out to look there were beans all over the ground but no Amao. He never went to the neighbours' houses[7] to play; and, sure enough, though I asked everywhere he wasn't there[8]. I got so worried[9], I begged people to help me find him. Not until that afternoon, after searching high and low[10], did they try the gully[11].

There they saw one of his little shoes caught on a bramble. 'That's bad,' they said. 'A wolf must have got him.' And sure enough, further on, there he was lying in the wolf's den, all his innards eaten away[12], still clutching that little basket tight in his hand..." At this point she broke down and could not[13] go on.

(Translated by Yang Xianyi and Gladys Yang)

解说：

1. 此处"接着说"是接着别人的话茬儿说，所以译作 put in, 而没有译作 continued。

★ 2. 此处是讲话，动词用了缩约式 didn't, 而没有用 did not。下面还用了 wasn't 和 That's, 也是同样的原因。

3. 这一句描写一连串的动作，译文用了几个并列的动词，但请注意译文是怎样用 and 连接的。此外，原文句末提到"剥豆"，但译文只说 shell them, 这是因为前面已经提到 beans, 为避免重复，这里用了代称。

★ 4. 译文在这里用了被动语态，用 he 作主语，保持前后主语一致。英语比较重视主语一致。若译作 he always did as I told him，语法上也是站得住的，但就不那么顺了。

★5．这一句译文加了 but，连接前后两个分句。

★6．此处译文加了 when，引导一个状语从句，否则句子就不通了。

7．"别家"单纯指邻居住的地方，因此译作 the neighbours' houses，而不用 family 或 home。family 强调家庭成员，home 感情色彩较重，用在这里都不合适。

★8．此处译文加了 though，其作用与注6所说的情况相似。

★9．这一句译文不是两个分句没有连接，而是中间省略了一个 that。这个 that 是可以用，也可以不用的。请看 *Oxford Advanced Learner's Dictionary*（OALD）所举的例子：She spoke so quietly (that) I could hardly hear her.

10．high and low 是一个固定词组，意思是 everywhere，经常与 search 连用。

11．did they try the gully 不是问句，却用了倒装语序，这是因为句子开头用了 Not until。

★12．这一句原文有三个主谓结构，译文只用一个简单句说明主要情况，其他情况用独立结构和分词短语表示了。

★13．这一句不是祥林嫂说的话，而是回到了作者的叙述，因此不能再用口语里使用的 couldn't，而用 could not。

Unit 7 Literature (2)

Lesson 13 (E—C)

Bilingual Reading

East of Eden
(An Excerpt)
by John Steinbeck[1]

    The Salinas Valley is in Northern California. It is a long narrow swale[2] between two ranges of mountains, and the Salinas River winds[3] and twists up the center until it falls at last into Monterey Bay.
    I remember my childhood names for grasses and secret flowers. I remember where a toad may live and what time the birds awaken in the summer—and what trees and seasons smelled like—how people looked and walked and smelled even. The memory of odors is very rich.
    I remember that the Gabilan Mountains to the east of the valley were light gay[4] mountains full of sun and loveliness and a kind of invitation,[5] so that you wanted to climb into their warm foothills almost as you want to climb into the lap of a beloved mother. They were beckoning mountains with a brown grass love. The Santa Lucias stood up against the sky to the west and kept the valley from the open sea, and they were dark and brooding[6]—unfriendly and dangerous. I always found in myself a dread[7] of west and a love of east. Where I ever got such an idea I cannot say, unless it could be that the morning came over the peaks of the Gabilans and the night drifted back from the ridges of the Santa Lucias. It may be that the birth and death of the day had some part in my feeling about the two

ranges of mountains.

From both sides of the valley little streams slipped out of the hill canyons and fell into the bed of the Salinas River. In the winter of wet years the streams ran full-freshet,[8] and they swelled the river until sometimes it raged and boiled, bank full, and then it was a destroyer. The river tore the edges of the farm lands and washed whole acres down; it toppled[9] barns and houses into itself, to go floating and bobbing[10] away. It trapped cows and pigs and sheep and drowned them in its muddy brown water and carried them to the sea. Then when the late spring came, the river drew in from its edges and the sand banks appeared. And in the summer the river didn't run at all above ground. Some pools would be left in the deep swirl places under a high bank. The tules and grasses grew back, and willows straightened up with the flood debris in their upper branches. The Salinas was only a part-time river. The summer sun drove it underground. It was not a fine river at all, but it was the only one we had and so we boasted about it—how dangerous it was in a wet winter and how dry it was in a dry summer. You can boast about anything if it's all you have. Maybe the less you have, the more you are required to boast.

(from John Steinbeck, *East of Eden*, Chapter 1)

提示:

第七单元：文学（2）。这里所选的作品主要是叙述和心理描写。有的对自然条件加以描述，有的讲述一件事情的过程。翻译这类作品，要注意连贯性，前后呼应。

关于第13课的对照阅读（BR13），请注意以下各点。

1. John Steinbeck was born in Salinas, California, in 1902 and died in December, 1968. His masterpiece, *The Grapes of Wrath*, won the Pulizer Prize in 1940. In 1962 he won the Nobel Prize for

Literature. His works include *Tortilla Flat* (1935), *Of Mice and Men* (1937), *The Moon Is Down* (1942), *The Pearl* (1948), *East of Eden* (1952), *The Winter of Our Discontent* (1961).

2. swale: a low place in a tract of land

3. wind [waind] (*v*.): go in a twisting manner

4. gay: suggesting happiness and joy

5. full of... loveliness and a kind of invitation: lovely and inviting you to go

6. brooding: melancholy/causing sadness

7. dread: fear

8. freshet: a sudden rise in the level of a stream due to heavy rains

9. topple: cause to fall down

10. bob: move quickly and repeatedly up and down, as on water

译文:

萨利纳斯河谷位于加利福尼亚州北部。那是两条山脉之间的一片狭长的洼地,萨利纳斯河蜿蜒曲折从中间流过,最后注入蒙特雷海湾。[1]

我记得儿时给各种小草和隐蔽的小花取的名字。[2] 我记得蛤蟆喜欢在什么地方栖身,鸟雀夏天早晨什么时候醒来——我还记得树木和不同季节特有的气息——记得人们的容貌、走路的姿态、甚至身上的气味。[3] 关于气味的记忆实在太多啦。

我记得河谷东面的加毕仑山脉总是阳光璀璨、明媚可爱,仿佛向你殷勤邀请,你不禁[4]想爬上暖洋洋的山麓小丘,正像爬到亲爱的母亲的怀里那样。棕色的草坡给你爱抚,向你召唤。西面的圣卢西亚斯山脉高耸入云,黑压压地挡在河谷和大海之间,显得不友好而危险。我发现自己一直对西方怀有畏惧,而对东方怀有喜爱。我说不出这种想法的根子在什么地方,也许是因为[5]黎明从加比仑山顶升起，夜晚从圣卢西亚斯山脊压下来。每一天的诞生和消亡也许使我对两条山脉产生了不同的感情。

　　洼地两面的小峡谷都有涧水流出，汇入[6]萨利纳斯河床。在多雨的年份，冬天水流充沛，引起河面暴涨，有时候汹涌翻腾，泛滥两岸，就成了祸害。[7]河水冲坏[8]农田边缘，毁掉大片大片的土地，使牲口棚[9]和房屋坍塌，卷入洪流，漂浮而去。牛、猪、羊走投无路，在黄褐色的泥水里眼睁睁地淹死，给带到海里。春末时分，河面变窄，露出[10]了沙岸。到了夏天，地上河水完全断流。[11]只有原先岸高漩涡深的地方才留下几个水塘。芦苇和茅草重新生长，柳树直起躯干，上部的枝桠还挂着洪水留下的枯枝败草。萨利纳斯只是一条季节性河流。夏天的太阳把它逼进了地底。它根本不是条了不起的河流，但是我们只有这一条，因此便为它吹嘘——说[12]它在多雨的冬天是多么危险，在干旱的夏天是何等枯竭。如果你别无他有，你可以为任何东西吹嘘。也许你有的东西越少，你就越要吹吹牛皮。[13]

(选自王仲年译《伊甸之东》)

解说：

　　1. until 不必译作"直到"。此处译文用并列谓语，中间并不需要用"直到"之类的词连接。

　　2. 原文 my childhood names for... 是一种很简洁的说法，汉语没有相对应的说法，因此译文略加发挥，译作"儿时给……取的名字"。

　　★3. 原文 remember 只出现一次，译文"记得"出现三次，这样才连贯。

　　★4. 原文 so that，此处译作"不禁"。后半句说"不禁"，前半句必定是有所感触，这正好表达了 so that 表达的联系。

　　5. unless 往往译作"除非"，但在这里译作"因为"。这句话的意思是：他说不出为什么有这种想法，除非是下面两件事使他产生这种想法。因此，译作"因为"是合适的。

6. fell 译作"汇入",反映了许多小溪流入萨利纳斯河的情景。

7. 在这一句里,until 又没有译。

★ 8. tore 是动词 tear 的过去式,其本意是"撕",在这里是一种形象的用法。译文没有用形象性词语,译作"冲坏",与主语"河水"是一个自然的搭配。

9. barn 一词,英国用法指谷仓,美国用法可以指谷仓,也可以指牲口棚。此处考虑到下文提到牛、猪等等,所以译作"牲口棚"。

10. appeared 在这里译作"露出",而不译作"出现"。

11. the river didn't run at all above ground,照字面可以译作"河水根本不在地面上流"。描写这种情景,汉语就说"断流"。因此这句话译作"地上河水完全断流"。

12. 译文在破折号后面加了一个"说"字,这就把前后的关系说清楚了,语气也连贯了。

13. 第3段和第4段,作者描述了故乡的山和水。在作者笔下,山成了有感情的东西,东边的山"给你爱抚,向你召唤",西边的山则"不友好而危险",作者也因此产生了他的爱与憎。那河水也成了有头脑有意志的东西,虽然每每造成水患,人们还要为它感到骄傲。通篇语言生动,情景交融。

———翻译理论简介———

郭沫若与茅盾

在我国,从 20 年代开始从事翻译工作,到 50 年代乃至 80 年代还在讨论翻译问题的,大概只有两个人,一个是郭沫若,一个就是茅盾。

郭沫若早在 1923 年就曾著文谈到理想的翻译。他说:"我们相信理想的翻译对于原文的字句、对于原文的意义,自然不许走转,而对于原文的气韵尤其不许走转。原文中的字句应该应有尽有,然不必逐字逐句的呆译,或先或后,或综或析,在不损及意义的范围以内,为气韵起见可以自由移易。这种译法并不是完全不可能的事情，它的先决条件是：（一）译者的语学知识要丰富，（二）对于原书要有理解，（三）对于作者要有研究，（四）对于本国文字要有自由操纵的能力。"[1]

1954年，郭沫若在全国文学翻译工作会议上讲话，对翻译工作的意义，翻译工作者应具备的条件，和应采取的态度作了详细的阐述。他说："翻译是一种创造性的工作，好的翻译等于创作，甚至还可能超过创作。这不是一件平庸的工作，有时候翻译比创作还要困难。"[2] 他还说："我们对翻译工作决不能采取轻率的态度。翻译工作者必须具有高度的责任感"[3]

1955年，他在致《俄文教学》编辑部的信中对翻译标准提出了他的看法。他说："原则上说来，严复的'信达雅'说，确实是必备的条件，但也要看所翻译的东西是什么性质。如果是文学作品，那要求就要特别严格一些，就是说你不仅要能够不走样，能够达意，还要求其译文同样具有文学价值。那就是三条件不仅缺一不可，而且是在信达之外，愈雅愈好。所谓'雅'，不是高深或讲修饰，而是文学价值或艺术价值比较高。"[4]

茅盾自20年代起，就对翻译问题发表过许多看法。他主张直译，同时又提倡保留"神韵"。他于1921年在一篇文章里说道："翻译文学之应直译，在今日已没有讨论之必要；但直译的时候，常常因为中西文字不同的缘故，发生最大的困难，就是原作的'形貌'与'神韵'不能同时保留。……就我的私见下个判断，觉得与其失'神韵'而留'形貌'，还不如'形貌'上有些差异而保留了'神韵'。"[5]

关于直译，他于1922年写道："直译的意义若就浅处说，只是'不妄改原文的字句'；就深处说，还求'能保留原文的情调与风格'。"[6]

1954年他在全国文学翻译工作会议上作了报告。他说："对于一般翻译的最低限度的要求，至少应该是用明白畅达的译文，忠实地传达原作的内容。……文学的翻译是用另一种语言，把原作的艺术意境传达出来使读者在读译文的时候能够像读原作时一样得到启发、感动和美的感受。……这样的翻译的过程,是把译者和原作者合而为一,好像原作者用另外一国文字写自己的作品。这样的翻译既需要译者发挥工作上的创造性,而又要完全忠实于原作的意图……。"[7]

1.《翻译论集》,商务印书馆,1984 年,第 331 页。
2.同上,第 498 页。
3.同上,第 499 页。
4.同上,第 500 页。
5.同上,第 337 页。
6.同上,第 343 页。
7.同上,第 343 页。

参考书目:
1.郭沫若,"理想的翻译之我见"。
2.郭沫若,"谈文学翻译工作"。
3.郭沫若,"关于翻译标准问题"。
4.茅盾,"译文学书方法的讨论"。
5.茅盾,"'直译'与'死译'"。
6.茅盾,"为发展文学翻译事业和提高翻译质量而奋斗"。

(以上各篇均载于《翻译论集》)

Exercise 13

将下列短文译成汉语:

The Sound of Music

(An Excerpt)

by Maria Augusta Trapp

Suddenly I heard quick footsteps behind me, and a full,

resonant voice exclaimed: "I see you are looking at my flag."

There he was—the Captain![1]

The tall, well-dressed gentleman standing before me was certainly a far cry from[2] the old sea wolf of my imagination. His air[3] of complete self-assurance and somewhat lordly[4] bearing would have frightened me, had it not been for[5] his warm and hearty handshake.

"I am so glad you have come, Fräulein..."[6]

I filled in, "Maria."

He took me in[7] from top to toe with a quick glance. All of a sudden I became very conscious of my funny dress, and sure enough, there I was diving under my helmet again. But the Captain's eyes rested on my shoes.

We were still standing in the hall when he said: "I want you to meet the children first of all."

Out of his pocket he took an odd-shaped, ornamented brass whistle, on which he piped[8] a series of complicated trills.

I must have looked highly amazed, because he said, a little apologetically: "You see[9] it takes so long to call so many children by name, that I've given them each a different whistle."

Of course, I now expected to hear a loud banging of doors and a chorus of giggles and shouts, the scampering feet of youngsters jumping down the steps and sliding down the banister. Instead, led by a sober-faced young girl in her early teens, an almost solemn little procession descended step by step in well-mannered silence—four girls and two boys, all dressed in sailor suits.[10] For an instant we stared at each other in utter amazement. I had never seen such perfect little ladies and gentlemen, and they had never seen such a helmet.

"Here is our new teacher, Fräulein Maria."

"*Grüss Gott, Fräulein Maria,*" six voices echoed in unison. Six perfect bows followed.

That wasn't real. That couldn't be true. I had to shove back that ridiculous hat again. This push, however, was the last. Down came the ugly brown thing, rolled on the shiny parquet floor, and landed[11] at the tiny feet of a very pretty, plump little girl of about five. A delighted giggle cut through the severe silence. The ice was broken.[12] We all laughed.

(from Maria Augusta Trapp, *The Sound of Music*)

提示:

1. Context shows that he was the captain of a warship.
★ 2. a far cry from: very different from
3. air: appearence/manner
4. lordly: (*adj.*) suitable for a lord
5. had it not been for ...: if it had not been for ...
6. The captain did not know the name of the young lady, so he left the sentence unfinished, waiting for the listener to complete it.
★ 7. He took me in: He looked at me, trying to find out what sort of person I was.
8. piped: blew (the whistle)
9. You see: a phrase used to introduce a remark, meaning "As I must explain to you".
10. "Procession", "descended" and "well-mannered silence" are formal words and phrases used here to add to the solemn atmosphere.
11. landed: stopped
★ 12. to break the ice: to overcome formality or reserve

Key to Exercise 13

参考译文:

音乐之声
(摘录)
玛丽亚·奥古斯塔·特拉普

我突然听见身后有急促的脚步声,接着就听见一个非常宏亮的声音说道:"看来[1]您是在看我的旗子哪!"

这个人,就是舰长。

站在我面前的是一位身材高大、衣着讲究的先生,与我先前想象的老海怪完全不同。他和我握手的时候是那样热情,那样真挚,要不然他那十分自信的神气和略为高傲的派头真会使我害怕呢。[2]

"你来了,我真高兴。[3]小姐您叫……"

我连忙说"玛丽亚"。

他以敏捷的眼光把我从头到脚打量了一番。我突然强烈地感到自己这身衣服非常可笑。我真的又拉了拉帽子,想在帽子底下躲一躲。[4]可是舰长的眼光却落到了我的鞋上。

这时我们还在大厅里站着。他忽然说:"我想让你先见见孩子们吧。"

他从口袋里掏出一个样子很怪但很精致的铜哨子,吹了一连串复杂的信号。

我一定是[5]显得很惊奇,因为他略带歉意地对我说:"你看,这么多孩子,要是一个个挨着叫名字,就得叫好半天,所以我就吹哨子,而且各有各的吹法。"[6]

这时我想一定会听到"砰!砰!"的关门声,叽叽嘎嘎的说笑声,孩子们下楼时嘈杂的脚步声,他们一定是连跑加跳,有的还要顺着扶手滑下来。可是看见的却是一支小小的队伍,在一个十来岁的沉静的女孩子带领下,规规矩矩不声不响地一磴磴走下来，简直可以说他们是非常严肃的。[7]他们是四个女孩子，两个男孩子，都穿着水手服。我们以非常惊奇的眼光彼此看了片刻。我从来没有见过这样出色的孩子，都像小女士、小先生一样，他们也从来没有见过我这样的帽子。

"这是我们新来的老师，玛丽亚小姐。"

"玛丽亚小姐，您好！"六个人齐声说道。接着又一本正经地鞠了六个躬。[8]

这不是真的。这不可能是真的。我不得不把那顶可笑的帽子又往后推一推。不过这一推可就完了。那棕色的丑东西一下子掉下来，在光亮的有图案的地板上滚了一会儿，在一个大约五岁的胖呼呼的漂亮姑娘那双小脚旁停了下来。[9]一阵咯咯的欢笑声打破了严肃而沉寂的气氛。谁也不拘束了，大家都笑了起来。[10]

解说：

1. 原文 I see 在这里的意思不是"我看见"，而是"我看得出"。所以译作"看来……"。

★ 2. 原文条件从句在后，译文将条件从句提前。原文可以用 warm 和 hearty 形容 handshake，如译作"热情真挚的握手"则不顺，所以把名词 handshake 译作动词，用"热情"、"真挚"形容主语"他"。

★ 3. 汉语一般先说具体的事，然后再说自己对这件事的看法或感受。

4. 原文用 dive 一词，是一种形象性的说法，意思是很快地钻到一个地方藏起来。译文无法保持原来的形象，所以译作"拉了拉帽子……"。

5. must 用在这里，意思不是"必须，"而是"必定"，表示一种推论。

6. 这句话不能译作"我给了他们每人一只不同的哨子"。

★ 7. 这一句比较文，所以译文用了"队伍"、"沉静"、"带领"、"严肃"等比较庄重的字眼。

8. 原文以 six voices 和 six bows 作主语，译文统一用"人"作主语，后面比较好处理。

★9. 原文 Down came ... 是一种加强语气的说法，landed 用在这里也显得过于庄重。作者用这种夸张的笔法来描写这顶帽子掉下来的情况，是为了引人发笑。译文用了"一下子"以加强语气，后面用了较长的定语，也是为了取得同样的效果。

10. 原文 The ice was broken，译文没有保留原文的形象，而是译出了它的具体含义。这样就可以和最后一句合并了。

Lesson 14 （C—E）

Bilingual Reading

找 点 活
新凤霞

在旧社会，我们评剧演员常常挣钱不够吃饭，艺人们大都是拉家带口，生活困难。演员们唱完戏还要各自找点儿活干，有人拉排子车，有人卖破烂，卖烟卷儿，当小工，拾烟头是普遍现象。

下雨或阴天回戏，不响锣就不给钱，是那时的规矩。腊月二十三封箱，把"祖师爷"请到前台去，后台冷冷清清，演员们就更苦了，要等到年初一开戏了，才能挣到钱。

我家里生活苦，父亲做小买卖，妈妈是家庭妇女，弟弟妹妹多；家里最大的是我，才十三岁，就唱戏养家了。真是一个钱撕成八瓣用，心里总想着怎样能够改善家里的困境。早晨去喊嗓子，我带着一个小篮拾煤核，为了回家取暖。拾煤核也要放聪明点儿，常常换地方，为的不受那些野男孩子的欺负。那些男孩子是成群结队的拾煤核，我是一个人，怕被他们欺负，我用换地方的办法，躲着他们。他们看见女孩拾煤核就捣乱，揪我的小辫，向我身上扔虫子，吓得我看见他们就躲。

腊月二十三灶王爷上天，后台封上戏箱，要等年初一开戏，封箱回戏，等于演员们封嘴，大家可苦了，各自找生活路子，我们女孩儿就做点女孩子能做的活。我同几个女孩子去东亚毛纺织厂当小工，分线头、扫地等干点杂活。每天天不亮戴着星星去排队，工厂没开大门就排上老长的队了。工头拿着皮鞭从大门出来，像轰牲口一样轰人，一个挨一个地用粉笔在人们背上写上号码，这个号码就是上工的证明。当这个小工真不容易。经常是排了一早晨队，大门才开；画了不多的号，工头就说："没号了！

没号了!"那种失望心情就别提多难受了!有一次是夏天,连阴天,连着回戏。我只好去排队找活干。还好,因为去得早,没等多久就画上号了。回家时忽然下了大雨,一路跑回家,我完全想不到自己被淋,只想着背上面的号,要是被雨淋掉,工就做不成了。我急着把衣服脱下来,大雨像飘泼一样。我把衣服紧紧抱在怀里,飞恰恰跑回家。回到家里打开一看就高兴了,号码一点也没有被淋湿;可我从头到脚淋成了落汤鸡了。(待续)

(选自《新凤霞回忆录》)

译文:

Looking for Work
by Xin Fengxia

In the old society, *pingju* players[1] seldom made enough to live on,[2] and as most were saddled with big families their life was hard. Apart from acting[3] they had to find other[4] work. Often[5] they pulled handcarts, sold junk or cigarettes, hired themselves out as coolies, or[6] collected cigarette stubs.

If a performance was cancelled because of bad weather, the rule in those days was: No show, no pay.[7] On the twenty-third of the twelfth lunar month, when theatres closed and the patron saint of actors*[8] was invited to the front stage, leaving the backstage deserted, actors were even worse off, unable to earn any more until the reopening on New Year's Day.[9]

My family was hard up, with[10] Father a peddler, Mother a housewife, and so many children to feed. At thirteen, as the eldest

---

* This was said to be the Tang emperor Minghuang, who founded the Pear Garden Company of actors. An altar for him was kept backstage, but moved to the front stage when the theatre closed.

child, I acted to help support the family.[11] Each single copper had to be eked out,[12] and I kept racking my brains for ways to improve our difficult conditions. Each morning when I went out to practise singing in the open air,[13] I took a little basket to scrounge for[14] cinders for our stove. Even when scrounging for cinders you had to have your wits about you and shift from place to place to avoid those mischievous boys who[15] banded together to collect cinders too. Being all on my own and afraid of being bullied by them, I shifted around to dodge them. Because when they found me scavenging they made trouble, pulling my plait or throwing insects at me, so that the sight of them frightened me away.[16]

On the twenty-third of the twelfth lunar month the Kitchen God went up to heaven, and the theatre shut down[17] until New Year's Day.[18] When that happened, actors' pay stopped[19] and they were hard put to it. Each had to fend for himself, and we young actresses did whatever work we could pick up. I went with some other[20] girls to the East Asia Woollen Mill to do odd jobs like unravelling strands of wool or sweeping the floor. We had to queue up before dawn when there were still stars in the sky.[21] A long queue formed before the mill's gate opened. The foreman came out with a whip, as if herding cattle, and chalked[22] a number on our backs, one by one. That number showed that we were taken on. But such small jobs were really hard to come by. Often, when we'd queued up for hours before the gate opened, after chalking a few numbers the foreman would say, "That's all! No more hands needed!"[23] At that we felt too disappointed for words![24] One summer a spell[25] of bad weather closed down our theatre, and I went to queue up. I was lucky. Becuase I went early, before long I had a number chalked on my back. By the time we knocked off[26] it was pouring with rain. As I ran home I didn't mind being soaked. I was only worried that if the rain washed off the number on my back I wouldn't be able to go to work the next day. I frantically took off my gown, while it rained cats and dogs.[27] Clutching my gown to my heart I flew home, and there, unfolding it, I was overjoyed to find that the number wasn't washed out, though I was drenched from head to foot like a drowned rat.[28] (to be continued)

(Translated by Gladys Yang)

解说：

1. "评剧"音译为 *pingju*，所以用斜体。"演员"译作 players，因为 actor 指男演员，actress 指女演员。

2. 原文"吃饭"在这里的意思是"维持生活"，所以译作 to live on。

★ 3. 原文"唱完戏"不是指每天唱戏之后，而是指不唱戏的时候，即在唱戏之外，所以译作 Apart from acting。

★ 4. 译文加了 other 一词，因为 acting 对他们来说也是工作，而且是他们的主要工作。

★ 5. "普遍现象"是用 often 一词来译的。phenomena 一词用在这里显得太大。

6. 请注意这个 or，表示有人干这个，有人干那个。

7. No show, no pay. 译文简洁，像是一条规矩，和原文也是吻合的。

8. 此处照字面译，然后加脚注说明细节。

★ 9. 这一句主要内容是 actors were even worse off，其余内容靠 when, leaving, until 等词串连起来。

★ 10. 请注意这个 with 的用法。

★ 11. 请注意这句译文里的主次关系。

★ 12. "一个钱撕成八瓣用"，这是一个形象性的说法。如照字面译，外国读者会感到莫名其妙，译文只能表其大意。to eke out 的意思是"通过节约的办法使（每一个铜板）花的时间更长一些"。

13. "喊嗓子"译文加了 in the open air，充分表达了原文的含义。

14. 如不熟悉 to scrounge for 这个短语，也可用 collect 代替。

★ 15. 此句译文用一个 who 引导的从句将原文一句话和下面一句的前半句结合起来，译文比较简洁。这样下一句译文就可集中说她如何害怕被欺负，躲着那些男孩子。

16. 这不是一个完整的句子，只是一个 because 引导的从句，相当于 I did this because … 或 This was because …，用来说明上句话里 I shifted to dodge them 的原因。

★ 17. "后台封上戏箱"，译作 the theatre shut down，既未提"后台"，也未提"戏箱"，这是一种概括的译法。

★ 18. "要等年初一开戏"，译作 until New Year's Day，在这个上下文里，这样译就包含着"开戏"的意思，不必说 until it opened again on New Year's Day。

19. "等于演员们封嘴"，译作 actors' pay stopped，也是概括的译法。

★ 20. 注意译文加了 other 一词，因为作者自己当时也是女孩。

21. 译文加了 in the sky，这是节奏上的需要，否则句子好像未完。

22. 注意动词 chalked,这一个词就表示"用粉笔写"的意思。

★ 23. "没号了！"不译作"No more numbers"，而译作"That's all!…"这样译更合乎在这种场合的说法。另外，用 hands 指"工人"，也是常见的一种说法。

24. 译文 too disappointed for words，意思是"找不到适当的字眼来形容我们失望的心情"，和原文是吻合的。

25. spell 一词在这里的意思是 a stretch of a specified type of weather。同样的天气持续一段时间，就可以用这个词来表示。

26. knocked off 意思是"下班"，是工人们常用的口语说法。

27. it rained cats and dogs，这是形容下大雨时一个常用的说法。

★28. "落汤鸡",译文没有保持原文里的比喻,而用了英语里的一个成语 like a drowned rat,其含义是一样的。

---------翻译理论简介---------

直译与意译

直译与意译这两种不同的译法,自古有之。然而自五四以来,人们围绕着这两种译法进行了激烈的争论。

1922 年,茅盾在"'直译'与'死译'"一文中写道:"近来颇有人诟病'直译';他们不是说'看不懂',就是说'看起来很吃力'。他们以为直译的东西看起来较为吃力,或者有之,却决不会看不懂。看不懂的译文是'死译'的文字,不是直译的。"[1]

1934 年,茅盾在"直译·顺译·歪译"一文中写道:"'直译'这名词,在'五四'以后方成为权威。这是反抗林琴南氏的'歪译'而起的。我们说林译是'歪译',可丝毫没有糟蹋他的意思;我们是觉得'意译'这名词用在林译身上并不妥当,所以称它为'歪译'。"[2]

1980 年,茅盾在《茅盾译文选集》序中回忆这一段往事,他写道:"后来有的译者随意增删原著,不讲究忠实原文的'意译',甚至'歪译',那就比林译更不如了。"[3]

从以上情况看,在二三十年代,反对直译的人所反对的是看不懂或看起来吃力的译文;反对意译的人所反对的是随意增删原著、不讲究忠实原文的译文。

鲁迅也是积极主张直译的。

后来有人提出直译和意译是一回事,二者是无法区分的。

1946 年,朱光潜在"谈翻译"一文中写道:"所谓'直译'是指依原文的字面翻译,有一字一句就译一字一句,而且字句的次第也不更动。所谓'意译'是指把原文的意思用中文表达出来,不必完全依原文的字面和次第。'直译'偏重对于原文的忠实,'意译'偏重译文语气的顺畅。哪一种是最妥当的译法,人们争执得很厉害。依我看,直译和意译的分别根本不应存在。……想尽量表达原文的意思,必须尽量保存原文的语句组织。因此直译不能不是意译,而意译也不能不是直译。"[4]

1953年,林汉达在"翻译的原则"一文中写道:"正确的翻译是直译,也就是意译。死译和胡译不同,呆译和曲译不同,这是可以划分的,它们都是错误的翻译。正确的翻译是分不出直译或意译的。"[5]

1959年,周建人为《外语教学与翻译》写了一篇文章,题目是"关于'直译'"。他在文中写道:"直译既不是'字典译法',也不是死译、硬译,它是要求真正的意译,要求不失原文的语气与文情,确切地翻译过来的译法。换一句话说,当时所谓直译是指真正的意译。"[6]

如果说四五十年代人们认为直译也就是意译,二者无法区分,那么到了七八十年代人们又对直译和意译分别作了分析。

1982年,周煦良在"翻译三论"一文中写道:直译可以分为三类:第一类是译音而不译意。如democracy译为"德谟克拉西",而不译为"民主"。第二类是照字面译。如crocodile tears译作"鳄鱼的眼泪",而不译作"虚伪的眼泪"。第三类是不按照中国语言习惯和词序而按照原文的结构或词序的翻译。如"'你来了,'她说"。最后,他指出"这样一些直译好像为数不少,但就一篇文章,一部书来看,直译的成分毕竟是少数。"[7]

1978年,许渊冲在"翻译中的几对矛盾"一文中也谈到直译与意译的问题,他说:"直译是把忠实于原文内容放在第一位,把忠实于原文形式放在第二位,把通顺的译文形式放在第三位的翻译方法。意译却是把忠实于原文的内容放在第一位,把通顺的译文形式放在第二位,而不拘泥于原文形式的翻译方法。"[8]最后他得出五点结论,归纳成两点就是:一、译文和原文相同的形式能表达和原文相同的内容时,可以直译,不能表达时就意译;二、原文的表达形式比译文精确、有力时,可以直译,译文的表达形式比原文精确、有力时，可以意译。

1979年，王佐良在"词义·文体·翻译"一文中写道："要根据原作语言的不同情况，来决定其中该直译的就直译，该意译的就意译。一个出色的译者总是能全局在胸而又紧扣局部，既忠于原作的灵魂，又便利于读者的理解与接受的。一部好的译作总是既有直译又有意译的：凡能直译处坚持直译，必须意译处则放手意译。"[9]

从以上情况看，七八十年代的译者对直译和意译作了分析和比较，采取了兼容并蓄的态度。这说明当代的译者比二三十年代乃至四五十年代的译者在理论上都更加成熟了。

1．《翻译论集》，商务印书馆，1984年，第343页。
2．同上，第351页。
3．同上，第518页。
4．同上，第453—454页。
5．同上，第592页。
6．同上，第652页。
7．同上，第981页。
8．同上，第798页。
9．同上，第834页。

Exercise 14

将下列短文译成英语：

找点活
（续）
新凤霞

这一淋可糟了！晚上发高烧，一会儿热，一会儿冷！脸上红得像抹了胭脂，周身疼，连翻身都疼，疼得像针扎！我想起来了：我人小，排队时常常被人挤出来，有些人又常常故意捣乱，工头举起鞭子就打，常常因为打别人而捎带上我。人多呀！一鞭子抽下来一大片，被捎上了背上就是一条子青一条子紫。这一病，发现被工头抽在身上的伤了！可疼坏了我了！可是幸亏这回只病了一夜，第二天早晨就退烧了，穿上带着号的衣服就赶快去上工了，虽然浑身酸软，可是不干活不行呀！晚上还得唱戏，一大家人都指着爸爸和我两个人挣钱吃饭呀！

我在东亚毛纺织厂当小工，那些女工大姐姐们都喜欢我，都说我好，[1]她们知道我是演员，[2]要我教她们唱，她们就教我织毛线，[3]还把工厂里印的毛线花样[4]的书送给我。从那以后我学会了很多毛衣[5]的花样，成了织毛衣的能手。

全国解放以后，我在我们自己的剧团，[6]中国评剧院工作了，我还是经常打毛衣；剧院里很多女演员学会打毛衣，大都是我教她们的。三十年来我爱人和孩子们身上穿的毛衣都是我织的，这都是我从东亚毛纺织厂学来的。

一九六二年我到天津中国大戏院演出，[7]一位中年女工[8]到后台来看我，原来是我当年在东亚厂熟识的王大姐，她已是工厂的干部[9]了。[10]她高兴地说："你可真是巧手呵！你现在不打毛线了，又换了纺线[11]了！"原来她是刚看了我演的《刘巧儿》。[12]

（选自《新凤霞回忆录》）

提示：

1. 都说我好：spoke well of me
2. 此处译文可用分词短语 Knowing ...
3. 织毛线：to knit
4. 花样：pattern
5. 毛衣：sweater
6. 剧团：opera troupe
7. 注意此处如何衔接。

8. 一位中年女工: a middle-aged woman worker

9. 干部: cadre

10. 这一句可以分作三句来译。

11. 纺线: to spin

12. 最后一句怎样译才能帮助外国读者了解这句话和前面一句的关系?

Key to Exercise 14

译文:

Looking for Work
(Continued)
by Xin Fengxia

That drenching nearly did for me![1] That evening I ran a fever,[2] burning hot one moment and icy cold the next.[3] My face was as red as if rouged, my whole body ached, and[4] turning over in bed[5] hurt like being needled! I remembered: Because I'm young, people often jostle me out of the queue; and when some of them make trouble and the foreman whips them, he often lashes me too.[6] In that crowd his whip falls on a whole lot of people, and it leaves blue and purple welts on your back.[7] Now that[8] I was ill I discovered the welts from his whip—they hurt so badly. But luckily I was only feverish one night, the next morning I felt well enough to put on my gown with the number and go to work.[9] Though I still ached all over, I had to work. And that evening I had to act. The whole family looked to Father[10] and me for food.

All the older women in the East Asia Woollen Mill liked me and spoke well of me. Knowing that I was an actress[11] they asked me to teach them to sing, and in turn they taught me to knit and gave me a book of patterns printed by the mill. After that I learned to knit sweaters of many kinds, acquiring a new skill.

After Liberation, I began to work in our own opera troupe, the China *Pingju* Theatre. Many other actresses in it learned to knit as well, mostly from me.[12] For over thirty years I've knit all the woollen clothes for my husband and children. I learned how to do this in the East Asia Woollen Mill.

In 1962, when I went to perform in the Grand Chinese Theatre in Tianjin, a middle-aged woman worker came backstage to see me. It turned out that she was Big Sister Wang whom I'd known in the East Asia Woollen Mill. She was now a cadre there.[13] She told me gaily, "You really have clever hands! You've stopped knitting now to take up spinning." She had just seen me playing in *Liu Qiaoer*, in which the heroine spins.[14]

(Translated by Gladys Yang)

解说：

1. 这里用了英语里的一个习语 do for somebody, 表示某事对某人十分有害。这一习语用于被动语态的情况较多。

2. 此处所用的 ran a fever 表示发烧, 是一个常用的搭配。说 have a fever 也是可以的。

3. 此处也可译作 now burning hot, now icy cold。但现在的译法 burning hot one moment and icy cold the next, 显得变化更为频繁。

4. 这一句有三个并列分句, 此处用 and 连接。

5. turning over in bed 是一个动名词短语, 用作主语。

★6. 这一句原文结构较松散, 先说自己如何, 再说有些人怎样, 最后说工头怎样。译文加了 because 和 when, 就是靠这些连词把句子组织起来的。

7. 译文 it leaves blue and purple welts on your back 具体地表

达了原文的含义。用英语表达身上青一块紫一块的意思，往往首先想到 black and blue 这一习语，但这一习语一般与动词 beat 连用，意思也显得比较笼统。

★8. now 在这里是连词，相当于 because，或 since，后面的 that 可以用，也可以不用。

★9. 译文在这里断句，如不断句，至少也要用分号，只靠逗号是连不起来的。

10. Father 第一个字母大写，和名字一样。若不大写，就要说 my father。

★11. 原文"知道我是演员"和"要我教他们唱"是两个并列谓语，有轻微的因果关系。这种关系在英语里恰恰是用分词短语来表示，因此译文用了 knowing that I was an actress they... 这一结构。

★12. "剧院里"只译作 in it，因为前面一句末尾刚说过 the China *Pingju* Theatre，此处用代称，以免重复。后半句"大都是我教她们的"，只译作 mostly from me，十分简洁。这里用了反译法，与前面的主语保持一致，而没有再引进一个主语，译文较顺。

★13. 原文是一句话，译文分成了三句。先说有人到后台来看她，再说这人的过去，最后说这人现在的情况。这样三句话是不能像原文那样用逗号连成一句话的。

★14. 译文加了 in which the heroine spins，这样外国读者就知道前面一句话的含义了。

Unit 8 Popular Science

Lesson 15 (E—C)

Bilingual Reading

Oil

(Excerpt 1)

by G.C. Thornley

There are three main groups of oils: animal, vegetable and mineral.[1] Great quantities of animal oil come from whales,[2] those enormous[3] creatures of the sea which are the largest remaining animals in the world. To protect the whale from the cold of the Arctic seas, nature has provided it with a thick covering[4] of fat called blubber.[5] When the whale is killed, the blubber is stripped off[6] and boiled down, either on board ship[7] or on shore. It produces a great quantity of oil which can be made into food for human consumption. A few other creatures yield oil, but none so much as the whale.[8] The livers of the cod[9] and the halibut,[10] two kinds of fish, yield nourishing oil. Both cod liver oil and halibut liver oil are given to sick children and other invalids who need certain vitamins.[11] These oils may be bought at any chemist's.[12]

Vegetable oil has been known from antiquity.[13] No household can get on without it, for it is used in cooking. Perfumes[14] may be made from the oils of certain flowers. Soaps are made from vegetable and animal oils.

To the ordinary man, one kind of oil may be as important as another. But when the politician or the engineer refers to oil, he almost always means mineral oil, the oil that drives tanks, aeroplanes and warships, motor-cars and diesel locomotives, the oil that is used to lubricate[15] all kinds of machinery. This is the oil that has changed the life of the common man. When it is refined[16] into petrol[17] it is used to drive the internal combustion engine.[18] To it we owe the existence of the motor-car,[19] which has replaced the private carriage drawn by the horse. To it we owe the possibility of flying. It has changed the methods of warfare on land and sea. This kind of oil comes out of the earth. Because it burns well, it is used as fuel and in some ways it is superior to[20] coal in this respect. Many big ships now burn oil instead of coal. Because it burns brightly, it is used for illumination; countless homes are still illuminated[21] with oil-burning lamps. Because it is very slippery, it is used for lubrication. Two metal surfaces rubbing together cause friction[22] and heat; but if they are separated by a thin film of oil, the friction and heat are reduced. No machine would work for long if it were not properly lubricated. The oil used for this purpose must be of the correct thickness; if it is too thin it will not give sufficient lubrication, and if it is too thick it will not reach all parts that must be lubricated.

(from *English Through Reading*)

提示：

第八单元：科普。这里所选的文章并不都是科普文章。第15课着重介绍了关于石油的知识。第16课选自一份介绍我国海洋事业发展战略的文件。它们都使用了科学术语，增长了人们的科学知识，但又不是谈得很专门，以至于只有科学家才能理解。所以放在这里，统称科普文章。虽然如此，我们仍可从中体会到一点科技文章的味道。除了学到一些科技术语，还可以看到被动语态，抽象名词的使用等。

王平在"科技英语的特点和翻译"一文中指出：科技文章属于严肃的书面语体，一般崇尚严谨周密，要求行文简练，语法正确，重点突出。科学叙述要按逻辑顺序精确地表达出概念的复杂体系，清楚地确定概念之间的相互关系。科技英语除上述各点外，还要求叙述开门见山，简短明快，使读者立即抓住问题的重点。"（见《科技翻译技巧文集》第 9 页）

关于第 15 课的对照阅读（BR15），请注意以下各点。

1. animal, vegetable and mineral = animal oil, vegetable oil and mineral oil

2. whale：鲸鱼

3. enormous：very large

4. covering：something that covers

5. blubber：鲸脂

6. strip off：take off

7. on board ship：in the ship

8. A few other creatures yield oil, but none so much as the whale = A few other creatures yield oil, but none of them yield so much oil as the whale does.

9. cod：鳕鱼

10. halibut：比目鱼

11. vitamin：维生素

12. chemist's（in British English）= drugstore（in American English）

13. antiquity：ancient times

14. perfume：香水

15. lubricate：put oil into（machine parts）to make（them）work easily

16. refine：make pure

17. petrol：汽油

18. internal combustion engine：内燃机

★ 19. To it we owe the existense of the motor-car = We owe the existense of the motor-car to it（mineral oil）= We have motor-cars today just because there is this kind of oil.

20. superior to: better than
21. illuminate: give light to
22. friction：摩擦

参考译文：

油

（摘录 1）

G.C. 索恩利

  油可以分为三大类：动物油，植物油，矿物油。[1]大量的动物油是从鲸鱼身上得来的。鲸鱼是海里的庞然大物，是世界上现有动物中最大的一种。[2]大自然为了保护鲸鱼，使它不致在北冰洋受冻，便让它长了厚厚的一层脂肪，叫做鲸脂。[3]鲸鱼杀死之后，[4]把鲸脂剥下来熬油，这项工作有的是在船上进行的，有的是在岸上进行的。这样，就能生产出大量的油，供人们食用。有些动物也出油，但都没有鲸鱼出得多。鳕鱼和比目鱼，这两种鱼的肝脏出的油营养丰富。[5]从这两种鱼得来的鱼肝油可以[6]给缺少某种维生素的患儿[7]或其他病人服用。[8]这两种鱼肝油在任何一家药房里都可以买到。

  植物油自古以来就为人们所熟悉。任何家庭都离不开它，因为做饭的时候就要用它。有些花儿产生的油可以用来制造香水。植物油和动物油还可以用来制作肥皂。[9]

  对一般人来说，这种油或那种油可能都是重要的。但是当政治家或工程师谈到油的时候，他所指的几乎总是矿物油。这种油可以用来开坦克，开飞机，开军舰，开汽车，开柴油机车，[10]可以用来润滑各种机械。就是这种油改变了普通人的生活。这种油经过提炼变成汽油以后，可以用来开动内燃机。就是因为有了这种油，我们才能用上汽车，[11]以代替马车。就是因为有了这种油，我们才有可能飞行。[12]它还改变了陆战和海战的方法。这种油来源于地下。因为它易于燃烧，可以用作燃料，而且在这方面比煤还有若干优越之处。现在许多大轮船就烧油而不烧煤。[13]因为它燃烧时非常明亮,也可以用来照明,许多家庭现在仍靠油灯照明。因为它非常滑润,可以用作润滑剂。[14]两个金属面相擦,就要产生摩擦和热;但如果在它们之间抹上薄薄的一层油,就可以减少摩擦,降低热度。[15]任何机械如果不使用一定的润滑剂,就不能持续工作。润滑油的浓度必须适当,太稀则起不到应有的润滑作用,太稠则流不到所有需要润滑的零件。

解说:

1. 原文用 animal, vegetable and mineral 这种省略的说法来说明三大类油。如果在每一类后面加上一个 oil,就显得非常累赘。汉语则不然,如译作"动物的、植物的、矿物的"则不顺,不如重复一个"油"字。

2. 这两句话在原文里是一句话。those enormous creatures of the sea . . . 是 whales 的同位语。这句话孤立来看,可以从后半句着手译,译作:"鲸鱼是海里的庞然大物,是世界上现有动物中最大的一种,大量的动物油就是从鲸鱼身上得来的。"译文也是一句话。但从上下文来考虑,上面要接前面提到的"动物油",下面要对鲸鱼作进一步的说明,因此参考译文作了那样的处理。

★3. 这句话原文一开头是一个很长的动词不定式短语,To protect . . . ,然后才出主语 nature。如果按照原文的结构译,就是:"为了保护鲸鱼,使它不致在北冰洋受冻,大自然便……",这样处理也是可以的。但是把主语"大自然"放在句首,更符合汉语的习惯说法。

★4. 此处原文是被动语态,但译文不一定说"鲸鱼被杀死以后",不用"被"字仍可表示被动的含义。"这种没有被动形式而有被动意义的格式,非常普遍;……如'信写好了'、'货送来了'。"(见吕叔湘、朱德熙著《语法修辞讲话》,第87页。)

★5. 这一句原文的主语是 The livers of the cod and the halibut,后面紧跟着一个同位语 two kinds of fish。作者怕有些读者不知道

the cod 和 the halibut 是什么动物，所以用了一个同位语加以说明。中国读者一看"鳕鱼和比目鱼"，自然知道这是两种鱼，就不需要用同位语来说明了。但是上面一句说"有些动物也出油……"，这一句如像原文那样一开始就说"鳕鱼和比目鱼的肝脏……"似觉突然。因此先说两种鱼的名字，然后再说"这两种鱼的肝脏……"比较自然。这种结构在汉语语法里叫做"外位成分"，"鳕鱼和比目鱼"是"外位语"，"这两种鱼"是本位语，在句子里作定语。(参看 BR11 解说 10。)

★6. 此处原文只是 are given，译文是"可以给……"，加了"可以"二字。这是因为在自然科学中，说明某种东西的用途时，往往用"可以"二字。《现代汉语词典》关于"鲸"一词的解释中就有这样一句话："肉可以吃，脂肪可以制油，用于医药和其他工业。"

7. sick children 在口语里可以译作生病的孩子。此处译作"患儿"，比较合乎文体。

8. 译文在这里加了"服用"二字。原文并无 to take 等字样，但意在其中。译文若不加字，句子难以煞住。

★9. 据统计，被动语态在科技英语里远比在一般英语里用得多。这一段共有四句话，就用了四个被动语态。译成汉语不一定都用被动式。第一句译为"……为人们所熟悉"，这是被动式。最后两句就只能算是没有被动形式而有被动意义的格式了。

10. 这里"开"字重复用了五次，比一个"开"字带五个宾语要顺一些。

★11. 原文 existense 是抽象名词，不必勉强译作"存在"。此处根据上下文译作"才能用上……"。

★12. possibility 也是抽象名词，也不必勉强译作"可能性"。此处译作"才有可能飞行"比较自然，也便于和前面一句话保持平衡。

13. instead of 不一定译作"代替"，此处就译作"而不"。

14. lubrication 是抽象名词，用在句末，可以煞住。此处如译作"……可以用来润滑"则煞不住，后面还要加宾语。所以译作"可以用作润滑剂"。

★ 15. 原文 the friction and heat are reduced，两个名词和一个动词搭配。在汉语里，既不能说"减少摩擦和热度"，也不能说"降低摩擦和热度"，因此译作"减少摩擦，降低热度"，用不同的动词来搭配。此外，这一句原文用了两个被动语态，译文用的是无主句。

————翻译理论简介————

傅 雷

"重神似不重形似"这是在讨论翻译问题时常说的一句话。最初提出这个观点的不是别人，而是傅雷。1951年，他在"《高老头》重译本序"一文中写道："以效果而论，翻译应当像临画一样，所求的不在形似而在神似。"

傅雷是一位勤奋的译者。他研究法国文学，翻译的作品达三十余种，其中包括巴尔扎克的《人间喜剧》和罗曼罗兰的《约翰·克利斯朵夫》。为向中国读者介绍法国文学，他作出了很大的贡献。

傅雷是一位严肃的译者。他热爱文艺，不愿作损害艺术品的事。他说："想译一部喜欢的作品要读到四遍五遍，才能把情节、故事，记得烂熟，分析彻底，人物历历如在目前，隐藏在字里行间的微言大义也能慢慢琢磨出来。但做了这些功夫是不是翻译的条件就具备了呢？不。因为翻译作品不仅仅在于了解与体会，还需要进一步把我所了解的，体会的，又忠实又动人的表达出来。"[1] 他对译文精益求精。《老实人》的译文前后改过八次。他不满足于自己已出的译本，有些书还要重译，出新的译本。包括《约翰·克利斯朵夫》这样的长篇巨著，他都重新译过。从这里可以看出他作为一个译者的责任感。

傅雷是一位有见地的翻译家。他认为"翻译重在实践"，[2] 然而他在中西语言对比，译者治学之道等方面也都有精辟的见解，对发展我国的翻译理论更是起了很大的作用。

他说："谈到翻译，我觉得最难应付的倒是原文中最简单最明白而最短的句子。例如 Elle est charmante = She is charming, 读一二个月英法文的人都懂，可是译成中文，要传达原文的语气，使中文里也有同样的情调，气氛，在我简直办不到。而往往这一类的句子，对原文上下文极有关系，传达不出这一点，上下文的神气全走掉了。……长句并非不困难，但难的不在于传神，而在于重心的安排。长句中往往只有极短的一句 simple sentence, 中间夹入三四个副句，而副句中又有 participle 的副句。在译文中统统拆了开来，往往宾主不分，轻重全失。为了保持原文的重心，有时不得不把副句抽出先放在头上，到末了再译那句短的正句。"[3]

他说："我们在翻译的时候，通常是胆子太小，迁就原文字面，原文句法的时候太多。要避免这些，第一要精读熟读原文，把原文的意义，神韵全部抓握住了，才能放大胆子。"[4]

他说："两国文字词类的不同，句法构造的不同，文法与习惯的不同，修辞格律的不同，俗语的不同，即反映民族思想方式的不同，感觉深浅的不同，观点角度的不同，风俗传统信仰的不同，社会背景的不同，表现方法的不同。以甲国文字传达乙国文字所包涵的那些特点，必须像伯乐相马，要'得其精而忘其粗，在其内而忘其外'。而即使是最优秀的译文，其韵味较之原文仍不免过或不及。翻译时只能尽量缩短这个距离，过则求其勿太过，不及则求其勿过于不及。……理想的译文仿佛是原作者的中文写作。那么原文的意义与精神，译文的流畅与完整，都可以兼筹并顾，不至于再有以辞害意，或以意害辞的弊病了。"[5]

关于"神似"，他说："传神云云，谈何容易！年岁经验愈增，对原作体会愈增，而传神愈感不足。领悟为一事，用中文表达为又一事。况东方人与西方人之思想方式有基本分歧，我人重综合，重归纳，重暗示，重含蓄；西方人则重分析，细微曲折，挖掘唯恐不尽，描写唯恐不周：此两种 mentalité 殊难彼此融洽交流。……愚对译事看法实甚简单：重神似不重形似；译文必须为纯粹之中文，无生硬拗口之病；又须能朗朗上口，求音节和谐，至节奏与 tempo，当然以原作为依归。"[6]

---

1. 《翻译论集》，商务印书馆，1984 年，第 626 页。
2. 同上，第 625 页。
3. 同上，第 545—546 页。
4. 同上，第 548 页。
5. 同上，第 558—559 页。
6. 同上，第 694 页。

参考书目：

1. 傅雷，"致林以亮论翻译书"。
2. 傅雷，"《高老头》重译本序"。
3. 傅雷，"翻译经验点滴"。
4. 傅雷，"论文学翻译书"。
5. 罗新璋，"读傅雷译品随感"。
6. 罗新璋，"我国自成体系的翻译理论"。
7. 刘靖之，"重神似不重形似"。

(以上各文均载于《翻译论集》)

Exercise 15

将下列短文译成汉语：

Oil

(Excerpt 2)

by G.C. Thornley

What was the origin of the oil which now drives our motor-cars and aircraft[1]? Scientists are confident about the formation of coal, but they do not seem so sure when asked about oil[2]. They think that the oil under the surface of the earth originated[3] in the distant past, and was formed from living things in the sea. Countless billions of minute[4] sea creatures and plants lived and sank to the sea bed. They were covered with huge deposits of mud, and by processes of chemistry, pressure and temperature were changed through long ages into what we know as oil[5]. For these creatures to become oil, it was necessary that they should be imprisoned[6] between layers of rock for an enormous length of time. The statement that oil originated in the sea is confirmed[7] by a glance at a map showing the chief oilfields of the world; very few of them are far distant from the oceans of today. In some places gas[8] and oil come up to the surface of the sea from its bed. The rocks in which oil is found are of marine origin too. They are sedimentary rocks,[9] rocks which were laid down by the action of water on the bed of the ocean. Almost always the remains of shells, and other proofs of sea life, are found close to the oil. A very common sedimentary rock is called shale,[10] which is a soft rock and was obviously formed by being deposited on the sea bed. And where there is shale there is likely to be oil.

Geologists[11], scientists who study rocks, indicate the likely places to the oil drillers.[12] In some cases oil comes out of the ground without any drilling at all and has been used for hundreds of years. In the island of Trinidad the oil is in the form of asphalt,[13] a substance[14] used for making roads. Sir Walter Raleigh* visited the famous pitch lake[15] of Trinidad in 1595; it is said to contain nine thousand million tons of asphalt. There are probably huge quantities of

---

* *Sir Walter Raleigh* English admiral and historian of Elizabethan times, born in 1552 and executed by James I in 1618.

crude oil[16] beneath the surface.

There is a lot of luck[17] in drilling for oil. The drill may just miss the oil although it is near; on the other hand, it may strike oil at a fairly high level. When the drill goes down, it brings up soil. The samples[18] of soil from various depths are examined for traces of oil[19]. If they are disappointed at one place, the drillers go to another. Great sums of money have been spent, for example in the deserts of Egypt, in "prospecting"[20] for oil. Sometimes little is found. When we buy a few gallons[21] of petrol for our cars, we pay not only the cost of the petrol, but also part of the cost of the search that is always going on.

When the crude oil is obtained from the field, it is taken to the refineries[22] to be treated[23]. The commonest form of treatment is heating. When the oil is heated, the first vapours[24] to rise are cooled and become the finest petrol. Petrol has a low boiling point; if a little is poured into the hand, it soon vaporizes. Gas that comes off the oil later is condensed[25] into paraffin[26]. Last of all the lubricating oils of various grades are produced. What remains is heavy oil that is used as fuel[27].

(from *English Through Reading*)

提示:

★ 1. aircraft: Please note that "aircraft" is the plural as well as the singular form.

2. when asked about oil = when they are asked about oil

3. originate: begin

4. minute [mai'nju:t]: very small

5. changed ... into what we know as oil = changed ... into the thing that we know as oil

6. be imprisoned: be kept

165

7. confirm: prove
8. "gas" here refers to "natural gas".
9. sedimentary rocks: 沉积岩
10. shale: 页岩
11. geologist: 地质学家
12. oil drillers: 钻探石油的人
13. asphalt: 沥青
14. substance: 物质
15. pitch lake: 沥青湖
16. crude oil: 原油
17. luck: chance, fortune
18. sample: 样品
19. traces of oil: signs showing that there is oil there
20. prospecting: 勘探
21. gallon: 加仑
22. refinery: place where oil is refined
23. treat: 处理
24. vapour: 蒸汽
25. condense: 浓缩
26. paraffin: kerosene 煤油
27. fuel: 燃料

Key to Exercise 15

参考译文：

油

(摘录2)

G.C. 索恩利

我们现在开汽车、开飞机使用的油是怎样形成的呢？科学家确知煤是怎样形成的,[1]但若问到石油是怎样形成的,[2]他们似乎就不那么有把握了。他们认为地下的石油在远古时期就已经开始形成,而且是由海中生物形成的。亿万个数不清的微小动物和植物在海水中生长并沉入海底,上面覆盖着大量沉积的泥沙,由于化学变化、压力和温度等因素,经过漫长的岁月,变成了现在我们所说的石油。[3]这些小动物必须在一层层岩石之间密封起来,经过极长的一段时间才能变成石油。石油是在海里形成的,这种说法,只要看一下世界主要油田分布图,[4]就可以得到证实;[5]大油田离开今日的海洋很远的极少。有些地方,天然气和石油从海底浮上水面。含有石油的岩层也是在海里形成的。这种岩层是沉积岩,是在海水的作用[6]之下沉积在洋底的。在有石油的地方,附近几乎总可以发现贝壳的残片以及海洋生物的其它遗迹。[7]有一种很普通的沉积岩,叫做页岩。这是一种松软的岩石,显然是在海底沉积而成的。凡是有页岩的地方,就可能有石油。

地质学家是研究岩石的科学家,他们可以为钻探石油的人指明哪些地方可能有油。[8]有些地方,根本未经钻探,石油就流出地面,而且已经使用了几百年。在特立尼达岛,石油以沥青的形式出现。沥青是一种可以用来铺路的物质。1595年,沃尔特·雷利爵士*曾参观过特立尼达有名的沥青湖。据说湖里储有沥青90亿吨。表层下面很可能储藏着极为丰富的原油。

钻探石油有很大的偶然性。钻头可能到了离油很近的地方而没有碰到油;另一方面,也可能在相当浅的地方[9]打出油来。钻头下去的时候,便把泥土送上来。从不同深度取出土样以后,便进行检验,看是否有含油的迹象[10]钻探石油的人如果在一个地方得不到预期的结果,便到另一个地方去钻探[11]。在石油"勘探"方面,已经花了大笔的钱[12],比如在埃及的沙漠里进行的勘探工作就是如此[13]。有时收效甚微。因此[14],当我们为自己的小汽车

---

* 沃尔特·雷利爵士是英国伊丽莎白时代的海军上将和历史学家,生于1552年,1618年被英王詹姆斯一世处决。——原注

买几加仑汽油的时候,我们所付的不只是汽油本身的费用,而且还有不断进行找油工作的一部分费用。

油田打出原油以后[15],便送到炼油厂去处理。最普通的处理办法是加热。石油经过加热[16],最先冒出来的蒸气冷却后就是质量最高的汽油。汽油的沸点低,倒一点在手上[17],很快就挥发了。随后从石油分离出来的气体可以浓缩成煤油。最后产生的是各种等级的润滑油。剩下的便是重油,可以用作燃料。[18] [19]

解说:

★1. 原文是 the formation of coal,包含着一个抽象名词,可以译作"煤的形成"。但在这个上下文里,译作"煤是怎样形成的",更顺一些。把带有抽象名词的词组译成分句,这是常见的一种译法。有时也只有这样译,意思才清楚。

2. 原文只说 when asked about oil,译文在"石油"后面重复了"是怎样形成的"几个字,这样更顺一些。

3. 这一句说明石油形成的过程。原文是两句话,译文合成了一句。原文在第一句末尾 sea bed 后面不可能用逗号点开,接着说 were covered...,而必须用 they 作主语,这样就只好另起一个句子,成了两句话。译文主语可以一直管到底,用一句话来简单地描述这个过程,也比较紧凑。

4. 此处如译作"世界主要油田的地图",可能被误解为各油田本身的地图。所以将 map 具体化,译作"分布图"。

★5. 这一句译文是外位结构。"石油是在海里形成的"是外位语,"这种说法"是本位语,在句子里作主语。关于这个问题,请参看王力著《中国语法理论》下册,第5章第37节复说法,和吕叔湘、朱德熙著《语法修辞讲话》第23页和第159—160页。

6. 原文 the action of water,如孤立地来看,可译作"水的作用"。但此处将 water 具体化,译作"海水的作用",意思比较清楚,文字也比较流畅。

★ 7. 原文 proofs of sea life，如译作"海洋生物的证据"，可能费解。其本意是 things that can prove that there was sea life here，所以译作"海洋生物的遗迹"。

★ 8. 原文 likely places，此处指 places where oil is likely to be found，即"可能找到油的地方"。因此不能译作"可能的地方"。

9. 原文 at a fairly high level，从上下文看，意思不是"在相当高的水平上"，而是指"不用打得很深，在较高的位置（即在离地面较近的位置）"，所以译作"在相当浅的地方"。

★ 10. 原文 for traces of oil 是一个介词短语，译成"看是否有含油的迹象"，加"看"、"有"、"含"三个动词，这可算是汉语比英语多用动词之一例。

★ 11. 在英语里，可以先出代词，后出实义词。在这个句子里，原文前半句中的 they 就是指后半句中的 the drillers。这种句子译成汉语，一定要先出实义词；如果需要的话，后面再用代词。此处译文用一个实义词作主语，管到底，后面便不需要再用代词了。

★ 12. 这一句原文是被动语态，但未说明谁是施动者。译文用了无主语句。这也是翻译被动语态常用的一个方法。

13. 原文 for example in the deserts of Egypt 是个插入语，放在句子中间。译文颠倒了语序，把这一部分放到了句末，因此最后加了"就是如此"四个字，否则句子就刹不住了。

★ 14. 此处译文加了"因此"二字。英语句子内部的关系一般都交待得很清楚，即所谓"形合"。但句子与句子之间的关系则往往不交待得很清楚。若仔细推敲一番，后面一句话可能说明前面一句话的原因，也可能说明其后果。汉语则恰恰相反，句子内部的关系一般不必交待得很清楚，即所谓"意合"。但句子与句子之间的关系则往往交待得很清楚。

★ 15. 这一句原文是被动语态，译文从地点状语中抽出 the field 作主语。

★16."石油经过加热",形式上是主动的,含义却是被动的,因此可以用"经过"来翻译被动语态。此外,when 没有译,不必一看见 when 就译作"当……的时候"。

★17. 原文 if a little is poured into the hand,在汉语里,if 不必译,自然意在其中。原文被动语态未提施动者,译为无主句,因为没有必要说明这件事是谁做的。

18. 原文 that is used as fuel 译作"可以用作燃料"。请参看 BR15,解说6。

19. 最后这一段并不长,原文共用了九个被动语态。被动语态用得多,是科技英语的一大特点。翻译科技文章时怎样处理好被动语态,是一个值得研究的题目。

Lesson 16 （C—E）

Bilingual Reading

海洋可持续发展战略

中国有12亿多人口，陆地自然资源人均占有量低于世界平均水平。根据中国有关方面的统计：中国有960万平方公里的陆地国土，居世界第三位，但人均占有陆地面积仅有0.008平方公里，远低于世界人均0.3平方公里的水平；全国近年来年平均淡水资源总量为28,000亿立方米，居世界第六位，但人均占有量仅为世界平均水平的四分之一；中国陆地矿产资源总量丰富，但人均占有量不到世界人均量的一半。中国作为一个发展中的沿海大国，国民经济要持续发展，必须把海洋的开发和保护作为一项长期的战略任务。

中国拥有大陆岸线18000多公里，以及面积在500平方米以上的海岛5000多个，岛屿岸线14000多公里；按照《联合国海洋法公约》的规定，中国还对广阔的大陆架和专属经济区行使主权权利和管辖权；中国的海域处在中、低纬度地带，自然环境和资源条件比较优越。中国海域海洋生物物种繁多，已鉴定的达20278种。中国海域已经开发的渔场面积达81.8万平方海里。中国有浅海、滩涂总面积约1333万公顷，按现在的科学水平，可进行人工养殖的水面有260万公顷，已经开发利用的有93.8万公顷。中国海域有30多个沉积盆地，面积近70万平方公里，石油资源量约250亿吨，天然气资源量约8.4万亿立方米。中国沿海共有160多处海湾和几百公里深水岸线，许多岸段适合建设港口，发展海洋运输业。沿海地区共有1500多处旅游娱乐景观资源，适合发展海洋旅游业。中国海域还有丰富的海水资源和海洋可再生能源。

（摘自《中国海洋事业的发展》第一部分）

译文：

Sustainable[1] Marine Development Strategy

China has a population of more than 1.2 billion, and[2] its land natural resources per capita are lower than the world's average.[3] Official[4] statistics show[5] that China has a land area of 9.6 million sq km, making it the third-biggest country in the world. However, the land area per capita is only 0.008 sq km, much lower than the world's average of 0.3 sq km per capita. In recent years China's average annual amount of freshwater resources has been 2,800 billion cu m, ranking sixth in the world;[6] but the amount of freshwater resources per capita is only one-fourth the world average. China is rich in land mineral resources, but the amount per capita is less than half the figure per capita worldwide.[7] As a major developing country with a long coastline, China, therefore, must take exploitation and protection of the ocean as a long term strategic task before it can achieve the sustainable development of its national economy.[8]

China boasts[9] a mainland coastline of more than 18,000 km. There are more than 5,000 islands in China's territorial waters, each with an area of more than 500 sq m, and the islands' coastlines total[10] more than 14,000 km. China also exercises sovereignty and jurisdiction over the vast continental shelves and exclusive economic zones (EEZs)[11], as defined by[12] the UN Convention on the Law of the Sea. Located in medium and low latitudes, China's sea areas have comparatively advantageous natural environmental and resource conditions. Some 20,278 species of sea creatures have been verified there. The fishing grounds[13] that have been developed in China's sea areas cover[14] 818,000 square nautical miles. The shallow seas and tidelands have a total area of 13.33 million ha, of which[15] 2.6 million ha of water surface are suitable for the raising of aquatic products in terms of the current scientific level. So far, 938,000 ha are being utilized for this purpose. Scattered in these offshore waters are more than 30 sedimentation basins, with[16] a total area of nearly 700,000 sq km. It is estimated that there are about 25 billion tons of oil resources and 8.4 trillion cu m of natural gas in these basins.[17] More than 160 bays are spread along China's coasts, plus the deepwater stretches of coast with a total length of several hundred kilometers. Many spots along the coastline are suitable for constructing harbors and developing marine transportation. There are more than 1,500 tourist, scenic and recreational spots[18] favorable for developing marine tourism. In addition, China's offshore areas abound[19] in seawater resources and regenerable marine energy resources.

(from *Beijing Review*)

解说:

★ 1. "可持续"是 sustainable, 而 sustained 的意思的"持续的", 这是两个不同的概念, 不可混用。

2. 这一句原文包含两个短句, 译文为两个并列分句, 中间用 and 相连。

★ 3. "平均水平"译作名词 average 一词就够了, 不必说 average level。

4. "有关方面的"可以译作 from departments concerned, 但与 statistics 连用时, official 一词就够了。

★ 5. 原文"统计"后面用冒号, 但英语在这种情况下不用冒号。即使译作 According to official statistics, 也只能用逗号, 而不用冒号。Official statistics show that... 比较自然。

★ 6. "居世界第六位"译作 ranking sixth in the world, 而前面的"居世界第三位"却译作 making it the third-biggest country in the world。同样的意思, 说法却不同, 这是因为英语不喜欢重复, 而喜欢变换说法。

7. 这一句原文说了三件事，陆地国土、淡水资源和陆地矿产资源，用分号隔开。译文分别用了独立的句子，这样比较清楚。

★8. 译文将 As ... 移至句首，将 before it can ... 移至句末，中间以 China must ... 作句子的主语和谓语，这样译恰当地突出了句子的重点。

★9. boast 相当于 possess，表示某地有什么东西，常用这个动词。但请注意，它在这里是个及物动词，后面不加 of。

10. total 在这里是动词。

11. "大陆架"译作 continental shelves，"专属经济区"译作 exclusive economic zones。这两个名词在谈到海洋发展时十分有用，值得牢记。

12. as defined by ... 是一个很有用的说法，和 in accordance with 的意思是一样的。

★13. ground 不一定指陆地。据 Collins Cobuild English Language Dictionary, a ground is an area of land, sea or air which is used for a particular purpose, 还有一个例子：This is one of the world's best fishing grounds. 可见"渔场"虽然是在水里，还是可以译作 fishing grounds。

14. 表示占多大面积，cover 是一个很有用的动词。

★15. 表示后面的数字是前面数字的一部分，用 of which 连接，是再方便不过了。

★16. "面积近 70 万平方公里"本是一个主谓俱全的小短句，译文只用一个 with 引导的介词短语就解决问题了。

17. 原文一句话，译文分成两句，因此末尾加了 in these basins, 以说明这一句与前一句的联系。

★18. 原文是"旅游娱乐景观资源"，译文却是 tourist, scenic and recreational spots, 把 scenic 提前，把 recreational 移后，大概是因为英语喜欢把短字放在前面，把长字放在后面。

19. 表示某地有大量的什么东西，abound 是一个很有用的动词,后面可以跟 in 或 with。

---翻译理论简介---

关于风格

关于风格能不能译,大体上有两种意见。

一种意见认为风格是能译的。1980年茅盾说过:"很重要的一点是能将他的风格翻译出来。譬如果戈理的作品与高尔基的作品风格就不同,肖伯纳的作品与同样是英国大作家的高尔斯华绥的作品的风格也不同。要将一个作家的风格翻译出来,这当然是相当困难的,需要运用适合于原作风格的文学语言,把原作的内容与形式正确无遗地再现出来。除信、达外,还要有文采。这样的翻译既需要译者的创造性,而又要完全忠实于原作的面貌。这是对文学翻译的最高要求。"[1]

茅盾的这个意见是他一贯坚持的。早在1922年他就曾写道:"直译的意义若就浅处说,只是'不妄改原文的字句';就深处说,还求'能保留原文的情调与风格'。"[2]

这个意见是有人支持的。1961年刘隆惠写道:"对于文学翻译,不仅要求通顺流畅,而且要求表达原作的风格。"[3] 他还说:"我认为风格并不是不能译,而是难译。其所以难是在于译者必须具备两个条件。其一是要有认识风格的水平;其二是要有表现风格的能力。"[4]

另一种意见认为风格是不能译的。1982年周煦良说过:"严复只提雅,而不提原文风格,我们现在提文学翻译要有风格,也不宜要求译出原文风格:原文风格是无法转译的。……我仍旧认为风格是无法翻译的,风格离不开语言,不同的语言无法表达同样的风格。"[5] 他认为,一部文学译品的风格是由四方面决定的:一、原作的风格;二、译者本人的文章风格;三、译者本国语言的特征;四、译者所处的时代。有后面三个因素掺杂其间,译者怎能正确反映出原作的风格呢?所以,他认为"只能要求它有个

风格。"⁶

周煦良的这个意见,他也是一贯坚持的。早在1959年他就曾写道:"有人自诩翻译哪一个作家就能还出这个作家的面目或风格,我看这只是英雄欺人语;据我所知,就有翻译家对本文还不大能弄懂得,就大吹自己的翻译是旨在表现原作诗一般美丽的风格。依我看,对一个作家或者风格的认识也还是根据对作品本文的理解而来的,否则便是空话。教外国文学的人最喜欢谈风格,但是,对于一个搞实际翻译的人来说,风格却是一个最难谈得清楚的东西。我觉得,在通常情形下,它好像只是在无形中使译者受到感染,而且译者也是无形中把这种风格通过他的译文去感染读者的,所以既然是这样情形,我看就让风格自己去照顾自己好了,翻译工作者大可不必为它多伤脑筋。……我觉得翻译工作者如果要花许多功夫去钻研作品的风格,还不如花点功夫去培养自己的外语感受能力好些,因为翻译工作究竟是和语言文字打交道的工作,而语言却不止是数字符号那样抽象而无情的东西。"⁷

这一种意见也是有人支持的。1961年张中楹写道:"在同一语言的领域里,尚且不易摹仿一个作者的风格;在翻译方面,把原作译成另一种语言而要保持同一风格,这是更不易做到的工作。……我是极为赞同周煦良同志的'不必多伤脑筋'的说法的。"⁸

1979年罗新璋在评论傅雷的译作时说过这样一句话:"服尔德的机警尖刻,巴尔扎克的健拔雄快,梅里美的俊爽简括,罗曼罗兰的朴质流动,在原文上色彩鲜明,各具面貌,译文固然对各家的特色和韵味有相当体现,拿《老实人》的译文和《约翰·克利斯朵夫》一比,就能看出文风上的差异,但贯穿于这些译作的,不免有一种傅雷风格。"⁹可见即使是名家的译作也难免既有原作的风格,又有译者的风格,而不可能是单纯的原作的风格。

以上所谈大都是讲的文学翻译。对于我们并非专门从事文学翻译的初学者来说,在表达方面只要做到两点就够了。第一,能区别口语与书面语,该文的时候文,该白的时候白,翻译对话像对话,翻译叙述像叙述;第二,能根据不同的文体使用不同的语言,翻译新闻像新闻,翻译文件像文件,翻译故事像故事,翻译诗歌像诗歌。如果在正确理解原文的基础上,能使译文做到这两点,这就很不错了。

1."《茅盾译文选集》序",《翻译论集》第 519 页。

2."'直译'与'死译'",《翻译论集》第 343 页。

3."谈谈文艺作品风格的翻译问题",《翻译研究论文集》(1949—1983)第 166 页。

4.同上,第 165 页。

5."翻译三论",《翻译论集》第 975—976 页。

6.同上,第 977 页。

7."翻译与理解",《翻译研究论文集》(1949—1983)第 138,140 页。

8."关于翻译中的风格问题",《翻译论集》第 669,672 页。

9.见"读傅雷译品随感",《翻译论集》第 992 页。

参考书目:

1.茅盾,"《茅盾译文选集》序"。

2.张中楹,"关于翻译中的风格问题"。

3.王佐良,"词义·文体·翻译"。

4.周煦良,"翻译三论"。

5.罗新璋,"读傅雷译品随感"。

(以上各篇载于《翻译论集》)

6.周煦良,"翻译与理解"。

7.刘隆惠,"谈谈文艺作品风格的翻译问题"。

8.冯世则,"风格的翻译:必要、困难、可能与必然"。

(以上各篇载于《翻译研究论文集》(1949—1983))

9. 翁显良,《意态由来画不成?》,中国对外翻译出版公司,1983年。

Exercise 16

将下列短文译成英语:

中国海洋事业的发展
前言[1]

海洋覆盖了地球表面的71%,是全球生命支持系统[2]的一个基本组成部分,也是资源的宝库,[3]环境的重要调节器。[4]人类社会的发展必然会越来越多地依赖海洋。

即将到来的二十一世纪是人类开发利用海洋的新世纪。维护《联合国海洋法公约》确定的国际海洋法律原则,维护海洋健康,保护海洋环境,确保海洋资源的可持续利用和海上安全,已成为人类共同遵守的准则[5]和共同担负的使命。[6]

中国是一个发展中的沿海大国。中国高度重视海洋的开发和保护,把发展海洋事业作为国家发展战略,加强海洋综合管理,不断完善海洋法律制度,积极发展海洋科学技术和教育。[7]中国积极参与联合国系统的海洋事务,推进国家间和地区性海洋领域的合作,并认真履行自己承担的义务,[8]为全球海洋开发和保护事业作出了积极贡献。[9]

1998年是联合国确定的国际海洋年,中国政府愿借此机会介绍中国海洋事业的发展情况。[10]

(摘自《中国海洋事业的发展》)

提示:

1. 前言: foreword
2. 生命支持系统: bio-support system
3. 宝库: treasure house

4. 调节器: regulator
5. 准则: norms
6. 使命: mission
7. 这两句话可统一考虑调整句子结构。
8. 义务: obligations
9. 这个句子的重点在哪里?
10. 这个句子中间怎样衔接?

Key to Exercise 16

译文:

The Development of China's Marine Programs
Foreword[1]

The ocean, which covers 71 per cent of the earth's surface[2], is a basic component of the global bio-support system[3]. It is also a treasure house of resources and[4] an important regulator of the environment. It is inevitable that the development of human society will come to depend more and more on the ocean.

In the coming 21st century mankind will have new opportunities to develop and utilize the ocean[5]. Upholding the principles of the international marine law as defined by[6] the United Nations Convention on the Law of the Sea, maintaining the wholesomeness[7] of the oceans, protecting the marine environment and guaranteeing the sustainable utilization of marine resources and maritime[8] safety have become common norms for all the people in the world to abide by, and a collective mission for all mankind to undertake.

As a major developing country with a long coastline[9], China attaches great importance to marine development and protection, and takes it as the state's development strategy[10]. It is constantly strengthening comprehensive marine management, steadily improving its marine-related laws[11], and actively developing science, technology and education pertaining to[12] the oceans. China has made positive contributions to international ocean development and protection by participating positively in UN marine affairs, promoting cooperation between countries and regions and conscientiously carrying out its obligations in this field[13].

The year 1998 has been designated by the United Nations as International Ocean Year, and on this occasion[14] the Chinese Government would like to introduce the progress of China's work in this particular field[15] to the world[16].

(from *Beijing Review*)

解说：

★1. foreword 一词是由 fore（前面的）和 word（话）构成的，意思是"前言"，不要把它和 forward 混淆。

★2. 在原文里，"覆盖了地球表面的 71%"和后面的"是……"是并列谓语，它说明的是一个客观情况。在英语里，这种说明客观情况的话，特别是说明人们已知情况的话，在句子里一般放在次要位置，这样可以突出句子主要想说的话。因此译文用了一个从句：which covers 71 per cent of the earth's surface。

3. 译文在这里断句，然后另起一句，处理"也是……"，干净利索。

4. a treasure house of resources 和 an important regulator of the environment，中间用 and 相连，而不能像汉语那样用逗号连接。

★5. 原文这句话里，"世纪"一词出现两次。如译作 The coming 21st centary is a century in which…，语法上是成立的，但重复 century 是不可取的。即使用代词 is one in which 也显得啰嗦。因此译文以时间状语开始，直接说 In the coming 21st century mankind will…，请注意 mankind 前面不用冠词。还有一点，原文有个"新"字,译文就用 new opportunities 处理了。

6. 这里又用了 as defined by,这是一个很有用的说法。

7. "健康"一词在这里很不好译。译作 health 恐怕是不行的,译作 quality 又显得远了一点,所以译作 wholesomeness。据 Oxford Advanced Learner's Dictionary,wholesome 一词有两个义项,一个是 good for one's health or well-being,一个是 suggesting a healthy condition,这第二个义项正是我们这里需要的意思。

8. maritime 与 marine 意思相近。谈论航海和海事活动时多用 maritime。

9. 此处原文是一个独立的句子,译文却只用了一个介词短语。理由见本文解说2。

10. 译文在这里断句,前面说的是总的情况,后面再说具体做的事情。

11. 此处可能译为 its marine laws 就够了。

12. pertaining to 是个很有用的说法,表示"与……有关的"。

★13. 这句话讲了四件事情,前三件是我国具体做的事,最后一件是总的评价。译文把最后一件用谓语动词来处理,然后用 by 引出三个动名词,处理三件具体的事,这就突出了句子的重点。

14. 这句原文说了两件事,译文用了 and on this occasion 把前后两部分连了起来。

★15. marine 一词已出现多次,为避免重复,此处用了 in this particular field。

★16. 此处如照原文只说 would like to introduce the progress of China's work in this particular field,句子好像没有完,刹不住,因此在句末加了 to the world。

Unit 9　Law

Lesson 17　(E—C)

Bilingual Reading

Environmental Law

(Excerpt 1)

As recently as the early 1960s, the phrase "environmental law" would probably have produced little more than a puzzled look,[1] even from many lawyers. Such issues as clean air, pure water and freedom from noise pollution[2] were not important public concerns.[3] There were, of course, numerous state[4] and some federal laws[5] intended to protect America's rivers and streams from excessive[6] industrial pollution and to guard wildlife[7] from the depredations[8] of man. But these regulations were generally ignored. With enforcement power[9] dispersed among many federal, state and local agencies, most of which were seriously undermanned,[10] and with noncompliance penalties[11] so slight as to have little more than harassment value,[12] there were few incentives to obey the laws. Indeed, many environmental statutes[13] were so little publicized and so vaguely worded that their existence was hardly known and their meaning was scarcely understood.

Then, in 1962, came a book called *Silent Spring* by Rachel Carson. A powerful indictment[14] of America's disregard[15] of ecology, *Silent Spring* was aimed chiefly at the wholesale[16] use of chemical pesticides, especially DDT. In 1965 a court action took place that ranks[17] in environmental importance with the publication of *Silent Spring*. That was the reversal by a court of appeals[18] of a

Federal Power[19] Commission decision to grant a license for a Consolidated Edison power plant at Storm King Mountain on the Hudson River in New York. The court ordered new proceedings[20] that were to "include as a basic concern the preservation of natural beauty and of national historic shrines."[21]

提示：

第九单元：法律。这里的选篇有论述，有条文，大量使用法律术语。法律条文内容周密，语言精确。翻译此类文章或文件，需特别强调忠实于原文。法律条文更要字斟句酌，以最精练的语言准确地传达原意。

施觉怀在"翻译法律文献的几个特点"一文中指出："法律文件的翻译，最主要的要求应当是'严谨'。因为法律文书直接影响到有关方面的权利义务，文字略有出入会产生严重后果。译文学作品所要求的文采，韵味，以至声调等等，在译法律文书中都不需要，译法律文书要求的是谨严和精确，甚至法学论著也是以谨严为宗。

"法律文书有正式法令、公约、合同与学术著作等，其具体要求又略有区别，法令、公约要求更严密一些，而法学著作可以在易解和流畅方面作一定的照应，但其根本要求还是严密，在严密与流畅之间有矛盾时，应牺牲流畅。翻译文学，同一作品可以有几种译本。但翻译法律（包括条约、法令、合同等，学术著作不在其内）就不应有几种译本，最理想的是只有一种译本，这才能体现出法律的严密性。"

他最后指出："根据以上选择的几个实例中所表明的问题，可以简单地归纳几点如下：

"（1）**条理清** 因法律文书往往繁复，不先弄清全文的条理，只是逐字或逐段跟着转，容易译乱，甚至译错。

"（2）**文字明** 因法律条文有其独特的表现方式，有时与汉语出入颇大，译文容易艰涩难懂，所以要在不影响原意的条件下,尽量使译文明确、严谨而不僵硬。

"(3) **意思全** 因在法律文书中,往往一个限制性短语,甚至一个字都涉及权利义务范围,不能含糊。当然有些意思重合,仅仅为了强调某种意思的并立字,可以不必一一跟着重复。需要的是意思完全而不是字字齐全。"(见《翻译论集》第1018,1025页)

关于第17课的对照阅读(BR17),请注意以下各点。

1. a puzzled look: a look on one's face that shows one is puzzled

2. freedom from noise pollution: the fact that there is no noise pollution

3. public concerns: worries of people in general

4. state laws: laws passed by the state (州)

5. federal laws: laws passed at the federal (联邦的) level

6. excessive: too much

7. wildlife: animals (and plants) which live and grow wild

8. depredations: destruction

9. enforcement power: the power to enforce the laws

10. undermanned: not having enough workers

11. noncompliance penalties: punishment for breaking a law

12. harassment value: the effect of making people worried

13. statute: law

14. indictment: accusation/charge

15. disregard: paying no attention to

16. wholesale: on a large scale

17. that ranks...with the publication of Silent Spring: that has equal importance with the publication of Silent Spring

18. court of appeals: 上诉法院

19. power: electric power

20. proceedings: an action taken in law

21. include as a basic concern the preservation of natural beauty

and of national historic shrines = include the preservation of natural beauty and of national historic shrines as a basic concern

译文：

环境保护法
（摘录1）

早在六十年代初[1]，甚至连许多律师接触到"环保法"这个词儿，大半也只会感到纳闷而已[2]。当时[3]，诸如空气清新、水质洁净、无噪声污染之类的问题[4]，都不是公众怎么了不起的关切所在。当然，已经有了许多州法和一些联邦法，其立法意图是保护美国的江河，使之免受过分的工业污染并保护野生生物不受人类的掠夺。可是对这些规定，人们一般都置之不理[5]。由于执法的权力分散在许许多多的联邦、州和地方等三级机关（而这些机关大多人手严重不足），也由于因违法而科处的罚款微不足道（从而只有恼人心烦的意义），人们就缺乏服从法律的劲头了[6]。说真的，许多环境法的宣传工作之薄弱与措词之含糊，使人简直不知道有环境法，而环境法的意义也就无人了解了[7]。

不久以后，在1962年雷切尔·卡森所著、名为《沉默的春天》一书问世了[8]。《沉默的春天》有力地控诉了美国之忽视生态[9]，它主要是针对大规模使用农药——特别是滴滴涕。1965年又发生了一件诉讼，其对环境之重要意义，不亚于《沉默的春天》之出版[10]：某上诉法院驳回了联邦电力委员会关于向纽约哈得逊河畔施多姆金山爱迪生联合发电厂颁发许可的决定。该法院命重新处理[11]该案并"以保护自然美和历史名胜为基本注意事项"。

（原文及译文均选自陈忠诚选编《法律英语五十篇》）

解说：

1. As recently as... 强调与本文的写作时间相隔很近，而不是很远。因此"早在六十年代初"似需改为"就在六十年代初"。

★2．原文以 the phrase "environmental law" 为主语。译文如像原文那样将even from many lawyers 保留在句末，句子无法安排，因此将"许多律师"提前作主语。

3．原文动词是were，这一时态表明这句话说的是过去的情况。译文加了"当时"二字，比较清楚。

4．clean air, pure water and freedom from noise pollution 译为"空气清新、水质洁净、无噪声污染"。名词短语译成了主谓结构或动宾结构。

5．这一句原文是被动语态，译文不必用被动式。但如译作"人们一般都不理采这些规定"，句子显得平淡。现在的译文把"置之不理"放在句末，重点比较突出。

6．这一句译文用了两个括号。遇到不好处理的句子，特别是定语从句，把次要内容放在括号里，也不失为一种译法。此句不用括号也可以。此外，have little more than harassment value 似可译作"只能起到让人心烦的作用"，或译作"只不过让人感到一阵心烦"。

★7．这一句译文避开了原文里的四个被动语态的动词和一个抽象名词，句子结构作了较大的变动。此外，"环境法"一词在句中出现三次，这种重复在汉语里是容许的。

8．came 一词译为"问世"，是上下文决定的。

9．请注意同位语 A powerful indictment of America's disregard of ecology 的译法。

★10．rank with… 意为"和……同样重要"。此处译文从反面入手，译为"不亚于……"，更为有力。

11．"处理"似可改为"审理"。

翻译理论简介

王佐良

著名翻译家王佐良教授以翻译英诗为主，兼及散文和戏剧。1980年出版的他的《英国诗文选译集》中，有他译的彭斯诗11首，雪莱诗8首，麦克迪儿米德诗10首，有他译的培根的散文3篇，科贝特的散文6篇。1985年出版了他译的《彭斯诗选》。此外他还曾将曹禺的《雷雨》译成英语。

王佐良教授不但是一位实践者，而且是一位翻译理论家。他不爱用抽像的字眼，而是以朴实、通俗的语言阐明深刻的道理。他的理论是他的经验总结。

王佐良教授关于翻译的论述，归纳起来，有以下12个要点：

1. 对翻译工作的认识。他说："文学翻译不是机械乏味的事，而是一种创造性的努力。"[1] "虽然困难不少，我却仍然喜欢译诗，也许是因为它毕竟是一种创造性的艺术活动，它的要求是严格的，而它的慰藉却又是甜蜜的。"[2] "……他们的努力使翻译工作变成一种英雄的事业。"[3]

2. 该用什么样的文字？他说"培根是一个善写警句的散文家，文字紧凑，又有一点古奥。问题是：译这样的作品该用什么样的文字？我做了一个试验，用浅近的文言译它，我的朋友们看了说喜欢我的译文。但是我觉得这里用文言是一种特殊情况，不足为训。通常情况下，我都是用白话文译。"[4]有人问他："你怎样译苏格兰方言，与译英文有什么不同？"他说："这确是一个问题。……我的回答是：仍然用我们中国的普通白话。译彭斯也有这个问题。我考虑过，也问过朋友，他们开玩笑说：不妨一试东北方言或四川方言。但是我做不到，我连北京方言也不会用。而且诗不比小说，小说里用方言是常见的，诗里就少。翻译更难办。……这里确实有一个值得深入研究的课题。我希望将来会有掌握地方方言较好的译者起来重译彭斯。现在我们这些人的译文毕竟只是过渡性的译文。"[5]

3. 关于直译与意译。他说:"近年来译成英语的外国文学作品在数量和质量上都进入一个新的繁荣时期。许多过去已有出色译文的各国名著被重新翻译出版,例如《企鹅古典丛书》(Penguin Classics)就是受到欢迎的,其主编人 E.V.Rieu 对译者只提出两个字的要求:'Write English!'这是以'顺'为主的翻译原则,但是这个"顺"必须用现代地道英语表现出来,Rieu 自己就以荷马史诗的新译实践了这个主张。针锋相对地,俄国血统的美国作家 Nabokov 则完全用直译的办法译了普希金的《叶甫盖尼·奥涅金》,提出了 maximal translation 的主张,亦即要:

...rendering as closely as the associative and syntactical capacities of another language allows the exact contextual meaning of the original.

……看来这存在已久的直译意译之争还要继续下去,但是最好的检验标准仍然是译文本身的质量。绝对的意译等于否定翻译,绝对的直译也被多次的尝试证明为此路不通。许多好的译者总是兼采直译意译之长,而且不论根据什么理论,好的译文才会受到读者欢迎,而只有为读者接受,译文才起了交流作用。"[6]

4. 关于风格。他说:"适合就是一切。文体学的灵魂在于研究什么样的语言适合什么样的社会场合。译者的任务在于再现原作的面貌和精神:原作是细致说理的,译文也细致说理;原作是高举想像之翼的,译文也高举想像之翼。一篇文章的风格只是作者为表达特定内容而运用语言的个人方式,它与内容是血肉一体,而不是外加的、美化的成分。因此从译文来说,严复的"信、达、雅"里的"雅"是没有道理的——原作如不雅,又何雅之可言?"[7]

5. 诗是否可译?他说:"我认为绝大多数的思想概念,即使不是所有的,都是能够翻译出来的;不易翻译的是原作的气氛,或者说力量。翻译诗词尤其如此。有一位美国诗人,我想是罗伯特·弗罗斯特吧,他不是说在翻译过程中会把诗味丢掉吗?也就是说诗歌几乎是无法翻译的。但是,歌德曾说过,一方面我们简直无法翻译诗歌;而另一方面却又非常需要翻译诗歌。这两者确实是很矛盾的。可是,事实上许多人在努力翻译诗歌。我确实感到翻译诗歌,其乐无穷。"[8]

6. 怎样译诗?他说:"此中的体会,主要一点是译诗须像诗。这就是说,要忠实传达原作的内容,意境,情调;格律要大致如原诗(押韵的也押韵,自由诗也作自由诗),但又不必追求每行字数的一律;语言要设法接近原作,要保持其原有的新鲜或锐利,特别是形象要直译。更要紧的,是这一切须结合诗的整体来考虑,亦即首先要揣摸出整首诗的精神、情调、风格,然后才确定细节的处理;译完之后,要把全诗从头到尾多读几遍,这时就会发现在注意细节时所不曾料到的一些问题(或全文不联贯,或重点不突出,或有套语待改,芜词可去,等等)。译者要掌握一切可能掌握的材料,深入了解原诗(这一点做到极为不易),又要在自己的译文上有创新和探索的勇气(不仅在用词方面,还有句子的排列组合,声韵的选择和调配等等方面,甚至全文的风格,都可以进行试验)。"[9]

7. 关于词语引起的联想。他说:"在翻译中,在区分短语的细微差别上,或是在处理某一短语所引起的各种联想方面,或在表达一首诗总的气氛方面,肯定会丢失原诗中的某些东西。在这一点上,我同意罗伯特·弗罗斯特的意见,他说在翻译诗的过程中总要丢掉一些东西。……只要我们中国人一用'江南'二字,表示'长江以南'的意思,江南秀丽的景色马上就会展现在我们的眼前,在那里可以看到最好看的园林,最漂亮的美人。同样,'塞外'这一短语会使人联想到一片白雪皑皑、荒无人烟的景象,想到历史上的游牧部落。所以,我认为这些东西都是很难翻译的。"[10]

8. 关于比喻。有人问:"你所谓保持比喻,究竟是什么意思?"他说:"我的意思是,如果在原诗里有某个比喻,应该把它直译过来,保持它原有的新鲜和气势。但这里有一个问题。有时一个比喻在原来语言中很新鲜,但是在译文中却类似套话,通常是因为译者用了一个意思大体相同的成语。在彭斯的《一朵红红的玫瑰》里,你记得,有一行诗表达主人公对一位姑娘的爱,说是即使所有的海洋干枯了,岩石都被太阳熔化了,他仍然忠于爱情。我想在原诗里这关于海和岩石的比喻一定是很新鲜很有力的。我们汉语里恰好有一个成语——'海枯石烂不变心'——可以说是完全的'对等词'。但是它在中国已经用得太久太广了,变成了陈词滥调。所以我在译文里避免用它,另外用了一个说法,文字不那么流利,但保存了原来的比喻。"[11]

9. 关于对等词。他说:"这一点很有意思,他触到了一个词义学所不常处理的问题,即同一意义的词(涕泗与 tears 是完全的等同语),在不同文化传统、不同社会里所引起的不同反应问题。某些词在一个语言里有强烈的情感力量,而其等同词在另一语言里却平淡无奇,上列'涕泗'便是一例。反过来,也有某一词在原文里近乎套语,而照字面直译到另一语言却显得生动、新鲜,'雨后春笋'便是一例。人们喜欢谈翻译中'对等词'的重要,殊不知真正的对应词应该包括情感力量,背景烘托,新鲜还是陈腐,时髦还是古旧,声调是和谐还是故意不协律,引起的联想是雅还是俗等等方面的'对等',而且在文学作品特别是诗的翻译中还有比词对词、句对句的对等更重要的通篇的'神似'问题。这一切使得翻译更为不易,但也正是这点不易使翻译跳出'技巧'的范畴而变为一种艺术,使它能那样强烈地吸引着无数世代的有志之士——他们明知其大不易而甘愿为之,而且精益求精,乐此不疲;他们是再创造的能人,他们在两种文化之间搭着桥梁,他们的努力使翻译工作变成一种英雄的事业。"[12]

10. 关于文化比较。他说:"他在寻找与原文相当的'对等词'的过程中,就要作一番比较,因为真正的对等应该是在各自文化里的含义、作用、范围、情感色彩、影响等等都相当。这当中,陷阱是不少的。……他处理的是个别的词,他面对的则是两大片文化。"[13]他又说:"翻译者必须是一个真正意义的文化人。

人们全说：他必须掌握两种语言；确实如此，但是不了解语言当中的社会文化，谁也无法真正掌握语言。不是说一个大概的了解，而是要了解使用这一语言的人民的过去与现在，这就包括了历史，动态，风俗习惯，经济基础，情感生活，哲学思想，科技成就，政治和社会组织，等等；而且了解得越细致、越深入，越好。"[14]

11．关于全文的重要性。他说："通常人们太多注意细节，不够注意整体。然而一首诗或一个故事有它自己的统一性。如果译者掌握了整个作品的意境、气氛或效果，他有时会发现某些细节并不直接促成总的效果，他就可以根据译文语言的特点作些变通。这样他就取得一种新的自由，使他能振奋精神，敢于创新。他将开始感到文学翻译不是机械乏味的事，而是一种创造性的努力。"[15]

12．关于怎样提高。他说："我以为更重要的还是翻译者本身要有长期的、多方面的实践，从中积累甘苦自知的经验，在一定时候同其他的翻译者交流一下，其好处远超过读任何语言学或翻译理论的著作。"[16] "世界文学里的好作品多得很，问题在于我们所知太少。翻译的作用，就是能帮助不懂外文的读者了解到更多关于外面世界的事情。首先，当然译者自己得大大打开眼界。"[17] "作为一个译者，我总是感到需要不断锻炼，要使自己的汉语炼得纯净而又锐利。"[18]他还说："翻译无论是当作艺术也好，科学也好，甚至叫它技术也好，它是有无限广阔的前途的。它是一个生长点，它正在生长。它也是一个开放的领域，有很多很多事情可以做。我们必须不断地学习，不断地深入观察，不断地深入实践。翻译者是一个永恒的学生。"[19]

1．《翻译：思考与试笔》，第 74 页。

2．"《英国诗文选译集》序"。

3．《翻译：思考与试笔》，17 页。

4．同上，第 69 页。

5．同上，第 70 页。

6．"现代英语的多功用"，《英语文体学论文集》，第 5—6 页。

7．《翻译：思考与试笔》，第 15—16 页。

8．同上，第 86 页。

9．"《英国诗文选译集》序"。

10．《翻译：思考与试笔》，第 87 页。

11．同上，第 72—73 页。

12．同上，第 17 页。

13．同上，第 19 页。

14．同上，第 18 页。

15．同上，第 74 页。

16．同上，第 16 页。

17．同上，第 71 页。

18．同上，第 73 页。

19．同上，第 36 页。

参考书目：

1．王佐良，《英国诗文选译集》，外语教学与研究出版社，1980 年。

2．王佐良，《英语文体学论文集》，外语教学与研究出版社，1980 年。

3．王佐良，《彭斯诗选》，人民文学出版社，1985 年。

4．王佐良，《论契合》，外语教学与研究出版社，1985 年。

5．王佐良，《翻译：思考与试笔》，外语教学与研究出版社，1989 年。

Exercise 17

将下列短文译成汉语：

Environmental Law
(Excerpt 2)

Today concern for the environment extends into such areas as chemical pollution of the air we breathe and the water we drink, strip mining,[1] dam and road building, noise pollution, offshore oil drilling, nuclear energy, waste disposal,[2] the use of aerosol cans and nonreturnable beverage containers and a host of[3] other issues. In fact, there is hardly a realm[4] of national life[5] that is not touched by the controversy[6] that often pits those who style[7] themselves environmentalists against proponents of economic growth[8] in our energy-consuming society. The problem is to balance the needs of the environment against those of the economy or consumers trying to cope with the high cost of living without destroying the earth on which we all depend.

In the late 1960s both state and federal governments began enacting legislation[9] and establishing new agencies to set and enforce standards of clean air and water and to protect America's remaining open land[10] from abuse by overzealous developers. The federal Clean Air Act[11] of 1967, the Clean Air Act Amendment[12] of 1970 and the 1972 amendments to the federal Water Pollution Control Act set new high standards for environmental quality. In many cases states have followed suit[13] by setting their own tough standards of air, water and land use. At every session of Congress and at most sessions of state legislatures[14] new bills[15] are brought forth, either to strengthen or weaken environmental standards, and hearings[16] are held in which groups with different interests battle through private lobbies,[17] industrial associations, labor unions and citizens' organizations to effect the legislation to their liking.[18] Inevitably, trade-offs[19] are made—such as a lowering of mandated auto pollution standards for the immediate future against a raising of overall air quality requirements—and the degree to which long-term environmental considerations are taken into account usually depends upon the ability of environmental groups to bring their pressure to bear in the hearings.

提示：

1. strip mining: mining in an open pit after removal of the earth and rock covering a mineral deposit

2. waste disposal: disposal of waste material

3. a host of: a large number of

4. realm: area

5. national life: people's livelihood

6. controversy: dispute/debate

7. style (v.): call/regard...as

8. proponents of economic growth: people who are for economic growth

9. enacting legislation: making laws

10. open land: land that is not fenced in

11. Act: 法

12. amendment: 修正案

13. follow suit: do the same as someone else has

14. legislature: law making body

15. bill: 议案

16. hearings: 听证会

17. lobby: 院外活动集团

18. to their liking: which suits their ideas or expectations

19. trade-off: the exchange of one thing for another, esp. to bring about a compromise

Key to Exercise 17

译文：

环境保护法
（摘录2）

今天，环境问题[1]已扩大到了下列领域：人们呼吸的空气和饮用的水之化学污染、露天采矿、堤坝和道路之修建、噪声污染、近海石油钻探、核能、三废处理、溶胶罐和不回收饮料容器之利用和一系列其它问题。事实上，国民生活的任何一个方面都没有不涉及这样一种争议[2]——这种争议往往使以环境论者自居的人[3]同美国耗能社会经济增长主张者对立起来。问题在于把保护环境的需要同经济需要和试图既能应付昂贵的生活费用而又不致破坏人们所赖以为生的地球的消费者的需要平衡起来。[4]

六十年代末，各州政府和联邦政府都曾开始立法并建立新的机构，来制定并执行保持空气和水洁净的标准，来保护美国现有的尚未开发的土地免受过分积极的开发商的糟蹋。[5] 1967年联邦《空气洁净法》、1970年《修正空气洁净法》和1972年联邦《水污染防治法》修正条款都给环境质量规定了新的标准。在许多情况下，各州也追随效尤，纷纷提出其对利用空气、水和土地的严格标准。[6]美国国会的每次会议和各州州议会的大多数会议上，都提出了许多不是要提高便是要降低环境标准的新议案；还举行了听证会，会上不同利益的集团通过私人院外集团、工业联合会、工会和公民组织，使立法合自己的胃口。（利益不同的各方）必然要互相作出让步才能取得进展——如，以在不久的将来降低强制规定的汽车污染标准来换取[7]提高空气质量的整体要求；而照顾到长期环境考虑的程度如何，[8]则一般取决于各环境利益集团对

195

听证会施加有效压力的能耐了。

（原文及译文均选自陈忠诚选编《法律英语五十篇》）

解说：

1．concern for the environment 没有译作"对环境的关心"，而译作"环境问题"，比较清楚。

2．there is hardly a realm...that is not... 是双重否定结构，可译作"几乎没有……不……"，或"无不……"。

3．who style themselves... 有贬义，译文"以……自居的人"恰当地表达了原文的语气。

4．这一句译文似可在中间用逗号点开，重复"平衡起来"，改为"问题在于把保护环境的需要同经济需要平衡起来，同试图既能应付昂贵的生活费用而又不致破坏人们所赖以为生的地球的消费者的需要平衡起来"。

5．这一句虽很长，但译文与原文结构相近，用了两个并列的"来……"表示两个目的。

6．"追随效尤，纷纷提出……"，据《现代汉语词典》，"效尤"的意思是："明知别人的行为是错误的而照样去做"，因此有贬义。译文似可改为"纷纷效法，提出……"

7．against 译作"换取"，这是因为前面提到 trade-offs。在这个上下文里，这样译是可以的。

8．the degree to which... 译作"……的程度如何"是好的。long-term environmental considerations 似可译得更灵活一点。这一部分可译作"而对环境方面的长远考虑能够照顾到什么程度"。

Lesson 18 (C—E)

Bilingual Reading

中华人民共和国中外合资经营企业法

(1979年7月1日第五届全国人民代表大会第二次会议通过，根据1990年4月4日第七届全国人民代表大会第三次会议《关于修改〈中华人民共和国中外合资经营企业法〉的决定》修正)

第一条 中华人民共和国为了扩大国际经济合作和技术交流，允许外国公司、企业和其它经济组织或个人（以下简称外国合营者），按照平等互利的原则，经中国政府批准，在中华人民共和国境内，同中国的公司、企业或其它经济组织（以下简称中国合营者）共同举办合营企业。

第二条 中国政府依法保护外国合营者按照经中国政府批准的协议、合同、章程在合营企业的投资、应分得的利润和其他合法权益。

合营企业的一切活动应遵守中华人民共和国法律，法令和有关条例规定。

国家对合营企业不实行国有化和征收；在特殊情况下，根据社会公共利益的需要，对合营企业可以依照法律程序实行征收，并给予相应的补偿。

第三条 合营各方签订的合营协议、合同、章程，应报国家对外经济贸易主管部门（以下称审查批准机关）审查批准。审查批准机关应在三个月内决定批准或不批准。合营企业经批准后，向国家工商行政管理主管部门登记，领取营业执照，开始营业。

第四条 合营企业的形式为有限责任公司。

在合营企业的注册资本中，外国合营者的投资比例一般不低于百分之二十五。

合营各方按注册资本比例分享利润和分担风险及亏损。

合营者的注册资本如果转让必须经合营各方同意。

第五条 合营企业各方可以现金、实物、工业产权等进行投资。

外国合营者作为投资的技术和设备，必须确实是适合我国需要的先进技术和设备。如果有意以落后的技术和设备进行欺骗，造成损失的，应赔偿损失。

中国合营者的投资可包括为合营企业经营期间提供的场地使用权。如果场地使用权未作为中国合营者投资的一部分，合营企业应向中国政府缴纳使用费。

上述各项投资应在合营企业的合同和章程中加以规定，其价格（场地除外）由合营各方评议商定。

第六条 合营企业设董事会，其人数组成由合营各方协商，在合同、章程中确定，并由合营各方委派和撤换。董事长和副董事长由合营各方协商确定或由董事会选举产生。中外合营者的一方担任董事长的，由他方担任副董事长。董事会根据平等互利的原则，决定合营企业的重大问题。

董事会的职权是按合营企业章程规定，讨论决定合营企业的一切重大问题：企业发展规划、生产经营活动方案、收支预算、利润分配、劳动工资计划、停业，以及总经理、副总经理、总工程师、总会计师、审计师的任命或聘请及其职权和待遇等。

正副总经理（或正副厂长）由合营各方分别担任。

合营企业职工的雇用、解雇，依法由合营各方的协议、合同规定。

第七条 合营企业获得的毛利润，按中华人民共和国税法规定缴纳合营企业所得税后，扣除合营企业章程规定的储备基金、职工奖励及福利基金、企业发展基金，净利润根据合营各方注册资本的比例进行分配。

合营企业依照国家有关税收的法律和行政法规的规定，可以享受减税、免税的优惠待遇。

外国合营者将分得的净利润用于在中国境内再投资时，可申请退还已缴纳的部分所得税。

第八条 合营企业应凭营业执照在国家外汇管理机关允许经营外汇业务的银行或其他金融机构开立外汇帐户。

合营企业的有关外汇事宜，应遵照中华人民共和国外汇管理条例办理。

合营企业在其经营活动中，可直接向外国银行筹措资金。

合营企业的各项保险应向中国的保险公司投保。

第九条 合营企业生产经营计划，应报主管部门备案，并通过经济合同方式执行。

合营企业所需原材料、燃料、配套件等，应尽先在中国购买，也可由合营企业自筹外汇，直接在国际市场上购买。

鼓励合营企业向中国境外销售产品。出口产品可由合营企业直接或与其有关的委托机构向国外市场出售，也可通过中国的外贸机构出售。合营企业产品也可在中国市场销售。

合营企业需要时可在中国境外设立分支机构。

第十条 外国合营者在履行法律和协议、合同规定的义务后分得的净利润，在合营企业期满或者中止时所分得的资金以及其它资金，可按合营企业合同规定的货币，按外汇管理条例汇往国外。

鼓励外国合营者将可汇出的外汇存入中国银行。

（待续）

译文：

LAW OF THE PEOPLE'S REPUBLIC OF CHINA ON CHINESE-FOREIGN EQUITY JOINT VENTURES

(Adopted at the Second Session of the Fifth National People's Congress on July 1, 1979, and revised in accordance with the Decision of the National People's Congress Regarding the Revision of the

Law of the People's Republic of China on Chinese-Foreign Equity Joint Ventures adopted at the Third Session of the Seventh National People's Congress on April 4, 1990)

Article 1 With a view to expanding international economic cooperation and technological exchange, the People's Republic of China[1] permits foreign companies, enterprises, other economic organizations or individuals (hereinafter referred to as "foreign joint venturers")[2] to establish equity joint ventures[3] together with Chinese companies, enterprises or other economic organizations (hereinafter referred to as "Chinese joint venturers") within the territory of the People's Republic of China on the principle of equality and mutual benefit and subject to approval by the Chinese Government.[4]

Article 2 The Chinese Government protects, according to the law, the investment of foreign joint venturers, the profits due them and their other lawful rights and interests in an equity joint venture, pursuant to the agreement, contract and articles of association approved by the Chinese Government.[5]

All activities of an equity joint venture shall comply with[6] the provisions of the laws, decrees and pertinent regulations of the People's Republic of China.

The State shall not nationalize or requisition any equity joint venture. Under special circumstances, when public interest requires, equity joint ventures may be requisitioned by following legal procedures and appropriate compensation shall be made.

Article 3 The equity joint venture agreement, contract and articles of association signed by the parties to the venture[7] shall be submitted to the State's competent department in charge of foreign economic relations and trade (hereinafter referred to as the examination and approval authorities) for examination and approval. The examination and approval authorities[8] shall decide to approve or disapprove the venture within three months. When approved, the equity joint venture shall register with[9] the State's competent department in charge of industry and commerce administration, acquire a business licence and start operations.

Article 4 An equity joint venture shall take the form of a limited liability company.

The proportion of the foreign joint venturer's investment in an equity joint venture shall be, in general, not less than 25 percent of its registered capital.

The parties to the venture shall share the profits, risks and losses[10] in proportion to their contributions to the registered capital.

If any of the joint venturers wish to assign[11] its registered capital, it must obtain the consent of the other parties to the venture.

Article 5 The parties to an equity joint venture may make their investment in cash, in kind or in industrial property rights, etc.

The technology and equipment contributed by a foreign joint venturer as its investment must be really advanced technology and equipment that suit China's[12] needs. In case of losses caused by a foreign joint venturer in its practising deception through the intentional provision of outdated technology and equipment, it[13] shall compensate for the losses.

A Chinese joint venturer's investment may include the right to the use of a site provided for the equity joint venture during the period of its operation. If the right to the use of the site is not taken as a part of the Chinese joint venturer's investment, the equity joint venture shall pay the Chinese Government for its use.

The above-mentioned investments shall be specified in the contract and articles of association of the equity joint venture and their value (excluding that of the site) shall be assessed by all parties to the venture.[14]

Article 6 An equity joint venture shall have a board of directors;[15] the number of the directors thereof from each party and composition of the board shall be stipulated in the contract and articles of association after consultation among the parties to the venture; such directors shall be appointed and replaced by the relevant parties. The chairman and the vice-chairman (vice-chairmen)[16] shall be determined through consultation by the parties to the venture or elected by the board of directors. If the Chinese side or the foreign side assumes the office of the chairman, the other side shall assume the office(s) of vice-chairman (vice-chairmen). The board of directors shall decide on important problems concerning the joint venture on the principle of equality and mutual benefit.[17]

The functions and powers of the board of directors are, as stipulated in the articles of association of the equity joint venture, to discuss and decide all major issues concerning the venture, namely,[18] the venture's development plans, proposals for production and business operations, the budget for revenues and expenditure, the distribution of profits, the plans concerning manpower and wages, the termination of business, and the appointment or employment of the general manager, the vice-general manager(s), the chief engineer, the treasurer and the auditors, as well as the determination of their functions, powers and terms of employment, etc.

The offices[19] of general manager and vice-general manager(s) (or factory manager and deputy manager(s)) shall be assumed by the respective parties to the venture.

The employment and discharge of the workers and staff members of an equity joint venture shall be stipulated in accordance with the law in the agreement and contract concluded by the parties to the venture.

Article 7 The net profit of an equity joint venture shall be distributed among the parties to the joint venture in proportion to their respective contributions to the registered capital, after payment out of its gross profit of the equity joint venture income tax,[20] pursuant to the provisions of the tax laws of the People's Republic of China, and after deductions from the gross profit of a reserve fund, a bonus and welfare fund for workers and staff members and a venture expansion fund,[21] as stipulated in the venture's articles of association.[22]

An equity joint venture may, in accordance with provisions of the relevant laws and administrative rules and regulations of the State on taxation, enjoy preferential treatment for tax reductions or exemptions.

A foreign joint venturer that reinvests its share of the net profit within Chinese territory may apply for a partial refund of the income tax already paid.

Article 8 An equity joint venture shall, on the strength of its business licence, open a foreign exchange account with a bank or any other financial institution which is permitted by the State agency for foreign exchange control to handle foreign exchange transactions.

An equity joint venture shall handle its foreign exchange transactions[23] in accordance with the regulations on foreign exchange control of the People's Republic of China.

An equity joint venture may, in its business operations, directly raise funds from foreign banks.

The various kinds of insurance coverage of an equity joint venture shall be furnished by Chinese insurance companies.

Article 9 The production and business operating plans of an equity joint venture shall be submitted to the competent authorities for record and shall be implemented through economic contracts.

In its purchase of required raw and processed materials, fuels, auxiliary equipment, etc., an equity joint venture should first give priority to purchases in China.[24] It may also make such purchases directly on the world market with foreign exchange raised by itself.

An equity joint venture shall be encouraged to market its products outside China.[25] It may sell its export products on foreign markets directly or through associated agencies or China's foreign trade agencies. Its products may also be sold on the Chinese market.

Whenever necessary, an equity joint venture may set up branches and subbranches outside China.

Article 10 The net profit which a foreign joint venturer receives as its share after performing its obligations under the laws, and the agreements or the contract, the funds it receives upon the expiration of the venture's term of operation or the suspension thereof, and its other funds may be remitted abroad in accordance with foreign exchange control regulations and in the currency or currencies specified in the contract concerning the equity joint venture.[26]

A foreign joint venturer shall be encouraged to deposit in the Bank of China foreign exchange which it is entitled to remit abroad.[27]

(to be continued)

解说：

★1. 译文先处理"为了……"，然后再出主语 the People's Republic of China。

★2. "以下简称"译作 hereinafter referred to as... 这是一个常用的套语。

3. venture 在这里是国际通用的术语，并无"冒险"之意。

★4. 这一句很长，译文将主要内容相对集中，状语有的放在句首，有的放在句末。

5. 状语"按照……章程"译作 pursuant to...，放在句末。

★ 6．"遵守"此处译作comply with。主语是activities，动词不能用obey, observe 或abide by。

7．"合营各方"译作the parties to the venture。作为一方参加某机构，party 后面要用介词 to。

★ 8．authorities 指"机关"或"部门"，均用复数。

9．"向……登记"译作register with...。请注意介词with。

★ 10．原文"分享"和"利润"连用。"分担"和"风险及亏损"连用。share 是一个中性词，后面既可以接profits，也可以接risks and losses。

★ 11．原文"资本如果转让"是以主动式表示被动的含义，英语很少用这种结构。因此译文以any of the joint venturers 为主语，这样才能与动词wish to assign 搭配。

★ 12．"我国"此处译作China，这是英语的习惯用法，提到自己的国家时，往往不说our country，而说自己国家的名称。

13．原文是无主句，但意思是清楚的。因此译文以 it（指a foreign joint venturer）为主语。

14．"加以规定"和"由……商定"都有被动的含义，因此译文用了被动语态。

★ 15．"合营企业设董事会"译作An equity joint venture shall have a board of directors。动词"设"不一定译作set up。

16．董事长只有一位，副董事长可以是一位，也可以不止一位，但汉语不必说明单复数。英语则不然，如只说the vice-chairman 则表示只有一位。法律条文必须说得很明确，而且要照顾到各种情况，所以加了(vice-chairmen)。

★ 17．"根据平等互利的原则"译作on the principle of equality and mutual benefit，这是一个标准的英语说法。"根据"不一定译作according to 或 in accordance with。

18．此处原文用冒号，译文用namely，这种译法更为多见。

★ 19．汉语可以说"正副总经理由……担任"，但英语不能直接把manager 和 assume 连用，因此加了 the offices。主语和谓语怎样搭配，这是翻译过程中经常遇到的一个问题。

20. 此处的介词短语 of the equity joint venture income tax，在语法上与前面的 payment 相连，而不与 gross profit 相连。

21. 这里的介词短语 of a reserve fund...and a venture expansion fund，在语法上与 deductions 相连，而不与 gross profit 相连。

★22. 这一句译文突出了净利润的分配，把 the net profit... 放在句首，其余内容均译作状语。

★23. "有关外汇事宜"译作 foreign exchange transactions, "办理"译作 handle，这在英语里是一个很好的搭配。动词和宾语怎样搭配，也是翻译过程中需要经常考虑的一个问题。

24. 原文以"合营企业所需原材料、燃料、配套件等"为主语，是一个有被动含义的主动句，译文以 an equity joint venture 为主语，就加了 in its purchase of 引出原来的主语。

25. 原文是个无主句，译文用了被动语态。

26. 这一句虽然很长，但并不复杂。其主要部分是 The net profit..., the funds..., and its other funds may be remitted abroad...，其余内容均译作定语或状语。

27. foreign exchange 后面还有定语从句，因此把 in the Bank of China 放在动词与宾语之间。在一般情况下，地点状语总是放在最后的。

―――― 翻译理论选读 ――――

Tytler's Three Principles *

---

　　* 这个标题是编者加的。本文作者泰特勒（Alexander Fraser Tytler, 1747—1814）于 1790 年在英国爱丁堡皇家学会宣读论文，题目为"论翻译的原则"（*Essay on the Principles of Translation*），随后出版单行本。他在文中提出了著名的翻译三原则。

　　泰特勒提出的三原则，在我国翻译界有很大影响。从二十年代直到最近，人们一直在议论。

　　1921 年郑振铎在《小说月报》发表文章，题为"译文学书的三个问题"（见《翻译论集》第 369—382 页），结合译文学书的方法详细评介了泰特勒的三原则。

　　1950 年罗书肆在《翻译通报》上著文介绍泰特勒的翻译理论（见《外国翻译理论评介文集》第 13—20 页），他认为"泰特勒的翻译理论大部分是正确的"。

　　1951 年傅雷在致林以亮的信中谈到泰特勒这部著作。他说："泰特勒一书，我只能读其三分之一，即英法文对照的部分……但他的理论大致还是不错的……例如他说凡是 idiom，倘不能在译文中找到相等的（equivalent）idiom，那么只能用平易简单的句子把原文的意义说出来，因为照原文字面搬过来（这是中国译者百分之九十九以上的人所用的办法），使译法变成 intolerable 是绝对不可以的。"（见《翻译论集》第 547—548 页）

　　1963 年徐永煐在《外语教学与研究》发表文章，题为"论翻译的矛盾统一"。他在文中对严复的信、达、雅和泰特勒的三原则作了比较。他认为"泰特勒的三原则，严复的信达雅，归根到底是不同程度的信。"（见《翻译论集》第 687 页）

　　1979 年刘重德在《湖南师院学报》著文，题为"试论翻译的原则"。他说："在翻译的原则方面，严复所定的信达雅，我认为，只要撇开他所讲的一些具体办法，'信''达'两字仍可沿用；而泰特勒所讲的三个总则，比较完善，可全部采纳。"（见《翻译论集》第 823 页）

　　1982 年周煦良在《翻译通讯》发表了题为"翻译三论"的文章，他说泰特勒"也提出三条翻译标准。其第二条就是要求翻译要反映原著风格，这是他不及严复的地方。严复只提雅，而不提原文风格，我们现在提文学翻译要有风格，也不宜要求译出原文风格；原文风格是无法转译的。"（见《翻译论集》第 975 页）

If it were possible accurately to define, or, perhaps more properly, to describe what is meant by a *good Translation*, it is evident that a considerable progress would be made towards establishing the Rules of the *Art*; for these Rules would flow naturally from that definition or description. But there is no subject of criticism where there has been so much difference of opinion...I would therefore describe a good translation to be, *That, in which the merit of the original work is so completely transfused into another language, as to be as distinctly apprehended, and as strongly felt, by a native of the country to which that language belongs, as it is by those who speak the language of the original work.*

Now, supposing this description to be a just one, which I think it is, let us exmaine what are the laws of translation which may be deduced from it.

It will follow,

Ⅰ. That the Translation should give a complete transcript of the ideas of the original work.

Ⅱ. That the style and manner of writing should be of the same character with that of the original.

Ⅲ. That the Translation should have all the ease of original composition.

(from A.F.Tytler: *Essay on the Principles of Translation*)

Exercise 18

将下列各条译成英语:

中华人民共和国中外合资经营企业法
(续)

第十一条　合营企业的外籍职工的工资收入和其它正当收

入，按中华人民共和国税法缴纳个人所得税[1]后，可按外汇管理条例汇往国外。

第十二条　合营企业的合营期限，按不同行业、不同情况，作不同的约定。有的行业的合营企业，应当约定合营期限；有的行业的合营企业，可以约定合营期限，也可以不约定合营期限。约定合营期限的合营企业，合营各方同意延长合营期限的，应在距合营期满六个月前向审查批准机关提出申请。[2]审查批准机关应自接到申请之日起一个月内决定批准或不批准。

第十三条　合营企业如发生严重亏损、一方不履行合同和章程规定的义务、不可抗力[3]等，经合营各方协商同意，报请审查批准机关批准，并向国家工商行政管理主管部门登记，可终止[4]合同。如果因违反合同[5]而造成损失的，应由违反合同的一方承担经济责任。

第十四条　合营各方发生纠纷，董事会不能协商解决时，由中国仲裁机构进行调解[6]或仲裁，[7]也可由合营各方协议在其它仲裁机构仲裁。

第十五条　本法自公布[8]之日起生效。[9]本法修改[10]权属于全国人民代表大会。

提示：

1. 个人所得税：individual income tax
2. 向……提出申请：file an application with...
3. 不可抗力：force majeure
4. 终止：terminate
5. 违反合同：breach the contract/a breach of contract
6. 调解：conciliation
7. 仲裁：arbitration
8. 公布：promulgation
9. 生效：enter into force
10. 修改：amend

Key to Exercise 18

译文：

Law of the People's Republic of China on Chinese-Foreign Equity Joint Ventures
(Continued)

Article 11 The wages, salaries or other legitimate income earned by a foreign worker or staff member of an equity joint venture, after payment of the individual income tax under the tax laws of the People's Republic of China,[1] may be remitted abroad in accordance with foreign exchange control regulations.

Article 12 Based on different lines of trade and different circumstances, arrangements for the duration of equity joint ventures may be made differently through agreement by the parties to the venture. Equity joint ventures engaged in certain lines of trade shall specify their duration in the contracts, while[2] equity joint ventures engaged in certain other lines of trade may choose to or not to specify their duration in the contracts.[3] Where[4] an equity joint venture has had its duration specified and the parties to the venture agree to extend the duration, the venture shall file an application for the purpose with the examination and approval authorities six months before its expiration. The examination and approval authorities shall, within one month after receipt of the application, decide on its approval or disapproval.

Article 13 In case of heavy losses, or failure of a party to perform its obligation under the contract and the articles of association[5], or force majeure, etc., the parties to the joint venture may, subject to their agreement through consultation, approval of their report by the examination and approval authorities and registration with the State's competent department in charge of industry and commerce administration[6], terminate the contract. In cases of losses caused by a breach of contract, the party that has breached the contract shall bear the economic responsibilities.

Article 14 Disputes arising between the parties to an equity joint venture which the board of directors has failed to settle through consultation may be settled through conciliation or arbitration by an arbitration agency of China or[7] through arbitration by another arbitration agency agreed upon by the parties.

Article 15 This Law shall enter into force as of the date of promulgation. The power to amend this Law[8] shall be vested in the National People's Congress.

解说：

1. 这一句译文把一个状语 after payment... 放在主语和谓语之间，这种译法也是常见的。

2. 此处原文用分号，而译文用 while 连接。

★3. 译文用了 choose to or not to..., 这样就可以避免重复 specify their duration in the contracts。

★4. 请注意这个句子用 where 来引导，表示"凡是这样的企业"。

★5. "不履行……"译作 failure to..., 而不译作 not to..., 是因为这里需要用名词。这也是一种常见的译法。

6. "经……"没有译作 through..., 而译作 subject to their agreement..., approval of... and registration with..., 表示"在……条件下"。

★7. "由……，也可由……"在译文里用 or 而不用 and 连接，值得注意。

★8. "本法"在第二句中重复出现时，译文也重复了 this

Law。在普通文章中，遇到这种情况，英语会用 it，而不重复。但在法律文件中，要尽力作到每句话都非常明确，以免发生歧义。

Unit 10　Speeches

Lesson 19　(E—C)

Bilingual Reading

Speech by President Nixon of the United States at Welcoming Banquet
21 February 1972

　　Mr. Prime Minister and all of your distinguished guests this evening,

　　On behalf of all of your American guests, I wish to thank you for the incomparable hospitality for which the Chinese people are justly[1] famous throughout the world. I particularly want to pay tribute, not only to those who prepared the magnificent dinner, but also to[2] those who have provided the splendid music. Never have I heard American music played better in a foreign land.

　　Mr. Prime Minister, I wish to thank you for your very gracious and eloquent remarks. At this very[3] moment through the wonder[4] of telecommunications, more people are seeing and hearing what we say than on any other such occasion in the whole history of the world. Yet, what we say here will not be long remembered. What we do here can change the world.

　　As you said in your toast[5], the Chinese people are a great people, the American people are a great people. If our two people are enemies the future of this world we share together is dark indeed. But if we can find common ground[6] to work together, the chance for world peace is immeasurably increased.

　　In the spirit of frankness which I hope will characterize our talks this week, let us recognize at the outset[7] these points: we have at times in the past been enemies. We have great differences[8] today. What brings us together is that we have common interests which transcend those differences. As we discuss our differences, neither of us will compromise[9] our principles. But while[10] we cannot close the gulf between us, we can try to bridge it so that we may be able to talk across it.

So, let us, in these next five days, start a long march together, not in lockstep[11], but on different roads leading to the same goal, the goal of building a world structure of peace and justice in which[12] all[13] may stand together with equal dignity and in which each nation, large or small, has a right to determine its own form of government, free of outside interference or domination[14]. The world watches. The world listens. The world waits to see what we will do. What is the world? In a personal sense, I think of my eldest daughter whose birthday is today. As I think of her, I think of all the children in the world, in Asia, in Africa, in Europe, in the Americas, most of whom were born since the date of the foundation of the People's Republic of China.

What legacy shall we leave our children? Are they destined[15] to die for the hatreds which have plagued[16] the old world, or are they destined to live because we had the vision[17] to build a new world?

There is no reason for us to be enemies. Neither of us seeks the territory of the other; neither of us seeks domination over the other, neither of us seeks to stretch out our hands and rule the world.

Chairman Mao has written, "So many deeds cry out to be done, and always urgently; the world rolls on, time presses. Ten thousand years are too long, seize the day, seize the hour!"

This is the hour. This is the day for our two peoples[18] to rise to the heights of greatness which can build a new and a better world.

In that spirit, I ask all of you present to join me in raising your glasses to Chairman Mao, to Prime Minister Chou, and to the friendship of the Chinese and American people which can lead to friendship and peace for all people in the world.

提示:

第十单元：演讲。演讲的范围广，一篇演讲可能涉及各方面的内容，语言正式而生动，有时带有强烈的感情色彩。翻译此类文章，句子结构不要过于复杂，语言宜正式而又能上口，并要考虑听众听的效果。

关于第 19 课的对照阅读（BR19），请注意以下各点。

1. justly: deservedly
★ 2. 请注意，这里只重复 to，不需要重复 pay tribute to。
★ 3. very 在这里是形容词，用以加强语气。
4. wonder: miracle
5. toast: 祝酒词
6. common ground: 共同点
7. at the outset: at the beginning
8. differences: 分歧
★ 9. compromise: weaken or give up
★ 10. while: although
11. in lockstep: together and at the same pace
12. What does "which" refer to?
13. What does "all" stand for?
14. "the goal...domination" is an appositive to "the same goal".
15. be destined to do something: to do something that is predetermined
16. plague: trouble
17. vision: foresight

18. "two peoples" and "two people" are both correct.

译文：

美国总统尼克松在欢迎宴会上的讲话
1972年2月21日

总理先生，今天晚上在座的诸位贵宾：

我谨代表你们的所有美国客人向你们表示感谢[1]，感谢你们的无可比拟的盛情款待。中国人民以这种盛情款待而闻名世界[2]。我们不仅要特别赞扬那些准备了这次盛大晚宴的人，而且还要赞扬[3]那些为我们演奏[4]美好音乐的人。我在外国从来没有听到过演奏得这么好的[5]美国音乐。

总理先生，我要感谢你的非常盛情和雄辩的讲话。此时此刻[6]，通过电讯的奇迹，看到和听到我们讲话的人比在整个世界历史上任何其他这样的场合都要多。不过，我们在这里所讲的话，人们不会长久地记住，但我们在这里所做的事却能改变世界。

正如你在祝酒时讲的那样，中国人民是伟大的人民，美国人民是伟大的人民。如果我们两国人民互相为敌，那么我们共同居住的这个世界的前途就的确很暗淡。但是，如果我们能够找到进行合作的共同点，那么实现[7]世界和平的机会就将无可估量地大大增加。

我希望我们这个星期的会谈将是坦率的[8]。本着这种坦率的精神，让我们在一开始就认识到这样几点：过去一些时候我们曾是敌人。今天我们有巨大的分歧。使我们走到一起的，是我们有超越这些分歧的共同利益。在我们讨论我们的分歧时，我们哪一方都不会在自己的原则上妥协。但是，虽然我们不能弥合双方之间的鸿沟，我们却能够设法搭一座桥，以便我们能够越过它进行会谈。

因此，让我们在今后的五天里一起开始一次长征吧，不是在一起迈步，而是在不同的道路上向同一个目标前进⁹。这个目标就是建立一个和平和正义的世界结构¹⁰，在这个世界结构中，所有的人都可以在一起享有同等的尊严；每个国家，不论大小，都有权利决定它自己政府的形式，而不受外来的干涉或统治。全世界在注视着。全世界在倾听着。全世界在等待着看我们将做些什么。这个世界是怎样的呢？就我个人来讲，我想到我的大女儿，今天是她的生日¹¹。当我想到她的时候，我就想到全世界所有的儿童，亚洲、非洲、欧洲以及美洲的儿童，¹²他们大多数都是在中华人民共和国成立以后出生的。¹³

我们将给我们的孩子们留下什么遗产呢？他们的命运是要为那些使旧世界蒙受苦难的仇恨而死亡呢，还是由于我们有缔造一个新世界的远见而活下去呢？

我们没有理由要成为敌人。我们哪一方都不企图取得对方的领土；我们哪一方都不企图统治对方。我们哪一方都不企图伸出手去统治世界。

毛主席写过："多少事，从来急；天地转，光阴迫。一万年太久，只争朝夕。"¹⁴

现在就是只争朝夕的时候了¹⁵，是我们两国人民攀登那种可以缔造一个新的、更美好的世界的伟大境界的高峰的时候了。¹⁶

本着这种精神¹⁷，我请求诸位同我一起举杯，为毛主席，为周总理，为能够导致全世界所有人民的友谊与和平的中国人民同美国人民之间的友谊¹⁸，干杯。

解说：

★ 1. 这一句较长，先说"向你们表示感谢"，停顿一下，再说"感谢你们的……"，而不直接说"感谢你们的……"

★ 2. 原文 which 引导的定语从句，在译文里单独成句。justly 若一定要译出，可译作"是理所当然的"，放在句末，但不能像原文那样放在句子中间某个地方。

★ 3. 虽然原文只重复介词 to，译文还是要重复动词"赞扬"。

★4．原文 provide 一词比较笼统，译文用"演奏"一词，比"提供"具体，好与"音乐"搭配。

5．此处也可译作"演奏得比这更好的"。

6．"此时此刻"用在这里非常合适。very 是个加强语气的词，常可以用"就"字来表示。但此处若译作"就在此刻"，就显得平淡了。

★7．原文 the chance for world peace，有了介词 for，就不需要再加动词了。但译文加了动词"实现"，否则句子就不通了。

★8．原文 which 引导的定语从句在译文里单独成句，而且放在前面，然后再说"本着这种坦率的精神……"。这是处理定语从句的一个很好的办法。

9．译文在这里断句。在原文里，the goal of... 是同位语，译文另起一句，具体说明"这个目标"的具体内容。

10．下面两个 in which 引导的定语从句，在译文里无须提前，可以留在后面，在原地处理。

11．whose 引导的定语从句虽然很短，在译文里也没有提前，而是留在后面，在原地处理。

12．此处译文重复了"儿童"。

13．most of whom 引导的从句，也是留在后面，在原地处理的。

14．这段引文必须用毛主席的原话，不能根据英文自己译。

15．This is the hour 借用了前段末句 seize the hour 里面的话，因此译文也借用前面的话，译作"现在就是只争朝夕的时候了"。

16．这句译文意思准确，句法平稳，是很不错的译文，只是定语上面加定语，而且都比较长，不甚好读。似可改为："……是我们两国人民攀登伟大境界的高峰，以缔造一个新的、更美好世界的时候了。"

★17．原文 in that spirit，指上面所说的话，译文仍要说"本着这种精神"。

★18．这一句也有很长的定语，"能够导致全世界所有人民的友谊与和平的"修饰"中国人民同美国人民之间的友谊"。这句话的上下文是为此而干杯，为了保持语气上的连贯，再长的定语也要把它一口气说完。

---翻译理论选读---

A New Concept of Translating*
by Eugene A. Nida and Charles R. Taber

Each language has its own genius.[1]

In the first place, it is essential to recognize that each language has its own genius. That is to say, each language possesses certain distinctive characteristics which give it a special character, e.g.,

---

* 这个标题是编者加的。尤金·奈达(Eugene A. Nida)博士是美国圣经学会翻译部主任。他不仅在美国主持《圣经》的英译工作，还在世界各地指导许多其他语言的翻译工作。1969年出版了他与查尔斯·泰伯(Charles R. Taber)合写的《翻译理论与实践》(*The Theory and Practice of Translation*)。他们在书中对翻译工作提出了一套新的概念，虽以《圣经》翻译为基础，但对其他翻译工作也有参考价值。

奈达认为，过去人们在翻译过程中过于重视与原文在形式上保持一致，而他主张着重考虑读者对译文的反应，应使译文的读者和原文的读者产生同样的感受。

关于原语，就《圣经》而言，也就是希伯来语和希腊语，奈达认为它们既不是天国的语言，也不是圣灵使用的语言，它们和世界上的其他语言一样，有自己的美妙之处，也有各种不足之处，它们也不过是工具，被人们用来表达《圣经》里包含的意思而已。因此，它们既不神圣，也不神秘。

关于译语，奈达认为每一种语言都有自己的特点，在构词法、语序、句子结构、谚语诸方面各不相同。各个民族的文化背景不同，对各自的语言也产生不同的影响。译者不必因为译语缺少某种表达方式而抱怨；相反地，他应该尊重这一语言的特点，最大限度地发挥其潜力，以找出适当的表达方式。他认为一个能干的译者不会把一种语言的形式强加于另一种语言，非要以名词译名词，以动词译动词，在结构方面保持原来的语序，而是随时准备在形式上作一切必要的变动，以求用符合译语特点的表达方式来表现原作的内容。他的结论是，要想使译文保持原作的内容，就必须在形式上有所改变。

word-building capacities, unique patterns of phrase order, techniques for linking clauses into sentences, markers of discourse,[2] and special discourse types of poetry, proverbs, and song. Each language is rich in vocabulary for the areas of cultural focus, the specialities of the people, e. g., cattle (Anuaks in the Sudan), yams (Ponapeans in Micronesia), hunting and fishing (Piros in Peru), or technology (the western world). Some languages are rich in modal particles.[3] Others seem particularly adept in the development of figurative language, and many have very rich literary resources, both written and oral.

To communicate effectively one must respect the genius of each language.

Rather than bemoan the lack of some feature in a language, one must respect the features of the receptor language[4] and exploit the potentialities of the language to the greatest possible extent. Unfortunately, in some instances translators have actually tried to "remake" a language. For example, one missionary in Latin America insisted on trying to introduce the passive voice of the verb into a language which had no such form. Of course, this was not successful. One must simply accept the fact that there are many languages which do not have a passive voice. They merely choose to report actions only as active.

Rather than force the formal structure of one language upon another, the effective translator is quite prepared to make any and all formal changes[5] necessary to reproduce the message in the distinctive structural forms of the receptor language.

To preserve the content of the message the form must be changed.

If all languages differ in form (and this is the essence of their being different languages), then quite naturally the forms must be altered if one is to preserve the content. For example, in Mark 1:4,[6] the Greek employs a nominal construction,[7] "baptism of repentance," but translated literally into English the resulting phrase really does not convey the meaning of the original. The average person is simply unable to describe clearly what is the relationship between "baptism" and "repentance." Moreover, in a high percentage of languages, terms which express events (and both "baptism" and "repentance" are events, not objects) are expressed more naturally as verbs, rather than as nouns. Even this Greek noun expression is really only a nominalization (or adaptation) of what occurs in Acts 2:38 in verbal form, namely, "repent and be baptized." In languages which either require that such events be expressed as verbs or normally use verb rather than noun phrases, it is not only right, but essential, that the nominal form of this Greek phrase be changed into a corresponding verbal expression.

(form Eugene A. Nida and Charles R. Taber, *The Theory and Practice of Translation*, Ch.1)

---

1. genius：特点
2. markers of discourse：话语标志
3. modal particles：情态小品词
4. receptor language：接受语，即"译语"，与"原语"（source language）相对。
5. formal changes = changes in form
6. Mark 1:4：《马可福音》第一章第四节
7. nominal construction：名词结构

Exercise 19

将下列短文译成汉语：

Speech by Former U.S. President Carter at Welcoming Banquet
29 June 1987

Permit me first to thank our Chinese hosts for your extraordinary arrangements and hospitality. My wife and I, as well as our entire party,[1] are deeply grateful. In the short period of six days, we have gone a longer distance than the Long March. We have acquired a keen sense of the diversity, dynamism[2], and progress of China under your policies of reform and opening to the outside world.

More than eight years have passed since Vice Premier Deng Xiaoping and I joined hands to establish full[3] diplomatic relations between our two great nations. Our hope and vision was to forge a Sino-American relationship which would contribute to world peace and the welfare of our two peoples. I personally looked upon the forging of firm Sino-American ties[4] as a historically significant experiment.

We faced the question in 1978, as to some extent we still do today: Can two nations as different as ours—yours one of the oldest civilizations on earth, mine one of the youngest; yours a socialist state and mine committed to capitalism; yours a developing country and mine a developed one—can two nations surmount[5] and indeed draw upon[6] these differences to build an unprecedented and distinctive[7] relationship in world affairs? If we are successful, in one great step our two nations will have been able to ease one of the greatest sources of tension in international affairs: that between the developing and developed worlds. We still have a long way to go, and it is still too early to conclude that our experiment will culminate[8] in success, but certainly the results of the first ten years are promising. Sino-American ties have become extensive, affecting all aspects of our national lives: commerce, culture, education, scientific exchange, and our separate national security policies.

I am most proud of the large number of Chinese students being educated in our country—now about 18,000. I teach some of them and see the benefits that come from this exchange. At the same time we are learning valuable lessons[9] from you. Nonetheless, problems remain[10] in our economic, educational and strategic relations.

As a private[11] American citizen I recognize that many of the burdens[12] and opportunities of our relationship have now passed to the non-governmental sectors of our two societies: to individuals, our corporations, universities, research institutes, foundations[13], and so on. There is no doubt that Sino-American relations have reached a new stage. In this context,[14] it is important for our two societies to search for areas of cooperation which clearly add to our mutual benefit.

In that regard, I am delighted that Global 2000—BCCI[15] is launching two projects in the area of public health. Although ours[16] is relatively quite small, such activities, when combined with our common foreign policy interests and a growing commercial relationship, should help to remove the lingering[17] fragility[18] in Sino-American relations.

提示：

1. party: group
2. dynamism: the quality of being vigorous
3. full: of the highest regular rank

4. ties: relations

5. surmount: get round/settle

6. draw upon: make use of

7. distinctive: having special features of its own

8. culminate: reach its highest point

9. lessons: experience

10. problems remain: there are still problems

11. private: not holding an official position

12. burdens: heavy load, as of work, duty, responsibility, etc.

13. foundations: 基金会

14. context: circumstances/background

15. BCCI: Bank of Credit and Commerce International 国际商业信贷银行

16. ours: our project

17. lingering: remaining too long

18. fragility: fragile nature

Key to Exercise 19

译文:

美国前总统卡特在欢迎宴会上的讲话
1987 年 6 月 29 日

首先, 请允许我对中国主人十分出色的[1]安排和款待表示感谢。我的夫人和我[2]以及全体随行人员都深为感激。在过去短短六天里, 我们所走的路程比长征的路程[3]还长。我们强烈地感受到你们执行的改革和对外开放政策给中国带来的多样化、活力和进步。

自从邓小平副总理和我共同建立我们两个伟大国家之间的正

式外交关系[4]以来,已经八年多了。建立一种有利于世界和平和我们两国人民幸福的中美关系是我们当时的希望和憧憬。我本人把建立牢固的中美关系看作是具有历史意义的尝试。

我们在1987年乃至今天在某种程度上面临的问题仍然是:我们两国迥然不同[5],贵国[6]是地球上最老的文明古国之一,而我国是最年轻的国家之一;贵国是社会主义国家,而我国致力于[7]资本主义;贵国是发展中国家,而我国是发达国家;像这样的两个国家是否能够超越这些差异并利用它在世界事务中建立一种前所未有的、独具特色的关系?如果我们取得成功,我们两国就能迈出一大步缓和国际事务中最大的一个造成紧张的因素,即发展中世界与发达世界的关系。我们面前还有很长的路,现在断言我们的尝试将会圆满成功还为时过早,但是头十年肯定是富有成效的。中美关系现在非常广泛,涉及我们人民生活的各个方面:商业、文化、教育、科学交流,以及我们各自的国家安全政策。

我感到十分自豪的是大量的中国学生——现在大约有18,000人——正在美国学习[8]。我也教过他们中一些人,并看到了这种交流所带来的益处。同时我们也从你们那里学到非常宝贵的经验[9]。尽管如此,在我们的经济、教育和战略关系中仍然存在着问题。

作为一个普通的[10]美国公民,我知道我们关系中的许多责任[11]和机会现在已经转到了我们两个社会的民间部门[12],即转到了个人、公司、大学、研究机构、基金会等等。毫无疑问,中美关系已达到了一个新的阶段。在这种情况下,我们两个社会应该寻求那些对我们两国确实互利的合作领域,这是很重要的。[13]

我很高兴"全球2000年"——国际商业信贷银行正在公共卫生领域从事两个项目。虽然我们的项目比较小,但这些活动同我们共同的外交政策利益以及不断增长的商业关系结合起来,就会有助于消除中美关系中仍然存在的脆弱性。

解说：

1．extraordinary 译作"十分出色的"，好与"安排和款待"搭配。

2．汉语一般把"我"放在前面。此处照原文顺序译作"我的夫人和我"，也是可以的。

★3．译文在这句话里重复"路程"，这样较顺。

4．full diplomatic relations 译作"正式外交关系"。参看 BR1，full member 译作"正式党员"。

★5．原文 as different as ours 是一个定语，修饰 two nations。译文把这一部分变为一个分句，下面从容展开，论述两国之不同，而不给人以谓语迟迟不出来的感觉。

6．"贵国"是汉语特有的一种客气的说法。在英语里还是说 your country。

★7．committed to 译作"致力于"，这是常见的一种译法。

8．原文 the large number of Chinese students being educated…是一个短语，译文用了一个主谓结构。

9．lessons 在这里没有贬义，所以译作"经验"。

10．private 表示"不在官方任职"，所以译作"普通的"。

11．burdens 指需要完成的繁重的事务，此处译作"责任"。也可译作"任务"。

★12．non-governmental sectors 译作"民间部门"。"民间"一词，在英语里往往找不到合适的对应词，一般就译作 non-governmental。

13．英语 it is important 放在句首，译文"这是很重要的"一般放在句末。

Lesson 20 （C—E）

Bilingual Reading

增进相互了解　加强友好合作
——江泽民主席在美国哈佛大学的演讲
（1997年11月1日）
（摘录1）

校长先生，
女士们，先生们：

　　我感谢陆登庭校长的邀请，使我有机会在这美好的金秋时节，来到你们这座美国古老而又现代化的学府。

　　哈佛建校三百六十年来，培养出许多杰出的政治家、科学家、文学家和企业家，曾出过六位美国总统，三十多位诺贝尔奖获得者。先有哈佛，后有美利坚合众国，这说明了哈佛在美国历史上的地位。

　　哈佛是最早接受中国留学生的美国大学之一。中国教育界、科学界、文化界一直同哈佛大学保持着学术交流。哈佛为增进中美两国人民的相互了解作出了有益的贡献。

　　相互了解，是发展国与国之间关系的前提。惟有相互了解，才能增进信任，加强合作。中美建交以来，我们两国人民之间的相互交流与了解在逐渐扩大和加深，但还不够。为了推动中美关系的发展，中国需要进一步了解美国，美国也需要进一步了解中国。

　　……

　　中国在自己发展的长河中，形成了优良的历史文化传统。这些传统，随着时代变迁和社会进步获得扬弃和发展，对今天中国人的价值观念、生活方式和中国的发展道路，具有深刻的影响。这里，我想就以下一些方面谈些看法，希望有助于诸位对中国的了解。

一是团结统一的传统。中华民族是由五十六个民族组成的大家庭。从遥远的古代起，我国各族人民就建立了紧密的政治经济文化联系，共同开发了祖国的河山，两千多年前就形成了幅员广阔的统一国家。悠久的中华文化，成为维系民族团结和国家统一的牢固纽带。团结统一，深深印在中国人的民族意识中。中国历史上虽曾出现过暂时的分裂现象，但民族团结和国家统一始终是中华民族历史的主流，是中国发展进步的重要保障。新中国的成立，标志着中华民族实现了空前的大团结。各民族之间建立了平等、团结、互助的新型关系。各民族人民依法享有各项权利和自由。在少数民族聚居的地方实行了区域自治。民族地区的经济社会获得不断的发展。所有这些，为巩固国家统一奠定了坚实的政治基础。

二是独立自主的传统。我们的先人历来把独立自主视为立国之本。中国作为人类文明发祥地之一，在几千年的历史进程中，文化传统始终没有中断。近代中国虽屡遭列强欺凌，国势衰败，但经过全民族的百年抗争，又以巨人的姿态重新站立起来。这充分说明，中国人独立自主的民族精神具有坚不可摧的力量。今天，我们在探索自己的发展道路时，坚持从中国国情出发，来解决如何进行经济政治文化建设的问题，而不照搬别国的模式。在处理国际事务中，我们采取独立自主的立场和政策。中国人民珍惜同各国人民的友谊与合作，也珍惜自己经过长期奋斗而得来的独立自主权利。

三是爱好和平的传统。我国先秦思想家就提出了"亲仁善邻，国之宝也"的思想，反映了自古以来中国人民就希望天下太平、同各国人民友好相处。今天，专心致志进行现代化建设的中国人民，更需要有一个长期的和平国际环境和良好的周边环境。我国的对外政策，是以和平为宗旨的。我们坚持在和平共处五项原则，特别是在相互尊重、平等互利、互不干涉内政的原则基础上，同世界各国建立和发展友好合作关系。我们绝不会把自己曾经遭受欺凌的苦难加之于人。中国的发展与进步，不会对任何人构成威胁。将来中国富强起来了，也永远不称霸。中国始终是维护世界和平与地区稳定的坚定力量。

四是自强不息的传统。我们的先哲通过观察宇宙万物的变动不居，提出了"天行健，君子以自强不息"的思想，成为激励中国人民变革创新、努力奋斗的精神力量。中国古代文明的发展，是中华民族艰苦奋斗、自强不息的结果。近百年来，为了摆脱半殖民地半封建的历史境遇，中国人民进行了艰苦卓绝、奋发图强的斗争。中国民主革命的先行者孙中山首先提出"振兴中华"的口号，他领导的辛亥革命，推翻了在中国延续几千年的君主专制制度。在毛泽东思想指引下，中国共产党领导中国人民实现了民族独立和人民解放，并把中国建设成为初步繁荣昌盛的社会主义国家。今天，在邓小平理论指引下，我国人民坚定不移地实行改革开放，在现代化建设中取得举世瞩目的成就。中国进入了百年来发展最快最好的历史时期。

译文：

Enhance Mutual Understanding and Build Stronger Ties of Friendship and Cooperation

Address by President Jiang Zemin at
Harvard University of
the United States of America
1 November 1997
(Excerpt 1)

Mr. President,

Ladies and Gentlemen,

I wish to thank President Rudenstine for inviting me to this old yet modern institution of the[1] United States in this golden fall.[2]

Since its founding some 360 years ago, Harvard[3] has nurtured a great number of outstanding statesmen, scientists, writers and businessmen, including six of the American Presidents and over thirty Nobel Prize winners. The fact that Harvard was founded before the United States of America testifies to its position in the American history.

Harvard is among the first American universities to accept Chinese students. The Chinese educational, scientific and cultural communities have all along maintained academic exchanges with this university.[4] Harvard has thus made useful contribution to the enhanced mutual understanding[5] between the Chinese and American peoples.

Mutual understanding is the basis for state-to-state relations. Without it[6], it would be impossible for countries to build trust and promote cooperation with one another. Since the establishment of diplomatic ties between China and the United States, the exchanges and mutual understanding between our two peoples have broadened and deepened steadily. However, this is not enough. To promote the development of China-U.S. relations, China needs to know the United States better and vice versa.[7]

......

In the prolonged course of its development, China[8] has formed its fine historical and cultural traditions, which[9] have been either developed or sublated with the changes of the times and social progress. These traditions have exerted a profound impact on the values and way of life of the Chinese people today, and on China's road of advance. Here, I would like to make some observations on the following aspects, which[10] I hope will help you know China better.

First, the tradition of solidarity and unity. The Chinese nation is a big family composed of 56 nationalities. Since time immemorial, people of all our nationalities have established close-knit political, economic and cultural links and joined hands in developing the vast land of our country. China became a vast unified country more than 2,000 years ago. The age-old Chinese culture becomes a strong bond for ethnic harmony[11] and national unity. Solidarity and unity are deeply inscribed in the hearts of the Chinese people as part of their national identity. Despite occasional divisions[12], ethnic harmony and national unity have remained the main stream in the history of the Chinese nation, and an important guarantee for China's development and progress. The founding of the People's Republic of China in 1949[13] marked an unprecedented great unity of the Chinese nation.[14] A new type of relationship of equality, solidarity and mutual assistance among all our nationalities has been established. People of all our nationalities enjoy full rights and freedoms provided for by the law. In places where there is a high concentration of ethnic minorities, regional autonomy is in practice. These regions have witnessed continued economic and social development.[15] All these have laid a solid political foundation for consolidated national unity.[16]

Second, the tradition of maintaining independence.[17] Our ancestors always regarded the spirit of maintaining independence as the foundation of a nation. As one of the cradles of human civilization, China has all along maintained its cultural tradition without letup in its history of several thousand years. In modern times, the frequent bullying and humiliation by imperialist powers once weakened China. However, after a hundred years' struggle of the entire Chinese nation, China has stood up again as a giant. This fully testifies to the indestructible strength of this independent national spirit of the Chinese people.[18] Today, in finding a road of advance suited to us, we will proceed from our own national conditions to address the problems[19] of how to attain economic, political and cultural development without blindly copying other countries' models. In handling international affairs, we decide our positions and policies from an independent approach. The Chinese people cherish its friendship and cooperation with other peoples, and they also cherish their right to independence, which they have won through protracted struggles.[20]

Third, the peace-loving tradition. Chinese thinkers of the pre-Qin days (over 2,000 years ago)[21] advanced the doctrine "loving people and treating neighbors kindly are most valuable to a country".[22] This is a reflection[23] of the aspiration of the Chinese people for a peaceful world where[24] people of all countries live in harmony. Today, the Chinese people who are committed to modernization[25] need more than ever[26] a long-term international environment of peace and a favorable neighboring environment. China's foreign policy[27] is peace-oriented. We will establish and develop friendly relations and cooperation with all countries in the world on the basis of the Five Principles of Peaceful Coexistence,[28] especially the principles of mutual respect, equality and mutual benefit and non-interference in each other's internal affairs. We will never impose upon others the kind of sufferings we ourselves once experienced. A developing and progressing China[29] does not pose a threat to anyone. China will never seek hegemony[30] even if it grows rich and strong in the future. China is always a staunch force for world peace and regional stability[31].

Fourth, the tradition of constantly striving to strengthen oneself. Through observing the changing nature of the universe and of all things, ancient Chinese philosophers proposed the following doctrine: "Heaven operates vigorously, and gentlemen exert to strengthen themselves unceasingly." This idea has become an important moral force[32] spurring the Chinese people to work hard for change and innovation. The fruits of China's ancient civilization were brought about by the tireless efforts and hard work of the Chinese nation. In the past one hundred years or so, the Chinese people waged arduous struggles to lift themselves from their historical plight under semi-colonial and semi-feudal rule. Dr. Sun Yat-sen[33], China's forerunner in the democratic revolution, was the first to put forward the slogan of "rejuvenation of China". He led the Revolution of 1911 to overthrow the autocratic monarchy lasting several millennia in China. Under the guidance of Mao Zedong Thought, the Communist Party of China led the Chinese people in achieving[34] China's national independence and people's liberation and in building China into a socialist country with initial prosperity. Today, guided by Deng Xiaoping Theory, the Chinese people are firmly pressing ahead with reform and opening-up and have achieved remarkable successes in the modernization drive. China has entered a period of its fastest and healthiest growth in this century.

(原文及译文均选自《努力建立中美建设性的战略伙伴关系》，世界知识出版社。)

解说：

★ 1. the United States, 此处一定要用定冠词，不能省略。

2. fall 表示"秋季"，美国人用得多。

★ 3. 此处先说 its founding, 然后再出 Harvard, 是英语可以先出代词后出实词之一例。

4. 这一段三句话，原文三次提到"哈佛"，译文第二句用了 this university, 以免过于重复。

★ 5. 此处没有译作 contribution to enhancing mutual understanding, 而译作 contribution to the enhanced mutual understanding, 这样译更合乎英语的说法。

★ 6. 此处两句话接连提到"相互了解"，译文第二句用了代词

it，以免重复。

★7．这一句包含两个结构相同的并列分句，第二句重复第一句，只是把第一句的主语和宾语颠倒一下。这种情况在英语里是不重复的，可以用英语里一个现成的说法：vice versa。

8．此处又是先出代词 its，后出实词 China。

★9．原文前面一句以"传统"结束，后面一句紧接着说"这些传统"，译文用 which 相连，最为方便。

10．这里又用了一个 which 引导的从句。

★11．"团结"一词，前面译作 solidarity，此处译作 harmony，交错使用，以免过于重复。

12．此处"中国历史上"没有译，这是可以的。有后半句衬托，不会产生歧义。

★13．译文加了 in 1949，这是为外国读者提供方便。

★14．marked 后面直接跟 unity of the Chinese nation，动词"实现了"可以不译。英译汉时，在一连串的名词中间增加一个动词，会使译文更加通顺。

★15．原文以"民族地区的经济社会"为主语，译文以 these regions 为主语，这样更合乎英语的说法。

16．这里没有译作 foundation for consolidating national unity，而译作 foundation for consolidated national unity，与注 5 所说的情况相同。

★17．"独立自主"译作 independence 一个词就够了。

18．testifies to 后面直接跟 the indestructible strength，原文里的动词"具有"就可以不译了。与注 14 所说的情况相同。

19．"解决……的问题"译作 address the problems of... 这是一个常见的搭配。参看 Ex.7，I believe Chinese economic authorities recognise the problem and the next Five-Year Plan will address it effectively.

20．定语"自己经过长期奋斗而得来的"译作 which 引导的定语从句，放在后面。

21. 译文加了（over 2,000 years ago），这也是为读者着想。

22. 这里引了一句古语。如有现成的译文，而且用在这里合适，就用现成的译文。否则译者可以自译。

23. 虽然原文用的是动词"反映了"，译文不说 this reflects, 而说 this is a reflection of... 这是地道的英语。

★24. where 巧妙地把前后连接起来。

★25. "现代化建设"译作 modernization 一词就够了。也可以说 modernization drive, 但不用 construction。

26. "更需要"译作 need more than ever, 也是很巧妙的。

27. "对外政策"译作 foreign policy, 作为一个整体，总是用单数，不用复数。

28. the Five Principles of Peaceful Coexistence, 第一个字母要大写。

★29. 原文的主语是"中国的发展与进步"，译文以 China 为主语。

30. "不称霸"译作 will never seek hegemony, 不用 hegemonism。

★31. a staunch force for 后面直接跟 world peace and regional stability, 原文里的动词"维护"可以不译。

32. "精神力量"译作 moral force, 不同 spiritual force。

33. "孙中山"译作 Dr. Sun Yat-sen, 不用汉语拼音。

★34. "领导中国人民实现了……"译作 led the Chinese people in achieving..., 不说 to achieve...

---翻译理论选读---

Guard Against Chinglish[*]
by Sol Adler

Now to come to the more specific topics.

To begin with what is still the most important and difficult problem, namely Chinglish.[1] Of course it would be best to think in English, try to formulate the thought as though it were being written in English (but even that rule is not universal). This is quite a problem because it's often not a question of grammar or of obviously incorrect usage, it's usually something more subtle.[2] It's often a question of collocation.[3] There are no simple rules, Chinese and English have different uses of verbs, nouns, adjectives and pronouns, different uses with regard to duplication,[4] emphasis[5] and so on.

There's also the question of word and clause order. Chinese and English are very similar in being quite flexible[6] in their order ... sometimes the order coincides,[7] which is very convenient,[8] but often it doesn't coincide and then there are more problems.

And there are other examples of Chinglish, of Chinese usages which you don't have in English. Chinese often uses a strong adverb with a strong verb. Here you need emphasis in Chinese, but in English it results in over-emphasis and has the opposite effect. One common example in the past which has largely been eliminated[9] is 'completely smash',[10] though 'smash' means to break completely. So

---

* 美国专家爱德乐参加了《毛泽东选集》第五卷的英译改稿和润饰工作。他作了一篇报告,题为 *A Talk on the Translation of Volume V of Chairman Mao's Selected Works*,载于《翻译通讯》1980 年第 1,2 期。本文是这篇报告的一部分。本文的标题是编者加的。

it's using completely twice. But even here there are exceptions. Sometimes, especially in a speech, you might say 'to smash to smithereens'. So, to repeat myself, I try to avoid formulating universal rules. There are always exceptions. I want to warn you in advance.

There is another problem we have which is an example of Chinglish. You use spatial and temporal adverbs,[11] and spatial and temporal adverbial phrases, more frequently than we do in English, especially where the context makes it clear. In English it's just clumsy.[12] For instance, we struggled in earlier volumes with 'in the world', 'in this world' and 'in our country'. In general I think in volume V it's been smoother in this respect. Or take 'at this time' which may be merely an indication of tense in Chinese. I think I've got one example of 'in our country' being superfluous[13] in English. At one stage 'Considerable progress has been made in the last few years by the various nationalities, democratic classes, democratic parties and people's organizations **in our country**'. Well, it couldn't possibly be anywhere else. So 'in our country' was just deleted.[14]

（选自《翻译通讯》）

---

1. Chinglish：中文式的英文（取 Chinese 与 English 二词的首尾拼合成的新词，带有谐谑意味，尚未被收入辞典。）
2. subtle：隐晦
3. collocation：搭配
4. duplication：重复
5. emphasis：强调
6. flexible：灵活
7. coincide：碰巧一致
8. convenient：方便

9. eliminate：消灭
10. completely smash：彻底粉碎
11. spatial and temporal adverbs：表示空间的副词和表示时间的副词
12. clumsy：别扭
13. superfluous：多余
14. delete：删去

Exercise 20

将下列短文译成英语：

增进相互了解　加强友好合作
——江泽民主席在美国哈佛大学的演讲
（一九九七年十一月一日）
（摘录 2）

改革开放，是中华民族自强不息和变革创新[1]精神在当代的集中体现[2]和创造性发展。我们把改革开放叫作社会主义改革开放，因为它是中国社会主义制度的自我完善[3]和发展。近二十年的实践已充分证明，我们进行改革开放的方向是正确的，信念是坚定的，步骤是稳妥的，方式是渐进的，取得的成就是巨大的[4]。虽然在前进中也遇到这样和那样一些困难和风险，但我们都顺利地解决了，不仅没有引起大的社会震动[5]，而且极大地解放和发展了社会生产力，保持了社会稳定和全面进步。

现在，我们正在满怀信心地全面推进改革。在经济上，要加快建立社会主义市场经济体制，实现工业化和经济的社会化、市场化、现代化；在政治上，要努力发展社会主义民主政治[6]，依法治国，建设社会主义法治国家[7]，保证人民充分行使管理国家和社会事务的权力；在文化上，要积极建设面向[8]现代化、面向世界、面向未来的，民族的科学的大众的社会主义文化，实行科教兴国战略，不断提高全民族的思想道德素质和科学文化素质。总起来说，就是要把中国建成富强民主文明的[9]现代化国家。

中国作为疆域辽阔、人口众多、历史悠久的国家，应该对人类有较大的贡献。中国人民所以要进行百年不屈不挠的斗争[10]，所以要实行一次又一次的伟大变革、实现国家的繁荣富强，所以要加强民族团结、完成祖国统一大业，所以要促进世界和平与发展的崇高事业，归根到底[11]就是为了一个目标：实现中华民族的伟大复兴，争取对人类作出新的更大的贡献。

提示：

1. 创新：innovation
2. 体现：embodiment
3. 自我完善：self-improvement
4. 这一句包含许多分句，怎样保持语气连贯？
5. 社会震动：social unrest
6. 民主政治：democracy
7. 社会主义法治国家：a socialist country under the rule of law
8. 面向……：be oriented to...
9. 文明的：culturally advanced
10. 不屈不挠的斗争：dauntless struggle
11. 归根到底：in the final analysis

Key to Exercise 20

译文:

Enhance Mutual Understanding and
Build Stronger Ties of Friendship and Cooperation

Address by President Jiang Zemin at
Harvard University of
the United States of America
1 November 1997
(Excerpt 2)

The reform and opening-up endeavour is an embodiment and a creative development of the Chinese spirit of constantly striving to strengthen oneself and change and innovation in modern times. We refer to our reform and opening-up as socialist reform and opening-up because it is a self-improvement and development of the socialist system in China. Practice in the last twenty years has eloquently proved[1] that we are going in the right direction, firm in conviction, steady in our steps and gradual in our approach[2] when carrying out the reform and opening-up and that we have achieved tremendous successes.[3] We have successfully overcome various difficulties and risks in the course of our advance without causing great social unrest. Rather, we have succeeded in greatly releasing and developing social productive forces and maintained social stability and an all-round progress.

We are conducting a comprehensive reform[4] with full confidence. Economically,[5] we will speed up the establishment of a socialist market economy[6] and realize industrialization, and the socialization, marketization and modernization of the economy. Politically, we will endeavor to develop socialist democracy[7], govern the country according to law, build a socialist country under the rule of law and ensure the full exercise of people's rights to govern the country and manage social affairs. Culturally, we will work hard to develop a socialist culture that is national, scientific and popular, a culture that is oriented to modernization, to the world and to the future[8], adopt a strategy of rejuvenating China through science and education,[9] and strive to raise the political and moral standards as well as scientific and cultural level[10] of the entire nation. In a word, it is to build China into a prosperous, strong, democratic, and culturally advanced[11] modern country.

A country with a vast territory, a big population and a long history, China should make greater contribution to humanity. The Chinese people waged a dauntless struggle for one hundred years. They have effected great reforms and changes one after another to build China into a strong and prosperous country. They have worked to strengthen ethnic solidarity[12] and achieve national reunification and to promote the lofty cause of world peace and development. In the final analysis, they have done all these for just one objective, that is, the great rejuvenation of the Chinese nation and China's new and greater contribution to humanity[13].

(原文及译文均选自《努力建立中美建设性的战略伙伴关系》,世界知识出版社。)

解说:

1. "充分证明"译作 eloquently proved, 比 amply proved 更为有力。

★2. 原文四个分句, 分别以"方向"、"信念"、"步骤"、"方式"为主语, 译文统一以 we 作主语, 语气比较顺。

3. 和前面四个分句并列的"取得的成就是巨大的", 单独译作一个以 that 引导的从句，与前面一个 that 引导的从句并列。

4．"全面推进改革"译作 conducting a comprehensive reform，原文里的状语在译文里改为定语。

5．"在经济上"用 economically 一词即够，不必译成短语。

★6．"社会主义市场经济体制"，译作 socialist market economy，"体制"的意思包含在 economy 一词之中。

★7．"社会主义民主政治"，译作 socialist democracy。democracy 一词就有"政治制度"的含义。

8．"社会主义文化"有两组定语，"民族的科学的大众的"更能说明社会主义文化的本质，在译文中与 socialist culture 结合得较紧，三个面向则作为同位语来处理。

9．"科教兴国"译作 rejuvenating China through science and education。

10．"素质"一词很不好译。"思想道德素质"译作 political and moral standards。"科学文化素质"译作 scientific and cultural level。

★11．"文明的"译作 culturally advanced，不要译作 civilized。

12．"民族团结"译作 ethnic solidarity。

13．这一句原文较长，先说四个"所以要"，最后说"归根到底……"逐渐形成气势。译文分成四句，比较有力。

Part II English and Chinese Compared

1. 实称、代称与重复

(1) 代词

代词的使用，在英语和汉语里有很大的不同。总的说来，英语代词用得多，汉语代词用得少。在文学作品里，在描述生活细节时，这种情况尤其明显。因此，英译汉时，有些代词可以不译。汉译英时则要在适当的地方增加代词，特别是物主代词。

1. Permit me first to thank our Chinese hosts for *your* extraordinary arrangements and hospitality. My wife and I, as well as *our* entire party, are deeply grateful.

首先，请允许我对中国主人十分出色的安排和款待表示感谢。我的夫人和我以及全体随行人员都深为感激。

2. When both visitors had told *their* stories, Chou smiled a little...

两位来客把经历说完后，周恩来微笑着说……

3. ... and every boat that passed sounded *its* siren in salutation.

……从旁边驶过的每一条船都拉响汽笛，表示敬意。

4. I was at once interested in this finger play and tried to imitate *it*.

我马上对这种用手指在手心里写字的游戏产生了兴趣，接着就模仿起来。

5. When Chou En-lai's door opened they saw a slender man of more than average height with gleaming eyes and a face so striking that *it* bordered on the beautiful.

周恩来的房门打开时，他们看到的是一个身材瘦长、比普通人略高一点的人，两眼闪着光辉，面貌很引人注意，称得上清秀。

以上五个例子，原文中的代词 your, our, their, its, it 都没有译。

6. Chu Teh remembered *his* age. He was thirty-six...

朱德想起自己的年龄，他已 36 岁……

例 6 说明，代词 his 如果要译，也不一定译作"他的"，而可译作"自己的"。

英语有时在句子里先出代词，然后再出它所指的人或物。汉语一般总是先出实词，然后才用代词。

7. If *they* are disappointed at one place, the drillers go to another.

钻探石油的人如果在一个地方得不到预期的结果，便到另一个地方去钻探。

8. Ignoring the chair offered *him*, Chu Teh stood squarely before this youth more than ten years his junior and in a level voice told him who he was...

朱德顾不得拉过来的椅子，端端正正地站在这个比他年轻十几岁的青年面前，用平稳的语调说明自己的身份……

9. Several times on *his* trips to China, which *he* made as a guest of the Chinese Government, Bill's birthday occurred while he was in Beijing.

比尔做为中国政府的客人访问中国，好几次都赶上在北京过生日。

知道了英汉两种语言使用代词的差异，汉译英时便要随时想到在适当的地方增加代词。

10. 有一年的冬初，四叔家里要换女工，做中人的卫老婆子带她进来了，头上扎着白头绳，乌裙，蓝夹袄，月白背心，年纪大约二十六七，脸色青黄，但两颊却还是红的。卫老婆子叫她祥林嫂，说是自己母家的邻舍，死了当家人，所以出来做工了。四叔皱了皱眉，四婶已经知道了他的意思，是在讨厌她是一个寡妇。但看她模样还周正，手脚都壮大，又只是顺着眼，不开一句口,很像一个安分耐劳的人,便不管四叔的皱眉,将她留下了。试工期内,她整天的做,似乎闲着就无聊,又有力,简直抵得过一个男子,所以第三天就定局,每月工钱五百文。

  Early one winter, when *my* uncle's family wanted a new maid, Old Mrs. Wei the go-between brought her along. She had a white mourning band round *her* hair and was wearing a black skirt, blue jacket, and pale green bodice. *Her* age was about twenty-six, and though *her* face was sallow *her* cheeks were red. Old Mrs. Wei introduced her as Xianglin's Wife, a neighbour of her mother's family, *who* wanted to go out to work now that *her* husband had died. *My* uncle frowned at this, and *my* aunt knew that he disapproved of taking on a widow. She looked just the person for them, though, with her big strong hands and feet; and, judging by *her* downcast eyes and silence, *she* was a good worker who would know her place. So *my* aunt ignored *my* uncle's frown and kept her. During *her* trial period she worked from morning till night as if *she* found resting irksome, and proved strong enough to do the work of a man; so on the third day *she* was taken on for five hundred cash a month.

  这段话,原文用了6个"她",指祥林嫂,1个"他",指四叔,1个"自己",指卫老婆子。译文却增加了15个代词,有my,her和she。

  11. 拾煤核也要放聪明点儿,常常换换地方,为的不受那些野男孩子的欺负。

  Even when scrounging for cinders *you* had to have *your* wits about *you* and shift from place to place to avoid those mischievous boys who banded together to collect cinders too.

  12. 中国作为一个发展中的沿海大国,国民经济要持续发展,必须把海洋的开发和保护作为一项长期的战略任务。

  As a major developing country with a long coastline, China, therefore, must take exploitation and protection of the ocean as a long-term strategic task before *it* can achieve the sustainable development of *its* national economy.

13. 现阶段中国已经实现了粮食基本自给, 在未来的发展过程中, 中国依靠自己的力量实现粮食基本自给, 客观上具备诸多有利因素。

China has basically achieved self-sufficiency in grain at the present stage, and there are many favorable objective factors for *her* to maintain such achievement by *her* own efforts in the course of future development.

例12指国家, 用了代词 it 和 its。例 13 同样是指国家, 却用了 her。在英语里, 用代词来指国家和船只时, 是可以用 she 和 her 的。请看:

14. ...and the great ship, tense and anxious, groped *her* way toward the shore with plumment and sounding-line.

大船上的人又紧张又着急, 一面用铅锤探测深浅, 一面向岸边慢慢驶去。

例13还有一点值得注意。"实现粮食基本自给"在同一句话里出现两次, 但译文却不重复 achieve self-sufficiency in grain, 第二次出现时, 译作 maintain such achievement。由此可以看出, 汉语可以在一句话里重复某些词语, 英语却不喜欢重复, 而用其他简洁的说法来替代, 这就是我们要在下一节里讲的"代称"了。

Drill 1

Ⅰ. 根据原文, 用适当的代词填空:

1. 在旧社会, 我们评剧演员常常挣钱不够吃饭, 艺人们大都是拉家带口, 生活困难。

In the old society, *pingju* players seldom made enough to live on, and as most were saddled with big familes _____ life was hard.

2. 真是一个钱撕成八瓣用,心里总想着怎样能够改善家里的困境。

Each single copper had to be eked out, and _____ kept racking _____ brains for ways to improve _____ difficult conditions.

3. 早晨去喊嗓子,我带着一个小篮拾煤核,为了回家取暖。

Each morning when _____ went out to practise singing in the open air, I took a little basket to scrounge for cinders for _____ stove.

4. 中国将努力促进国内粮食增产,在正常情况下,粮食自给率不低于95%,净进口量不超过国内消费量的5%。

China endeavors to increase _____ grain production so that _____ self-sufficiency rate of grain under normal conditions will be above 95 percent and the net import rate 5 percent, or even less, of the total consumption quantity.

Ⅱ. 根据原文,在译文适当的地方加上代词:

5. 晚上发高烧,一会儿热,一会儿冷!脸上红得像抹了胭脂,周身疼,连翻身都疼,疼得像针扎!

That evening ran a fever, burning hot one moment and icy cold the next. Face was as red as if rouged, whole body ached, and turning over in bed hurt like being needled!

6. 中国作为人类文明发祥地之一,在几千年的历史进程中,文化传统始终没有中断。

As one of the cradles of human civilization, China has all along mainatined cultural tradition without letup in history of several thousand years.

7. 中国有12亿多人口,陆地自然资源人均占有量低于世界平均水平。

China has a population of more than 1.2 billion, and land

natural resources per capita are lower than the world's average.

8. 中国将努力提高现有水域的生产能力，保持水产品继续快速增长。

China will actively increase the productivity of waters so as to keep a continuous rapid increase of aquatic products.

Ⅲ. 将下列单句译成英语：

9. 中国在自己发展的长河中，形成了优良的历史文化传统。

10. 哈佛建校三百六十年来，培养出许多杰出的政治家、科学家、文学家和企业家，曾出过六位美国总统，三十多位诺贝尔奖获得者。

Key to Drill 1

1. In the old society, *pingju* players seldom made enough to live on, and as most were saddled with big families *their* life was hard.

2. Each single copper had to be eked out, and *I* kept racking *my* brains for ways to improve *our* difficult conditions.

3. Each morning when *I* went out to practise singing in the open air, I took a little basket to scrounge for cinders for *our* stove.

4. China endeavors to increase *its* grain production so that *its* self-sufficiency rate of grain under normal conditions will be above 95 percent and the net import rate 5 percent, or even less, of the total consumption quantity.

5. That evening *I* ran a fever, burning hot one moment and icy cold the next. *My* face was as red as if rouged, *my* whole body ached, and turning over in bed hurt like being needled!

6. As one of the cradles of human civilization, China has all along maintained *its* cultural tradition without letup in *its* history of several thousand years.

7. China has a population of more than 1.2 billion, and *its* land natural resources per capita are lower than the world's average.

8. China will actively increase the productivity of *its* waters so as to keep a continuous rapid increase of aquatic products.

9. In the prolonged course of *its* development, China has formed its fine historical and cultural traditions.

10. Since *its* founding some 360 years ago, Harvard has nurtured a great number of outstanding statesmen, scientists, writers and businessmen, including six of the American Presidents and over thirty Nobel Prize winners.

(2) 名词的重复与代称

英语不喜欢重复，如果在一句话里需要重复某个词语，则用代词来代替，或以其他手段来避免重复。汉语不怕重复，连续使用某个词语是常见的事。汉语也用代词，但不如英语用得多。所以汉译英时要千方百计避免重复，多用代称；英译汉时则要少用代称，多用实称。

上述这种现象有时不止出现在一句话里，而是出现在相连的几句话里。要想处理得好，就不能把视线局限在一个句子之内，而要照顾到上下文。请看下面这段话。

Egypt, wrote the Greek historian Hecataeus, is the gift of *the Nile*. No other country is so dependent on a single lifeline. Egypt's very soil was born in *the Nile's* annual flood; with the flood came the life-giving mud that made Egypt the granary of the ancient world. And as rain fell in the Ethiopian highlands and the snows melted in the Mountains of the Moon, *the river* was everlastingly renewed.

在第一句和第三句里，the Nile 出现两次。在第四句里再次出现时，使用了代词 the river。虽然这个代称并不比实称简短，按字母计算的话,还多一个字母,仍然用了这个代称,因为需要换一个说法,免得重复。

英语避免重复,最常见的办法是使用代词。

1. It may seem strange to put into the same packet an industrial revolution and two political revolutions. But the fact is that *they* were all social revolutions.

把一场工业革命同两次政治革命归作一类似乎有点奇怪,但事实上这三次革命都是社会革命。

2. Two things are outstanding in the creation of the English system of canals, and *they* characterise all the Industrial Revolution.

在修建英国的运河网的过程中,有两点是非常突出的,而这两点也正是整个工业革命的特点。

3. The canals were arteries of communication: *they* were not made to carry pleasure boats, but barges.

运河是交通的动脉,开运河不是为了走游艇,而是为了通行驳船。

4. James Brindley was a pioneer in the art of building canals or, as *it* was then called, 'navigation'.

布林德雷是开凿运河的先驱者,当时人们把开凿运河叫做 navigation。

5. Several factors accounted for this extraordinary achievement. *One* was the expansion into the west. *Another* was the application of machinery to farming.

取得这一特殊成就有几方面的原因:第一个原因是向西部的扩展,第二个原因是机器在农业上的应用。

6. .... for the establishment of agricultural and industrial colleges. *These* were to serve both as educational institutions and as centers for research in scientific farming.

……以便建立农业和工业学院。这些学校一方面是教育机关,另一方面,也是农业科学的研究中心。

有时在英语里避免重复,也不一定用代词,而用名词。用名词作代称,可能比实称简短,也可能并不简短,只是为了换一个说法。

7. 哈佛是最早接受中国留学生的美国大学之一。中国教育界、科学界、文化界一直同哈佛大学保持着学术交流。

Harvard is among the first American universities to accept Chinese students. The Chinese educational, scientific and cultural communities have all along maintained academic exchanges with *this university*.

8. 据专家测算,中国粮食在种、收、运、储、销和加工、消费等环节的损失率至少为10%,总损失量在4,500万吨以上。如果将各环节的损失降至合理范围,每年至少可节约粮食2,000万吨。

...So it will be possible to save at least 20 million tons of grain every year if *such losses* are reduced to within the rational limits.

在英语里,还可以采用部分重复的办法,或者加以简化,将重复的部分合并,以减少重复。

9. 五四运动是在当时世界革命号召之下,是在俄国革命号召之下,是在列宁号召之下发生的。

The May 4th Movement came into being at the call *of* the world revolution, *of* the Russian Revolution *and of* Lenin.

10. 五四运动是在思想上和干部上准备了1921年中国共产党的成立,又准备了五卅运动和北伐战争。

Both in ideology and in the matter of cadres, the May 4th Movement paved the way *for* the founding of the Chinese Communist Party in 1921 *and for* the May 30th Movement in 1925 and the Northern Expedition.

11. 五四运动是反帝国主义的运动,又是反封建的运动。五四运动的杰出的历史意义,在于它带着为辛亥革命还不曾有的姿态,这就是彻底地不妥协地反帝国主义和彻底地不妥协地反封建主义。

The May 4th Movement was an anti-imperialist as well as an anti-feudal *movement*. *Its* outstanding historical significance is to be seen in a feature which was absent from the Revolution of 1911, namely, its *thorough and uncompromising opposition* to imperialism as well as to feudalism.

(3) 其他词语的代称

英国语言学家 Randolph Quirk 等四位学者合编的 *A Grammar of Contemporary English* 在关于 substitution 的一节中指出：不仅名词短语可以有代称，状语、谓语乃至宾语从句，都可以有代称。该书把用作代称的替代词统称为 pro-forms。书中举了许多例子，如：

We saw John *at eight on Monday evening*. We told him *then* that we would be coming to the party.

Look *in the top drawer*. You'll probably find it *there*.

A: John drives a car.　　B: I think Bob *does* too.

A: John dirves a car.　　B: *So does* Bob.

Oxford is likely to win the next boat race. All my friends say *so*. (= that Oxford is likely to win the next boat race)

以上例子中的 then, there, does, so does, so 都可以说是 pro-forms。

请看以下几个例子。

1. ... This is nothing like back home in Colorado. We have rains *there*, too. Thunderstorms in spring and summer...

……这跟家乡科罗拉多的情况迥然不同。

科罗拉多也下雨。春夏两季雷雨交加……

2. 1962年我到天津中国大戏院演出，一位中年女工到后台来看我，原来是我当年在东亚厂熟识的王大姐，她已是工厂的干部了。

In 1962, when I went to perform in the Grand Chinese Theatre in Tianjin, a middle-aged woman worker came backstage to see me. It turned out that she was Big Sister Wang whom I'd known in the East Asia Woollen Mill. She was now a cadre *there*.

例1原文第二句用 there 代替 in Colorado,而译文重复"科罗拉多"。例2原文用了"东亚厂"、"工厂",都是实词,译文却用了 there。

3. We faced the question in 1978, as to some extent we still *do* today...

我们在1978年乃至今天在某种程度上面临的问题仍然是……

4. Almost at once the number of egg masses deposited on experimental goats began to decrease, as *did* their fertility.

在试验用的山羊身上产的卵块几乎立刻减少,其受精率亦下降。

例3的 do 和例4的 did 都是 pro-forms,用来代替动词。例3的译文把两个动词合并,没有重复。例4的译文考虑到主谓搭配,用了不同的动词。

有时一句话后半句表示的动作和前半句是一样的,只是把施事和受事颠倒一下。这在汉语里,后半句和前半句一般用同样的结构,略显重复。英语里则有一简单的说法:vice versa。

5. 为了推动中美关系的发展,中国需要进一步了解美国,美国也需要进一步了解中国。

To promote the development of China-U.S. relations, China needs to know the United States better and *vice versa*.

有时为了加强语气,取得一定的修辞效果,故意重复句中的某些词语。这无论是在英语里还是在汉语里都是常见的。遇到这种情况,即便是英语也照样重复,而不用代称。

6. *The world* watches. *The world* listens. *The world* waits

to see what we will do.

全世界在注视着。全世界在倾听着。全世界在等待着看我们将做些什么。

7. As you said in your toast, the Chinese people *are a great people*, the American people *are a great people*.

正如你在祝酒时讲的那样，中国人民是伟大的人民，美国人民是伟大的人民。

Drill 2

将下列单句译成英语：

1. 先有哈佛，后有美利坚合众国，这说明了哈佛在美国历史上的作用。
2. 要提倡科学，靠科学才有希望。
3. 第一次世界大战后，帝国主义对中国加强侵略，北洋军阀政府对外妥协投降，对内残酷压迫人民，给中国带来了深重的民族危机……北洋军阀政府出动军警镇压，捕去学生三十多名。
4. 革命是解放生产力，改革也是解放生产力。
5. 老科学家、中年科学家很重要，青年科学家也很重要。
6. 这五年，首先是农村改革带来许多新的变化，农作物大幅度增产，农民收入大幅度增加，乡镇企业异军突起。
7. 就我们国家来讲，首先是要摆脱贫穷。要摆脱贫穷，就要找出一条比较快的发展道路。
8. 中国愿与东盟各国永做好邻居、好伙伴、好朋友。
9. 每一个社会主义国家的改革又都是不同的，历史不同，经验不同，现在所处的情况不同，各国的改革不可能一样。
10. 不能把欧洲视为亚洲，也不能把亚洲视为欧洲。

Key to Drill 2

1. The fact that Harvard was founded before the United States of America testifies to its position in the American history.

2. We must promote science, for that is where our hope lies.

3. After World War I, the imperialists stepped up their aggression against China while the Northern Warlord government resorted to compromise and capitulation externally and to ruthless oppression of the people internally, thus landing China in a grave national crisis. ... The government called out troops and policemen to suppress the demonstrators and over thirty students were arrested.

4. Revolution means the emancipation of the productive forces, and so does reform.

5. Veteran and middle-aged scientists are important, and so are young ones.

6. During those five years rural reform brought about many changes: grain output increased substantially, as did the peasants' income, and rural enterprises emerged as a new force.

7. For China, the first thing is to throw off poverty. To do that we have to find a way to develop fairly rapidly.

8. China will forever be a good neighbor, a good partner and a good friend with ASEAN countries.

9. The particular reform to be carried out in each socialist country is different too. Since each has a different history, different experience and different current circumstances to confront, their reforms cannot be identical.

10. It is therefore not advisable to identify Europe with Asia or vice versa.

2. 搭配

(1) 主谓搭配——主语

为了叙述的方便,这里所说的"主谓搭配"是指主语和谓语动词的搭配。

英汉两种语言的主谓搭配,在大多数情况下是相通的。英语里一个主谓搭配,译成汉语后,可以保持原来的搭配。但有时却不行,汉译英时也是这样。一般说来,汉语的主谓关系没有英语那么密切。英语对于主语能否做后面的动作考虑较多。因此,译文以什么作主语,怎样和谓语搭配,是汉译英时经常需要斟酌的一个问题。

1. 合营企业的形式为有限责任公司。

An equity joint venture shall take the form of a limited liability company.

2. 合营者的注册资本如果转让必须经合营各方同意。

If any of the joint venturers wish to assign its registered capital, it must obtain the consent of the other parties to the venture.

3. 合营企业的有关外汇事宜,应遵照中华人民共和国外汇管理条例办理。

An equity joint venture shall handle its foreign exchange transactions in accordance with the regulations on foreign exchange control of the People's Republic of China.

4. 合营企业所需原材料、燃料、配套件等,应尽先在中国购买,也可由合营企业自筹外汇,直接在国际市场上购买。

In its purchase of required raw and processed materials, fuels, auxiliary equipment, etc., *an equity joint venture* should first give priority to purchases in China. It may also make such purchases directly on the world market with foreign exchange raised by itself.

以上四例,"合营企业"和"合营者"都是定语,但译文却把 an equity joint venture 和 joint venturer 作主语,这样后面比较好安排,所考虑的主要就是主谓搭配的问题。

5. 中国水域、草原、山地资源丰富,开发潜力巨大。

China has rich water, grassland and sloping land resources which have great potential for exploitation.

6. 中国的发展与进步,不会对任何人构成威胁。

A developing and progressing *China* does not pose a threat to anyone.

7. 在少数民族聚居的地方实行了区域自治。民族地区的经济社会获得不断的发展。

In places where there is a high concentration of ethnic minorities, regional autonomy is in practice. *These regions* have witnessed continued economic and social development.

8. ……我们进行改革开放的方向是正确的,信念是坚定的,步骤是稳妥的,方式是渐进的,取得的成就是巨大的。

... that we are going in the right direction, firm in conviction, steady in our steps and gradual in our approach when carrying out the reform and opening-up and that we have achieved tremendous successes.

以上四例都是以国家、地区或个人为主语,而没有依照原文,以"水域"、"发展"、"经济"、"方向"为主语。例8以 we 作主语还有一个好处。原文用了一连串并列的主谓结构,主语不断变换,而这是英语所不喜欢的。译文以 we 作主语,管住全句,比较合乎英语的习惯。

有时为了突出重点,译文需要保留原文的主语,那就需要考虑选用合适的动词了。

9. 合营企业的一切活动应遵守中华人民共和国法律、法令和有关条例规定。

All activities of an equity joint venture shall *comply* with the provisions of the laws, decrees and pertinent regulations of the People's Republic of China.

例9译文与原文一致,以activities为主语,问题在于怎样选一个合适的动词和它搭配。abide by 和observe都只能用于人或机构。这里选用了comply,这个动词用的范围比较广。

10. 正副总经理（或正副厂长）由合营各方分别担任。

The offices of general manager and vice-general manager(s)(or factory manager and deputy manager(s)) shall be assumed by the respective parties to the venture.

11. 合营各方发生纠纷,董事会不能协商解决时,由中国仲裁机构进行调解或仲裁,也可由合营各方协议在其它仲裁机构仲裁。

Disputes arising between the parties to an equity joint venture which the board of directors has failed to settle through consultation may be settled through conciliation or arbitration by an arbitration agency of China or through arbitration by another arbitration agency agreed upon by the parties.

例10和例11的结构有共同之处,都用"由"字引出谓语,而且译文都用了被动语态。例10译文加了the offices作主语,方能和后面的shall be assumed 搭配。例11则直接以disputes作主语了。

12. 鼓励合营企业向中国境外销售产品。

An equity joint venture shall be encouraged to market its products outside China.

13. 鼓励外国合营者将可汇出的外汇存入中国银行。

A foreign joint venturer shall be encouraged to deposit in the Bank of China the foreign exchange which it is entitled to remit abroad.

例12和例13,原文都是无主句,而在这样正式的场合,英语句子是一定要有主语的。译文用了被动语态,就以原文里的宾语作主语了。

Drill 3

填空：

1. 基本路线要管一百年，动摇不得。

　　_____ for a hundred years, with no vacillation.

2. 改革开放胆子要大一些，敢于试验。

　　_____ and have the courage to experiment.

3. 我国的经济发展，总要力争隔几年上一个台阶。

　　_____ should strive to reach a higher level every few years.

4. 我国经济发展分三步走，本世纪走两步，达到温饱和小康，下个世纪用三十年到五十年时间再走一步，达到中等发达国家的水平。

　　_____. Two steps will be taken in this century, to reach the point where our people have adequate food and clothing and lead a fairly comfortable life. The third step, which will take us 30 to 50 years into the next century, is to reach the level of the moderately developed countries.

5. 社会主义发展生产力，成果是属于人民的。

　　_____, the result belongs to the people.

6. 成功的经验鼓励了我们，增加了我们的信心。

　　_____ have inspired us and strengthened our confidence.

7. 现在提出党政分开，但不管怎样还是共产党领导，是为了更好地加强和改善党的领导。

　　We are now raising the question of separating _____. But no matter how that is done, it will still be the Party that leads, and _____ will be designed to strengthen its leadership.

Key to Drill 3

1. *We* should adhere to the basic line for a hundred years, with

no vacillation.

2. *We* should be bolder than before in conducting reform and opening to the outside and have the courage to experiment.

3. In developing the economy, *we* should strive to reach a higher level every few years.

4. *China* is developing its economy in three steps. Two steps will be taken in this century, to reach the point where our people have adequate food and clothing and lead a fairly comfortable life. The third step, which will take us 30 to 50 years into the next century, is to reach the level of the moderately developed countries.

5. Under socialism, when *the productive forces* are developed, the result belongs to the people.

6. *Our successes* have inspired us and strengthened our confidence.

7. We are now raising the question of separating *the functions* of the Party from those of the government. But no matter how that is done, it will still be the Party that leads, and *the separation* will be designed to strengthen its leadership.

(2) 主谓搭配——动词

动词在英语里，可以说是一个最活跃的词类。名词和形容词，相对说来意思比较固定，而动词往往可以表示各种不同的含义，用法也特别多。因此，英译汉时，动词处理起来弹性特别大，需要考虑的往往是怎样选择一个能够很好地与主语搭配的动词。

1. The city *contains* many fine examples of early Australian architecture.

市内有精美的澳大利亚早期建筑物多处。

2. Day by day the sea is *eating* the land—the dam has stopped

the sediment of the Nile from replenishing the shoreline.

海水一天天冲刷陆地——水坝已经使得尼罗河的泥沙无法沉积下来加固海岸了。

3. The flood does not *carry* away the salt as before.
现在不像从前了，河水不泛滥，盐分就冲不走了。

4. Adelaide *enjoys* a Mediterranean climate...
阿德莱德属地中海型气候……

5. The delta and the narrow Nile Valley to the south *make up* only 3 percent of Egypt's land but *are* home to 96 percent of her population.
三角洲和南边狭窄的尼罗河河谷只占埃及土地的百分之三，却有百分之九十六的人口住在这里。

不仅动词和主语之间有搭配问题，动词和宾语之间也有搭配问题，情况相近，一并在这里谈一谈，就不单独处理了。

6. James Brindley was a pioneer in the art of *building* canals or as it was then called, 'navigation'.
布林德雷是开凿运河的先驱者，当时人们把开凿运河叫作navigation。

7. As an early agricultural marketing centre, it *handled* wheat, wool, fruits, and wine.
这里是早期的一个农业贸易中心，经营过小麦、羊毛、水果和酒类。

例6中的build一词，译法很多，主要是取决于后面的宾语。我们常说"修建铁路"，"修筑公路"。和"运河"搭配，当然是"开凿"了。例7中的动词handle，前面的主语是it，指an early agricultural center，后面的宾语是wheat, wool, fruits, and wine，因此，handle译作"经营"比较恰当。

有时在原文里两个主语可以共用一个动词，或一个动词可以有两个并列的宾语，而在译文里却不能这样搭配。这就需要根据有关的主语或宾语，选用不同的动词，分别处理了。

8. Two metal surfaces rubbing together cause friction and heat; but if they are separated by a thin film of oil, the friction and heat are *reduced*.

两个金属面相擦,就要产生摩擦和热;但如果在它们之间抹上薄薄的一层油,就可以减少摩擦,降低热度。

9. My fingers lingered almost unconsciously on the familiar leaves and blossoms which had just *come forth* to greet the sweet southern spring.

我几乎是无意识地用手抚摸着我所熟悉的叶片和花朵,这新长的叶片和刚开的花朵在南方迎来了芬芳的春天。

10. 合营各方按注册资本比例分享利润和分担风险及亏损。

The parties to the venture shall *share* the profits, risks and losses in proportion to their contributions to the registered capital.

以上三个例子说明,由于主语或宾语的影响,一个动词可以译成两个,或两个动词可以译成一个。例8更从原来的主谓关系变成了动宾关系。例9的动词 come forth 因出现在定语从句中,译成"新长的"和"刚开的",便成了形容词。例10 "分享"用于好事,"分担"用于坏事,而 share 是中性词,两方面的含义都可以包括。可见无论是英译汉,还是汉译英,无论是主谓关系、动宾关系、还是修饰关系,都存在一个选择最佳搭配的问题。要用不同的词组成不同的搭配,而不要用同一个词勉强去管它管不住的东西。

有时英语用倒装句,主谓和谓语的顺序颠倒,或虽未用倒装句,但译文若保留原结构会很别扭,那就不能只在动词上作文章,挖空心思去找一个适当的动词,而是要考虑改变句子的结构了。

11. With the flood *came* the life-giving mud that made Egypt the granary of the ancient world.

河水泛滥带来了泥沙,万物得以生长,埃及就这样成了古代世界的粮仓。

12. The land is poorer, because the mud that used to *come* with the Nile flood has stopped.

土地更差了，因为过去尼罗河一泛滥就带来泥沙，可现在没有了。

13. At the edge of the fields, rising in dramatic hills or stretching flat to the horizon, *lay* the brown barren deserts.

田地外边是寸草不生的棕色沙漠，有的地方突然隆起像是小山，有的地方则平平地伸向地平线。

14. The road we have long been travelling is deceptively easy, a smooth superhighway on which we progress with great speed, but at its end *lies* disaster.

我们一直在走的这条路表面上很好走，是一条平坦的超级公路，我们可以高速前进，但是走到尽头却要遇到灾难。

15. Egyptian agriculture has been transformed, and industry is *benefiting* from power generated by the dam.

埃及的农业得到了改造，工业也用上了水坝发出的电力。

Drill 4

填空：

1. 一九八四年我来过广东。

_____ in Guangdong in 1984.

2. 革命是解放生产力，改革也是解放生产力。

_____ the emancipation of the productive forces, and so does reform.

3. 每年领导层都要总结经验，对的就坚持，不对的赶快改，新问题出来抓紧解决。

Every year leaders should _____, continuing those measures that have proved correct, acting promptly to change those that have proved wrong and tackling new problems as soon as they are identified.

4. 从我们自己这些年的经验来看,经济发展隔几年上一个台阶,是能够办得到的。

Judging from what we have accomplished in recent years, it should be possible for our economy _____.

5. 中央的方针是等待他们,让事实教育他们。

The Central Committee's policy was to wait for them _____.

6. 中央要求科技界面向经济建设。

The Central Committee of the Party has called for the work in science and technology _____.

7. 越老越不要最后犯错误,越老越要谦虚一点。现在还要继续选人,选更年轻的同志,帮助培养。不要迷信。

The older they are, the more modest they should be and the more careful not to make mistakes in their later years. We should go on selecting younger comrades for promotion and helping train them. Don't _____.

Key to Drill 4

1. I *was* here in Guangdong in 1984.

2. Revolution *means* the emancipation of the productive forces, and so does reform.

3. Every year leaders should *review what they have done*, continuing those measures that have proved correct, acting promptly to change those that have proved wrong and tackling new problems as soon as they are identified.

4. Judging from what we have accomplished in recent years, it should be possible for our economy *to reach a new stage* every few years.

5. The Central Committee's policy was to wait for them to *be convinced* by facts.

6. The Central Committee of the Party has called for the work in science and technology *to be geared to the needs of* economic development.

7. The older they are, the more modest they should be and the more careful not to make mistakes in their later years. We should go on selecting younger comrades for promotion and helping train them. Don't *put your trust only in old age*.

(3) 形容词与副词

形容词和副词在英语里是两个非常活跃的词类。其词义往往随前后搭配而变化，其用法也特别灵活。若与汉语相比较，则会发现有时是与汉语一致的，有时则有很大的差距。这两个词类有些共同的特点，而且翻译时往往可以互相转换，因此放在一起讨论。

首先要确定词义，根据上下文，找出适当的译法。

1. When the reply came a few months later they were enrolled as *full* members, but Chu's membership was kept a secret from outsiders.

过了几个月，回信来了，两人都被吸收为正式党员，但朱德的党籍对外界保持秘密。

2. More than eight years have passed since Vice Premier Deng Xiaoping and I joined hands to establish *full* diplomatic relations between our two great nations.

自从邓小平副总理和我共同建立我们两个伟大国家之间的正式外交关系以来，已经八年多了。

3. As a *private* American citizen I recognize that many of the burdens and opportunities of our relationship have now passed to the *non-governmental* sectors of our two societies: to individuals, our corporations, universities, research institutes, foundations, and so on.

作为一个普通的美国公民,我知道我们关系中的许多责任和机会现在已经转到了我们两个社会的民间部门,即转到了个人、公司、大学、研究机构、基金会等。

4. Yet it was a manly face, serious and intelligent, and Chu judged him to be in his *middle* twenties.

可是,那是个男子汉的面庞,严肃而聪颖,朱德看他大概是二十五六岁的年龄。

例1和例2,full都译作"正式"。例3,private 和 American citizen 连用,译作"普通的"。non-governmental 译作"民间",这是一个常见的译法。汉译英时,"民间的"也往往译作 non-governmental。例4,middle 这样用,在汉语里没有与之对应的词语,因此译文具体,译作"二十五六岁的年龄"。

汉译英也会遇到同样的情况。

5. 我感谢陆登庭校长的邀请,使我有机会在这美好的金秋时节,来到你们这座美国古老而又现代化的学府。

I wish to thank President Rudenstine for inviting me to this *old* yet modern institution of the United States in this golden fall.

6. 哈佛为增进中美两国人民的相互了解作出了有益的贡献。

Harvard has thus made *useful* contribution to the enhanced mutual understanding between the Chinese and American peoples.

7. ……成为激励中国人民变革创新、努力奋斗的精神力量。

This idea has become an important *moral* force spurring the Chinese people to work hard for change and innovation.

8. 总起来说,就是要把中国建设成富强民主文明的现代化国家。

In a word, it is to build China into a prosperous, strong, democratic, and *culturally advanced* modern country.

看到"古老"一词,往往首先想到 ancient,但用来形容1636年创立的哈佛大学,显然是不合适的,因此例5用了 old 一词。例6,"有益的"常译作 useful。例7,"精神力量"译作

moral force，因 spiritual 一词有宗教色彩。"精神文明"常译作 cultural and ethical progress。例 8，"文明的"常译作 culturally advanced，而不译作 civilized。

9."我真傻，真的，"祥林嫂抬起她没有神采的眼睛来，接着说。

"I was really too stupid, really..." put in Xianglin's Wife, raising her *lacklustre* eyes.

例 9 用 lacklustre 来描写眼睛，显然要比 listless 更为合适。

10. 近百年来，为了摆脱半殖民地半封建的历史境遇，中国人民进行了艰苦卓绝、奋发图强的斗争。

In the past one hundred years or so, the Chinese people waged *arduous* struggles to lift themselves from their historical plight under semi-colonial and semi-feudal rule.

汉语有时连用几个四字成语作定语，以加强语气。译文需考虑句子的整体结构，避免累赘，可以适当压缩。例 10 中的"艰苦卓绝、奋发图强的斗争"就只译作 arduous struggles。

11. It is a *long narrow* swale between two ranges of mountains, and the Salinas River winds and twists up the center until it falls at last into Monterey Bay.

那是两条山脉之间的一片狭长的洼地，萨利纳斯河蜿蜒曲折从中间流过，最后注入蒙特雷海湾。

12. That was because I saw everything with the *strange*, *new* sight that had come to me.

……因为我是用刚刚产生的这种新奇的视力来看待一切的。

几个形容词连用时，译文的顺序不一定与原文的顺序一样。例 11，long 在前，narrow 在后，译成汉语则只能说"狭长"。例 12，strange 在前，new 在后，译文则把 new 和 that had come to me 结合起来，译作"刚刚产生的"，放到前面去了。

这种颠倒顺序的现象在汉译英时也是常见的。例如"经济特区"译作 special economic zone；"国际经济新秩序"译作 the new international economic order。

13. We have acquired a *keen* sense of the diversity, dynamism, and progress of China under your policies of reform and opening to the outside world.

我们强烈地感受到你们执行的改革和对外开放政策给中国带来的多样化、活力和进步。

14. ... and the farther up the hills you went, the thinner grew the soil, with flints sticking through, until at the brush line it was a kind of dry flinty gravel that reflected the hot sun *blindingly*.

越往高处，土层越薄，硬石露了头；到了灌木都不生长的地方，只有干巴巴的硬卵石，反射出炙热炫目的阳光。

15. Chou was a *quiet* and *thoughtful* man...

周恩来举止优雅，待人体贴……

这几个例子说明原文里的形容词可以译成副词，原文里的副词可以译成形容词，或改变句式，用主谓结构。例13 的 have acquired a keen sense of 译作"强烈地感受到"。例14 的 reflected the hot sun blindingly 译作"反射出炙热炫目的阳光"。例15 quiet 和 thoughtful 译作"举止优雅"和"待人体贴"，这是合乎汉语描述人物的说法的。

汉译英也不乏这样的例子。例如："创造性地提出了农村包围城市的战略"，译作 proposing the *creative* strategy of encircling the cities from the countryside。"深化经济体制改革，相应地进行政治体制改革"译作 deepening the reform of the economic structure and carrying out a *corresponding* reform of the political structure。

16. On the *wide level* acres of the valley the topsoil lay deep and fertile. It required only a *rich* winter of rain to make it break forth in grass and flowers.

宽阔平坦的河谷，表土层厚而肥沃。一冬雨水充足，就能使花草萌发。

例 16 的原文，wide level 形容 acres，或者说形容 acres of the valley，原文 rich 形容 winter，或者说形容 winter of rain。在译文里，"宽阔平坦"却要直接形容"河谷"，"充足"也要直接形容"雨水"。

17. On entering the door I remembered the doll I had broken. I felt my way to the hearth and picked up the pieces. I tried *vainly* to put them together.

一进门，我就想起了被我摔碎的娃娃。我摸索着走到壁炉跟前，捡起了碎片。我想把这些碎片拼在一起，可是拼不起来了。

18. ... he now put aside an impulse to shake his head *negatively*, and observed: "But you haven't had any training in this work."

所以他本来打算摇摇头表示拒绝，现在却没有这么做，只是说："不过你对这种工作还没有什么经验呀。"

有时英语的形容词或副词在句中形成一定的搭配，译成汉语时，如保持原来的词类在原来的位置很难处理，这时便可把形容词或副词拿出来，放在后面，单独处理。例 17，vainly 译作"可是拼不起来了。"例 18，negatively 译作"表示拒绝"。译文加了动词，就好处理了。

Drill 5

Ⅰ. 填空：

1. 发展才是硬道理。

Development is the _____ principle.

2. 科学技术是第一生产力。

Science and technology are a _____ productive force.

3. 搞社会主义现代化建设是基本路线。

It is our _____ line to carry out socialist modernization.

4. 在整个改革开放的过程中，必须始终注意坚持四项基本原则。

Throughout the process of reform and opening, we must also adhere to the Four _____ Principles.

5. 社会主义本身是共产主义的初级阶段，而我们中国又处在社会主义的初级阶段。

Socialism itself is the _____ stage of communism, and here in China we are still in the _____ stage of socialism.

Ⅱ. 将下列单句译成英语：

6. 调动积极性是最大的民主。

7. 把权力下放给基层和人民……这就是最大的民主。

8. 依我看，科学技术是第一生产力。

9. 对科学技术的重要性要充分认识。

10. 悠久的中华文化，成为维系民族团结和国家统一的牢固纽带。

Key to Drill 5

1. Development is the *absolute* principle.

2. Science and technology are a *primary* productive force.

3. It is our *basic* line to carry out socialist modernization.

4. Throughout the process of reform and opening, we must also adhere to the Four *Cardinal* Principles.

5. Socialism itself is the *first* stage of communism, and here in China we are still in the *primary* stage of socialism.

6. When the people's initiative is aroused, that's the best manifestation of democracy.

7. Devolving authority to the localities and the people... is the height of democracy.

8. In my opinion, science and technology are a primary productive force.

9. We must recognize the full importance of science and

technology.

10. The age-old Chinese culture becomes a strong bond for ethnic harmony and national unity.

(4) 增词与减词

无论是英译汉,还是汉译英,有时为了行文的需要,都可以在译文里增加几个词,或减少几个词。增词可以使译文流畅,减词可以使译文简洁。这是因为有些词在一种语言里可能是必要的,而在另一种语言里就会显得多余了。

1. 1998年是联合国确定的国际海洋年,中国政府愿借此机会介绍中国海洋事业的发展情况。

The year 1998 has been designated by the United Nations as International Ocean Year, and on this occasion the Chinese Government would like to introduce the progress of China's work in this particular field to the world.

2. 我在东亚毛纺织厂当小工,那些女工大姐姐们都喜欢我,都说我好……

All the older women in the East Asia Woollen Mill liked me and spoke well of me...

3. 我进去看了,只记得门警是瑞士兵士,穿着黄色制服,别的没有印象了。

I went there to have a look. All I remember now is that the guards at the entrance were Swiss soldiers in yellow uniforms.

例1原文"介绍……的发展情况"句子是完整的。但在译文里却需要说明向谁介绍,因此加了 to the world。例2译文没有提"当小工"之事。这是因为上文已经说了"我同几个女孩子去东亚纺织厂当小工",这里就简化了。例3也是一个减词的例子。汉语为了加强语气,对于一件事,往往从一个方面说了之后,还要从另一个方面说一说。英语则不然。例3的译文,前面有了

All I remember now is...，后面如果再说 and I don't remember anything else，就显得多余了。

范畴词如"方面"、"方式"、"问题"、"情况"等，在汉语里用得很多。这类词在句子里没有多少实际意义，但很有用，可以使句子流畅。汉译英时，往往不需要译出来。

4．中国有12亿多人口，陆地自然资源人均占有量低于世界平均水平。

China has a population of more than 1.2 billion, and its land natural resources per capita are lower than the world's average.

5．中国民主革命的先行者孙中山首先提出"振兴中华"的口号，他领导的辛亥革命，推翻了在中国延续几千年的君主专制制度。

Dr. Sun Yat-sen, China's forerunner in the democratic revolution, was the first to put forward the slogan of "rejuvenation of China". He led the Revolution of 1911 to overthrow the autocratic monarchy lasting several millennia in China.

6．中国历史上虽曾出现过暂时的分裂现象，但民族团结和国家统一始终是中华民族历史的主流，是中国发展进步的重要保障。

Despite occasional divisions, ethnic harmony and national unity have remained the main stream in the history of the Chinese nation, and an important guarantee for China's development and progress.

7．近代中国虽屡遭列强欺凌，国势衰败，但经过全民族的百年抗争，又以巨人的姿态重新站起来。

In modern times, the frequent bullying and humiliation by imperialist powers once weakened China. However, after a hundred years' struggle of the entire Chinese nation, China has stood up again as a giant.

例4里的 average 作为名词，就包含着"水平"的意思。例5里的 the autocratic monarchy 就是一种制度，可以不加 system.

例6,"分裂现象"译作 divisions 就够了。例7,as a giant 就是"以巨人的姿态"的意思。

　　动词的增减也是翻译中常见的一种现象。英语名词、介词用得多,汉语则动词用得多。英译汉时,在英语没有出现动词的情况下,译文往往加上动词,可以使句子显得较为灵活。汉译英时,译文可以把原文使用的动词(不是谓语动词)删去,比较简洁。

　　8. But if we can find common ground to work together, the chance for world peace is immeasurably increased.

　　但是,如果我们能够找到进行合作的共同点,那么实现世界和平的机会就将无可估量地大大增加。

　　9. We have acquired a keen sense of the diversity, dynamism, and progress of China under your policies of reform and opening to the outside world.

　　我们强烈地感受到你们执行的改革和对外开放政策给中国带来的多样化、活力和进步。

　　10. 相互了解,是发展国与国之间关系的前提。

　　Mutual understanding is the basis for state-to-state relations.

　　11. 中国始终是维护世界和平与地区稳定的坚定力量。

　　China is always a staunch force for world peace and regional stability.

　　12.……归根到底就是为了一个目标:实现中华民族的伟大复兴,争取对人类作出新的更大的贡献。

　　In the final analysis, they have done all these for just one objective, that is, the great rejuvenation of the Chinese nation and China's new and greater contribution to humanity.

　　例8,the chance for world peace 译作"实现世界和平的机会",加了"实现"二字。例9,your policies of reform and opening to the outside world 译作"你们执行的改革和对外开放政策",加了"执行"二字。两处都在定语里加了一个动词,这是合乎汉语的说法的。这一点,看一下例10、例11和例12的原文就清楚了。例10里的"发展"、例11里的"维护"和例12里的"实现",在译文里都没有了。这也是合乎英语的说法的。例8和例9的原文就可以证明这一点。

13. 哈佛为增进中美两国人民的相互了解作出了有益的贡献。

Harvard has thus made useful contribution to the enhanced mutual understanding between the Chinese and American peoples.

14. 所有这些,为巩固国家统一奠定了坚实的政治基础。

All these have laid a solid political foundation for consolidated national unity.

还有一个值得注意的现象。例13,"为增进中美两国人民的相互了解"包含一个动宾结构,译文没有省略动词,若照原文的结构译,应是 to enhancing mutual understanding..., 但译文没有用动名词 enhancing,而用了过去分词 enhanced。例14,"为巩固国家统一"可译作 for consolidating national unity, 但译文却用了 consolidated。这是现在常见的一种说法。从结构上看,不用动宾结构,而用名词词组,结构简化了,也许这正是它可取的地方。

Drill 6

填空:

1. 正确的政治路线要靠正确的组织路线来保证。

_____ must be ensured by a correct organizational line.

2. 形式主义也是官僚主义。

Formalism is _____.

3. 我们非常关注非洲的发展与繁荣。

We are closely following Africa's development _____.

4. 我们最大的经验就是不要脱离世界,否则就会信息不灵。

The biggest lesson we have learned is that we should not isolate ourselves from _____, lest we become ill-informed.

5. 总结过去,面向未来,为了保障东亚各国人民的根本利益，为了促进人类和平与发展的崇高事业，必须进一步加强东亚合作。

When we review the past and look to the future, _____ it is necessary for us to further strengthen East Asian cooperation in order to ensure the fundamental interests of East Asian peoples and promote the lofty cause of peace and development of mankind.

6. 我去过一次深圳，那里确实是一派兴旺气象。

I visited Shenzhen a couple of years ago _____.

7. 他们自己总结经验，由内向型转为外向型。

The people in Shenzhen reviewed their experience _____ shift the zone's economy from a domestic orientation to an external orientation.

8. 改革开放以来，我们立的章程不少，而且是全方位的。

_____, we have drawn up many rules and regulations, covering all fields of endeavour.

9. 这标志着中美关系进入了一个新的发展阶段。

This will mark _____.

10. 我们真正干起来是1980年。1981、1982、1983这三年，改革主要在农村进行。

We actually started the reform in 1980. _____ it was carried out primarily in the countryside.

11. 总之，就全国范围来说，我们一定能够逐步顺利解决沿海同内地贫富差距的问题。

In short, taking the country as a whole, I am confident that _____.

12. 乡镇企业的发展，主要是工业，还包括其他行业，解决了占农村剩余劳动力百分之五十的人的出路问题。

This increase in village and township enterprises, _____, has provided jobs for 50 per cent of the surplus labour in the countryside.

Key to Drill 6

1. *The implementation of* the correct political line must be ensured by a correct organizational line.
2. Formalism is a *kind of* bureaucratism.
3. We are closely following Africa's development and *progress towards* prosperity.
4. The biggest lesson we have learned is that we should not isolate ourselves from *the rest of* the world, lest we become ill-informed.
5. When we review the past and look to the future, *we realize that* it is necessary for us to further strengthen East Asian cooperation in order to ensure the fundamental interests of East Asian peoples and promote the lofty cause of peace and development of mankind.
6. I visited Shenzhen a couple of years ago *and found* the economy flourishing.
7. The people in Shenzhen reviewed their experience *and decided to* shift the zone's economy from a domestic orientation to an external orientation.
8. Since *we introduced* the reform and the open policy, we have drawn up many rules and regulations, covering all fields of endeavour.
9. This will mark a new stage of development in China-U.S. relations.
10. We actually started the reform in 1980. In 1981, 1982 and 1983 it was carried out primarily in the countryside.
11. In short, taking the country as a whole, I am confident that we can gradually bridge the gap between coastal and inland areas.

12. This increase in village and township enterprises, particularly industrial enterprises, has provided jobs for 50 per cent of the surplus labour in the conntryside.

3. 并列与主从

(1) 并列——并列

汉语行文多用并列结构，一个句子里可以用几个并列分句，或一个主语带出几个并列谓语。英语行文，并列结构不如汉语用得多，但并列分句和并列谓语也是有的。因此翻译起来很方便。

1. The young man left, *and* Durbeyfield lay waiting on the grass in the evening sun.

小伙子走了。夕阳下，德贝菲尔躺在草地上等着。

2. The two older brothers then left, *and* the youngest entered the field.

两个哥哥走了，那最小的兄弟便走进场地里。

3. 四叔皱了皱眉，四婶已经知道了他的意思，是在讨厌她是一个寡妇。

My uncle frowned at this, *and* my aunt knew that he disapproved of taking on a widow.

4. 真是一个钱撕成八瓣用，心里总想着怎样能够改善家里的困境。

Each single copper had to be eked out, *and* I kept racking my brains for ways to improve our difficult conditions.

5. The young man stood before Durbeyfield, *and* looked at him from head to toe.

那小伙子站在德贝菲尔面前，把他从头到脚打量了一番。

6. So he took off his pack, put it on the grass *and* opened the gate.

所以他卸下行装，放在草地上，把栅门打开了。

7. ……便不管四叔的皱眉，将她留下了。

... so my aunt ignored my uncle's frown *and* kept her.

8. 今天，在邓小平理论指引下，我国人民坚定不移地实行改革开放，在现代化建设中取得举世瞩目的成就。

Today, guided by Deng Xiaoping Theory, the Chinese people are firmly pressing ahead with reform and opening-up *and* have achieved remarkable successes in the modernization drive.

例1至例4用的是并列分句。例5至例8用的是并列动词。汉语和英语几乎是一样的。但有一点区别，这一点区别虽不显眼，却非常重要。那就是英语里要用连词 and。这个 and 看上去很不起眼，你几乎感觉不到它的存在，英译汉时也不用费心处理，但它却体现了英汉两种语言之间的差异，而且在汉译英的时候，最容易被忽略。一般说来，and 一词在英语使用并列结构的句子里是必不可少的，这正体现英语的"形合"。但汉语重"意合"，句子成分之间的联系不一定在字面上表现出来。因此，汉译英时，不要忘记使用连词 and，就显得特别重要了。

Drill 7

填空：

1. 世界在变化，我们的思想和行动也要随之而变。

The world is changing, _____.

2. 第二个目标是在本世纪末达到小康水平，第三个目标是在下个世纪的五十年内达到中等发达国家水平。

The second objective is to secure a relatively comfortable life for our people by the end of the century, _____.

3. 对人民实行民主，对敌人实行专政，这就是人民民主专政。

Democracy is practised within the ranks of the people _____. This is the people's democratic dictatorship.

4. 我们搞社会主义才几十年，还处在初级阶段。

We have been building socialism for only a few decades _____.

5. 不发达地区又大都是拥有丰富资源的地区，发展潜力是很大的。

Most of the less developed areas are rich in resources _____.

6. 社会主义中国应该用实践向世界表明，中国反对霸权主义、强权政治，永不称霸。

Socialist China should show the world through its actions that _____.

7. 我们要埋头苦干。我们肩膀上的担子重，责任大啊！

We must immerse ourselves in hard work: we have difficult tasks to accomplish _____.

8. 从一九二九年到一九四八年这二十年中间，我写得快，也写得多。

In the twenty years between 1929 and 1948, I worte very quickly _____.

9. 我常常同主人公一起哭笑，又常常绝望地乱搔头发。

I both cried and laughed along with my principal characters, _____.

10. 大家都叫她祥林嫂；没问她姓什么……

Everybody called her Xianglin's Wife _____...

Key to Drill 7

1. The world is changing, *and* we should change our thinking and actions along with it.

2. The second objective is to secure a relatively comfortable life for our people by the end of the century, *and* the third is to reach the level of moderately developed countries in the first 50 years of the next century.

3. Democracy is practised within the ranks of the people *and* dictatorship over the enemy. This is the people's democratic dictatorship.

4. We have been building socialism for only a few decades *and* are still in the primary stage.

5. Most of the less developed areas are rich in resources *and* have great potential for development.

6. Socialist China should show the world through its actions that it is opposed to hegemonism *and* power politics *and* will never seek hegemony.

7. We must immerse ourselves in hard work: we have difficult tasks to accomplish *and* bear a heavy responsibility.

8. In the twenty years between 1929 and 1948, I wrote very quickly *and* wrote a great deal.

9. I both cried and laughed along with my principal characters, *and* often despondently scratched my head.

10. Everybody called her Xianglin's Wife *and* no one asked her own name...

(2) 从句

汉语有些句子,层次分明,关系清楚,译成英语,句子结构大体上一样。这种句子比较好译,在这里就不多说了。

和英语相比,汉语里用得更多的是并列结构,有的是并列分句,有的是并列谓语。王力在《中国语法理论》一书中论述复合句的一节中说:"中国的复合句往往是一种意合法……在平常的语言里不用连词的时候比用连词的时候更多。"因此有些句子比较复杂,各成分之间存在着各种不同的联系,但都不用文字表示出来,表面上只是一个并列结构。翻译这种句子,就要多用些心思了。

1. 这里,我想就以下一些方面谈些看法,希望有助于诸位对中国的了解。

Here, I would like to make some observations on the follwoing aspects, which I hope will help you know China better.

2.……反映了自古以来中国人民就希望天下太平、同各国人民友好相处。

This is a reflection of the aspiration of the Chinese people for a peaceful world where people of all countries live in harmony.

例1,原文主语后面有两个并列的谓语,译文用 which 相连。例2,"希望"后面有两个并列的宾语,译文用 where 相连。并列结构变成了主从结构,办法是在译文里使用从句。

3.海洋覆盖了地球表面的71%,是全球生命支持系统的一个基本组成部分,也是资源的宝库,环境的重要调节器。

The ocean, which covers 71 per cent of the earth's surface, is a basic component of the global bio-support system. It is also a treasure house of resources and an important regulator of the environment.

4.中国有浅海、滩涂总面积约1,333万公顷,按现在的科学水平,可进行人工养殖的水面有260万公顷。

The shallow seas and tidelands have a total area of 13.33 million ha, of which 2.6 million ha of water surface are suitable for the raising of aquatic products in terms of the current scientific level.

例3,主语后面有三个并列的谓语:覆盖了……,是……,也是……。但仔细分析起来,便可看出,"覆盖了地球表面的71%"说明了一个人们已知的客观事实,句子的重点在后面。因此译文用了一个从句:which covers 71 per cent of the earth's surface 修饰主语,而用谓语集中处理后半句的内容。例4,原文是两个并列分句,但很显然后面的分句所谈的范围包含在前面一个分句所谈的大范围之中。因此译文用了 of which。

5.中国在自己发展的长河中,形成了优良的历史文化传统。这些传统,随着时代变迁和社会进步获得扬弃和发展。

In the prolonged course of its development, China has formed its fine historical and cultural traditions, which have been either developed or sublated with the changes of the times and social progress.

例5的情况比较特殊。原文是两句话,第一句在句末提出"历史文化传统",第二句接着加以发挥。两句话虽在内容上紧密相连,但在形式上却是两个并列的句子,互相没有从属关系。但也正是因为二者紧密相连,译文有可能用which把两个句子连在一起,使之变成一个主从句。

6.……艺人们大都是拉家带口,生活困难。

...as most were saddled with big families their life was hard.

7.她是春天没了丈夫的;他本来也打柴为生,比她小十岁。

Her husband, who had died that spring, had been a woodcutter too, and had been ten years younger than she was.

8.我人小,排队时常常被人挤出来,有些人又常常故意捣乱,工头举起鞭子就打,常常因为打别人而捎带上我。

Because I'm young, people often jostle me out of the queue; and when some of them make trouble and the foremen whips them, he often lashes me too.

例6,"拉家带口"和"生活困难",在结构上可以说是并列的,但也有一点因果关系。因此译文用了一个从句as most were saddled with big families。例7,上文已说祥林嫂死了当家人,是个寡妇,因此译文用了一个从句who had died that spring,把句子的重点放在后半句。例8,内容较多,译文先用becuase,中间用分号,后面又用when和and才把这个句子组织起来。

9.有一年的冬初,四叔家里要换女工,做中人的卫老婆子带她进来了。

Early one winter, when my uncle's family wanted a new maid, Old Mrs. Wei the go-between brought her along.

10.拾煤核也要放聪明点儿,常常换换地方,为的不受那些野男孩子的欺负。那些男孩子是成群结队的拾煤核……

Even when scrounging for cinders you had to have your wits

about you and shift from place to place to avoid those mischievous boys who banded together to collect cinders too.

11. 一九六二年我到天津中国大戏院演出，一位中年女工到后台来看我。

In 1962, when I went to perform in the Grand Chinese Theatre in Tianjin, a middle-aged woman worker came backstage to see me.

例9和例11都是用when把前后两部分连接起来。例10用的是 even when。这样就把原文里的并列结构都变成了主从结构。汉语用并列结构，不用关联词，翻译时译者就要用心考虑用什么关联词最合适。比如例11，如果不加关联词，译作：In 1962, I went to perform in the Grand Chinese Theatre in Tianjin, a middle-aged woman..., 就不合乎英语的说法了。

Drill 8

填空：

1. 海南岛和台湾的面积差不多，那里有许多资源，有……

Hainan Island, _____, has abundant natural resources, such as...

2. 七年前，也是三月份，开过一次科学大会，我讲过一篇话。

Seven years ago, also in the month of March, we held another conference _____.

3. 计划经济不等于社会主义，资本主义也有计划；市场经济不等于资本主义，社会主义也有市场。

A planned economy is not equivalent to socialism, _____; a market economy is not capitalism, _____.

4. 要提倡科学，靠科学才有希望。

We must promote science, _____.

5. 将来中国富强起来了，也永远不称霸。

China will never seek hegemony _____.

6. 我就担心丧失机会。不抓呀，看到的机会就丢掉了，时间一晃就过去了。

The only thing I worry about is that we may lose opportunities. _____, they will slip through our fingers _____.

7. 深圳搞了七八年了，取得了很大的成绩。

But the Shenzhen Special Economic Zone has achieved remarkable successes _____.

8. 大错误没有犯，小错误没有断，因为我们没有经验。

However, _____, we have made many minor ones, because we have no experience.

9. 我们在总结这些经验的基础上，提出了整个社会主义历史阶段的中心任务是发展生产力，这才是真正的马克思主义。

On the basis of the analysis of our experience, we have proposed that the central task for the entire period of socialism should be to develop the productive forces, _____.

10. 我们的第一个目标是解决温饱问题，这个目标已经达到了。

Our first objective was to solve the problem of food and clothing, _____.

Key to Drill 8

1. Hainan Island, *which* is almost as big as Taiwan, has abundant natural resources, such as...

2. Seven years ago, also in the month of March, we held another conference *at which* I spoke.

3. A planned economy is not equivalent to socialism, *because* there is planning under capitalism too; a market economy is not capitalism, *because* there are markets under socialism too.

4. We must promote science, *for* that is where our hope lies.

5. China will never seek hegemony *even if* it grows rich and

strong in the future.

6. The only thing I worry about is that we may lose opportunities. *If* we don't seize them, they will slip through our fingers *as* time speeds by.

7. But the Shenzhen Special Economic Zone has achieved remarkable successes *since* it was established almost eight years ago.

8. However, *although* we haven't made any major mistakes, we have made many minor ones, because we have no experience.

9. On the basis of the analysis of our experience, we have proposed that the central task for the entire period of socialism should be to develop the productive forces, *which* is true Marxism.

10. Our first objective was to solve the problem of food and clothing, *which* we have now done.

(3) 分词短语

英语体现主从关系，除了使用从句，还可以使用分词短语。英语有现在分词，还有过去分词，而且用法灵活多变。分词引导的短语，可以放在句首，可以放在句中，也可以放在句末。英译汉时并不构成什么困难，往往可以和普通动词同样处理。大概也正因为如此，汉译英时我们往往想不到发挥英语的这一特点，使译文显出层次，而只知一味地使用并列动词。因此要想提高译文的质量，经常提醒自己用好分词短语，便是一件值得注意的事了。

1. 她们知道我是演员，要我教她们唱，她们就教我织毛线，还把工厂里印的毛线花样的书送给我。

Knowing that I was an actress they asked me to teach them to sing, and in turn they taught me to knit and gave me a book of patterns printed by the mill.

2. 我是一个人，怕被他们欺负，我用换地方的办法，躲着他们。

Being all on my own and afraid of being bullied by them, I shifted around to dodge them.

3. 中国的海域处在中、低纬度地带，自然环境和资源条件比较优越。

Located in medium and low latitudes, China's sea areas have comparatively advantageous natural environmental and resource conditions.

例1里的 Knowing that I was an actress, 例2里的 Being all on my own, 和例3里的 Located in medium and low latitudes, 都说明原因，说明为什么出现后面所说的情况。

4. 中国有960万平方公里的陆地国土，居世界第三位。

China has a land area of 9.6 million sq km, *making* it the third-biggest country in the world.

5. 全国近年来平均淡水资源总量为28,000亿立方米，居世界第六位。

In recent years China'a average annual amount of freshwater resources has been 2,800 billion cu m, *ranking* sixth in the world.

6. 从那以后我学会了很多毛衣的花样，成了织毛衣的能手。

After that I learned to knit sweaters of many kinds, *acquiring* a new skill.

例4里的 making it the third-biggest country in the world, 例5里的 ranking sixth in the world, 和例6里的 acquiring a new skill, 都说明结果，说明前面所说的情况产生的结果。

7. 她不很爱说话，别人问了才回答，答的也不多。

She said little, *only answering* briefly when asked a question.

8. 日子很快的过去了，她的做工却毫没有懈，食物不论，力气是不惜的。

Time passed quickly. She went on working as hard as ever, *not caring* what she ate, *never sparing* herself.

例7，主句很短，也很笼统，靠后面的分词短语来补充一些细节。例8也是靠后面的两个分词短语来提供细节。

从这几个例子看，英语使用分词短语，虽然不像使用连词说得那样明确，仍然可以体现出句中各成分的不同层次，和它们之间的关系，这才合乎英语的说法。

Drill 9

填空：

1. 中国始终不渝地奉行独立自主的和平外交政策，中国对外政策的最高宗旨是和平。

_____, China takes peace as the ultimate goal of its foreign policy.

2. 展望二十一世纪，可以坚信，中国与东盟各国的发展繁荣和友好合作，前景将更加美好。

_____, we are convinced that there lies an even brighter future for the development, prosperity, friendship and cooperation between China and ASEAN countries.

3. 在充分看到东亚经济发展取得成就的同时，也要正视前进中存在的困难和障碍。

_____, we must also look squarely into the difficulties and obstacles on the road ahead.

4. 这一地区拥有丰富的劳动力资源和自然资源，各国都在按照自己的实际情况确定发展战略……

_____, countries in this region have formulated their development strategies in light of their actual conditions...

5. 中国与东盟各国或山水相连，或隔海相望，在悠久的交往中，人民之间形成了深厚的传统友谊。

_____, China and ASEAN countries have developed a profound traditional friendship among the people in the course of their age-old contacts and exchanges.

6. 现在，中国和东盟各国都在抓住历史机遇，按照各自的国情制定发展战略，不断发展社会生产力，保持经济的持续增长。

At present, both China and ASEAN countries, _____, have formulated development strategies in light of their own national conditions and continued to develop the productive forces and maintain a sustained economic growth.

7. 农村改革的成功增加了我们的信心，我们把农村改革的经验运用到城市，进行以城市为重点的全面经济体制改革。

Our success in rural reform increased our confidence, and, _____, we began a reform of the entire economic structure, focused on the cities.

8. 它们在国际和地区事务中发挥积极作用，不断推进自己的经济发展和社会进步，为亚洲和世界的和平、稳定与发展作出了重要贡献。

They have played a positive role in international and regional affairs and constantly advanced their own economic development and social progress,_____.

9. 我们的改革和开放是从经济方面开始的，首先又是从农村开始的。

We introduced reform and the open policy first in the economic sphere,_____.

Key to Drill 9

1. Unswervingly *pursuing* an independent foreign policy of peace, China takes peace as the ultimate goal of its foreign policy.

2. *Looking* into the 21st century, we are convinced that there lies an even brighter future for the development, prosperity, friendship and cooperation between China and ASEAN countries.

3. While fully *recognizing* the economic achievements in East

Asia, we must also look squarely into the difficulties and obstacles on the road ahead.

4. *Endowed* with rich human and natural resources, countries in this region have formulated their development strategies in light of their actual conditions...

5. *Joined* together by mountains and rivers or facing each other across the sea, China and ASEAN countries have developed a profound traditional friendship among the people in the course of their age-old contacts and exchanges.

6. At present, both China and ASEAN countries, *seizing* opportunities presented by history, have formulated development strategies in light of their own national conditions and continued to develop the productive forces and maintain a sustained economic growth.

7. Our success in rural reform increased our confidence, and, *applying* the experience we had gained in the countryside, we began a reform of the entire economic structure, focused on the cities.

8. They have played a positive role in international and regional affairs and constantly advanced their own economic development and social progress, thus *making* important contributions to peace, stability and development in Asia and the world at large.

9. We introduced reform and the open policy first in the economic sphere, *beginning* with the countryside.

(4) 介词短语

汉语里的并列成分，译成英语，除了用从句和分词短语之外，还可以使用介词短语，使句子重点突出，层次分明。

1. 中国是一个发展中的沿海大国。中国高度重视海洋的开发和保护，把发展海洋事业作为国家发展战略。

As a major developing country with a long coastline, China attaches great importance to marine development and protection, and takes it as the state's development strategy.

2. 家里最大的是我,才13岁,就唱戏养家了。

At thirteen, *as* the eldest child, I acted to help support the family.

3. 我家里生活苦,父亲做小买卖,妈妈是家庭妇女,弟弟妹妹多。

My family was hard up, *with* Father a peddler, Mother a housewife, and so many children to feed.

4. 中国海域有三十多个沉积盆地,面积近70万平方公里。

Scattered in these offshore waters are more than 30 sedimentation basins, *with* a total area of nearly 700,000 sq km.

5. 中国积极参与联合国系统的海洋事务,推进国家间和地区性海洋领域的合作,并认真履行自己承担的义务,为全球海洋开发和保护事业作出了积极贡献。

China has made positive contributions to international ocean development and protection *by* participating positively in UN marine affairs, promoting cooperation between countries and regions and conscientiously carrying out its obligations in this field.

这几个例子有一个共同的特点,原文都是并列结构,有的是并列的句子,有的是并列分句,有的是并列谓语,但译文都根据其含义而分出了层次。

例1,原文有两句话,第一句说明一个已知的客观情况,这样的话,英语不需要单独用一个句子来表示。因此译文将两句合并,前面用一个 as 引导的短语,这样就突出了后面的内容。例2,也是先说明当时的情况,再说她做了什么事,译文作了和例1同样的处理。

例3和例4,原文都是并列分句,第一个分句说明总的情况,后面的分句补充一些细节。在译文里,补充细节没有用分句，而用了 with 引导的短语。

例 5，原文有四个并列的谓语，前三个说明具体做的事情，最后一个说明做这些事情的重大意义。译文为了突出最后一点，便把它提前，用主要动词来表示，而把三件具体的事情放在 by 引导的短语之中。这也是翻译中常用的办法。下面再举几个例子：

解决的办法之一，就是先富起来的地区多交点利税，支持贫困地区的发展。

One way is for the areas that become prosperous first to support the poor ones *by* paying more taxes or turning in more profits to the state.

有些理论家、政治家，拿大帽子吓唬人。

Some theorists and politicians try to intimidate people *by* pinning political labels on them.

运用人民民主专政的力量，巩固人民的政权，是正义的事情。

It is right to consolidate the people's power *by* employing the force of the people's democratic dictatorship.

Drill 10

填空：

1. 制定一切政策，要从实际出发。

_____, we have to proceed from realities.

2. 亚欧两大洲都是古代文明的摇篮，对人类文明的进步和科学文化的发展都做出过不可磨灭的贡献。

_____, both Asia and Europe have made indelible contribution to the progress of human civilization and the advancement of science and culture.

3. 中国是世界上最大的发展中国家，社会生产力水平总的还比较低，还要经过几十年的艰苦奋斗才能实现现代化，需要有长期的和平国际环境特别是良好的周边环境。

_____, China needs a long-term peaceful international environment and a good neighborly environment in particular to realize its modernization program through decades of arduous struggle.

4. 我们正处在世纪之交的重要历史时刻,应该以长远的战略眼光审视和处理双方关系,建立中国与东盟面向二十一世纪的睦邻互信伙伴关系。

_____, we should approach and handle our bilateral relations from a long-range strategic perspective and forge a Chinese-ASEAN good-neighborly partnership of mutual trust oriented to the 21st century.

5. 人类即将步入新的纪元,下个世纪人们将生活在什么样的国际秩序之中,这一课题已日益尖锐地摆在各国人民的面前。

_____, under what kind of an international order will people live in the next century? This question has been put before the people of all countries in all its seriousness.

6. 长期以来,我们百分之七十至八十的农村劳动力被束缚在土地上,农村每人平均只有一两亩土地,多数人连温饱都谈不上。

For a long time 70 to 80 per cent of the rural work force was tied to the land, _____, and most peasants did not even have adequate food and clothing.

Key to Drill 10

1. In short, *in* formulating a policy, we have to proceed from realities.

2. *As* cradles of ancient civilization, both Asia and Europe have made indelible contribution to the progress of human civilization and the advancement of science and culture.

3. *As* the largest developing country in the world *with* a rela-

tively low level of productive forces on the whole, China needs a long-term peaceful international environment and a good neighborly environment in particular to realize its modernization program through decades of arduous struggle.

4. *At* this important historical juncture on the eve of the new century, we should approach and handle our bilateral relations from a long-range strategic perspective and forge a Chinese-ASEAN good-neighborly partnership of mutual trust oriented to the 21st century.

5. *With* a new era quickly approaching, under what kind of an international order will people live in the next century? This question has been put before the people of all countries in all its seriousness.

6. For a long time 70 to 80 per cent of the rural work force was tied to the land, *with* an average of only about 0.1 hectare per person, and most peasants did not even have adequate food and clothing.

4. 断句与并句

汉英两种语言的句子结构各有自己的特点，因此翻译的时候，原文里的一句话在译文里可能分成两句或三句，使译文意思清楚，文字干净利落，也可能把两句话合成一句话，为的是照顾意思的完整和语气的连贯。

就汉译英而论，断句的情况是很多的，而并句的情况是个别的。

1. 海洋覆盖了地球表面的71%，是全球生命支持系统的一个基本组成部分，也是资源的宝库，环境的重要调节器。

The ocean, which covers 71 per cent of the earth's surface, is a basic component of the global bio-support system. It is also a treasure house of resources and an important regulator of the environment.

2. 目前，中国的粮食单产水平与世界粮食高产国家相比也是比较低的，中国要在短时间内达到粮食高产国家的水平难度较大，但经过努力是完全可以缩小差距的。

At present, China's per unit area yield of grain is low compared with countries with high grain yields. It will be difficult for China to reach the level of countries with high grain production in a short period of time, but the gap can certainly be narrowed through earnest efforts.

3. 合营企业所需原材料、燃料、配套件等，应尽先在中国购买，也可由合营企业自筹外汇，直接在国际市场上购买。

In its purchase of required raw and processed materials, fuels, auxiliary equipment, etc., an equity joint venture should first give priority to purchases in China. It may also make such purchases directly on the world market with foreign exchange raised by itself.

4. 国家对合营企业不实行国有化和征收；在特殊情况下，

根据社会公共利益的需要,对合营企业可以依照法律程序实行征收,并给予相应的补偿。

The State shall not nationalize or requisition any equity joint venture. Under special circumstances, when public interest requires, equity joint ventures may be requisitioned by following legal procedures and appropriate compensation shall be made.

例1、例2和例3都是在中间断句,例4是在原文用分号的地方断句。断句以后,每个句子重点突出,意思清楚。

有时也可以在靠近句首或靠近句末的地方断句,这要看句子的内容而定。

5. 但看她模样还周正,手脚都壮大,又只是顺着眼,不开一句口,很像一个安分耐劳的人,便不管四叔的皱眉,将她留下了。

She looked just the person for them, though, with her big strong hands and feet; and, judging by her downcast eyes and silence, she was a good worker who would know her place. So my aunt ignored my uncle's frown and kept her.

6. 日子很快的过去了,她的做工却毫没有懈,食物不论,力气是不惜的。

Time passed quickly. She went on working as hard as ever; not caring what she ate, never sparing herself.

7. 然而她反满足,口角边渐渐地有了笑影,脸上也白胖了。

And she for her part was quite contented. Little by little the trace of a smile appeared at the corners of her mouth, while her face became whiter and plumper.

例5先用一个长句说明四婶怎样衡量她这个人,后用一个短句说明决定用她。例6先用一个短句说明时间过得快,再说她的工作情况。例7先用一个短句说明她的心情,再说她容貌上的变化。断句的地方有前有后。

8. 有一年的初冬,四叔家里要换女工,做中人的卫老婆子带她进来了,头上扎着白头绳,乌裙,蓝夹袄,月白背心,年纪大约二十六七,脸色青黄,但两颊却还是红的。

Early one winter, when my uncle's family wanted a new maid, Old Mrs. Wei the go-between brought her along. She had a white mourning band round her hair and was wearing a black skirt, blue jacket, and pale green bodice. Her age was about twenty-six, and though her face was sallow her cheeks were red.

9. 直到十几天之后,这才陆续的知道她家里还有严厉的婆婆;一个小叔子,十多岁,能打柴了;她是春天没了丈夫的;他本来也打柴为生,比她小十岁:大家所知道的就只是这一点。

Thus it took them a dozen days or so to find out bit by bit that she had a strict mother-in-law at home and a brother-in-law of ten or so, old enough to cut wood. Her husband, who had died that spring, had been a woodcutter too, and had been ten years younger than she was. This little was all they could learn.

例8和例9内容都比较多,分成两句还不够,就分成三句了。例8的译文一句话说来了人,一句话说她的穿戴,一句话说她的容貌。例9的译文一句话说她的婆婆和小叔子,一句话说她死去的丈夫,最后一句话加以概括。

10. 中国是一个发展中的沿海大国。中国高度重视海洋的开发和保护,把发展海洋事业作为国家发展战略,加强海洋综合管理,不断完善海洋法律制度,积极发展海洋科学技术和教育。

As a major developing country with a long coastline, China attaches great importance to marine development and protection, and takes it as the state's development strategy. It is constantly strengthening comprehensive marine management, steadily improving its marine-related laws, and actively developing science, technology and education pertaining to the oceans.

例10是一个有分有合的例子。原文第二句话前半句说明国家对海洋事业的总的态度,后半句说明三项具体工作。译文把前半句分出来，与前面一句合并，后半句话就单独成句了。

英译汉时，绝大多数情况下可以一句译一句；需要超出句子的范围处理时，需要断句的情况居多，需要并句的情况是很个别的。这和上面所说汉译英时遇到的情况是一样的。

11. Today, being driven by the necessity of doing something for himself, he entered the drug store which occupied the principal corner, facing 14th street at Baltimore, and finding a girl cashier in a small glass cage near the door, asked of her who was in charge of the soda fountain.

今天他因为急于要给自己想个办法，迫不得已，便走进了那家杂货店。这家店铺座落在巴尔第摩街路口，正面是十四号街，地位正当要冲。他看见靠近门口的一座小玻璃柜房里有一个女出纳员，就去向她打听卖汽水的柜台归谁负责。

12. Interested by his tentative and uncertain manner, as well as his deep and rather appealing eyes, and instinctively judging that he was looking for something to do, she observed: "Why, Mr. Secor, there, the manager of the store."

这个姑娘一看他那试探和踌躇的神情和他那双深沉的、相当讨人喜欢的眼睛，便对他发生了兴趣。她直觉地揣测到他是要找事做，便说："噢！塞科尔先生，在那儿，他是本店的经理。"

13. She nodded in the direction of a short, meticulously dressed man of about thirty-five, who was arranging an especial display of toilet novelties on the top of a glass case.

她朝一个三十五岁上下的矮个子男人那边点点头。那个人穿得很讲究，一点也不马虎。他正在布置一只玻璃柜上的一些新奇化妆品，要摆成一种特别的式样。

14. Clyde approached him, and being still very dubious as to how one went about getting anything in life, and finding him engrossed in what he was doing, stood first on one foot and then on the other, until at last, sensing some one was hovering about for

something, the man turned:"Well?" he queried.

克莱德走到他身边,不过心里还在犹疑不定,不知道应该怎样才能找个出路,同时他又看出人家正在全神贯注地干他手头的事情,于是便站在一边,两只脚替换着歇一歇。到后来,那个经理觉得仿佛有人在他身边守着,想找他谈什么事,这才转过身来说:"有事吗?"

例 11,一句译成了三句,分出来的,一个是 which 引导的从句,一个是分词短语 finding... 和第二个谓语 asked...。例 12,一句译成了两句,分出来的是一个分词短语 interested...。例 13,又是一句译成了三句,分出来的,一个是定语 meticulously dressed,一个是 who 引导的从句。例 14,又是一句译成了两句,分出来的是 until 引导的从句。

15. On behalf of all of your American guests, I wish to thank you for the incomparable hospitality for which the Chinese people are justly famous throughout the world.

我谨代表你们的所有美国客人向你们表示感谢,感谢你们的无可比拟的盛情款待。中国人民以这种盛情款待而闻名世界。

16. In the spirit of frankness which I hope will characterized our talks this week, let us recognize at the outset these points: we have at times in the past been enemies.

我希望我们这个星期的会谈将是坦率的。本着这种坦率的精神,让我们在一开始就认识到这样几点:过去一些时候我们曾是敌人。

17. So, let us, in these next five days, start a long march together, not in lockstep, but on different roads leading to the same goal, the goal of building a world structure of peace and justice in which all may stand together with equal dignity and in which each nation, large or small, has a right to determine its own form of government, free of outside interference or domination.

因此,让我们在今后的五天里一起开始一次长征吧,不是在一起迈步,而是在不同的道路上向同一个目标前进。这个目标就是建立一个和平和正义的世界结构,在这个世界结构中,所有的人都可以在一起享有同等的尊严;每个国家,不论大小,都有权利决定它自己政府的形式,而不受外来的干涉或统治。

18. Neither of us seeks the territory of the other; neither of us seeks domination over the other, neither of us seeks to stretch out our hands and rule the world.

我们哪一方都不企图取得对方的领土;我们哪一方都不企图统治对方。我们哪一方都不企图伸出手去统治世界。

例15,分出来的是定语从句。例16,分出来的也是定语从句,放在前面,先处理。例17,也是一句译成两句,分出来的是一个同位语加两个定语从句。例18,分出来的是一个并列分句。

19. Yet, what we say here will not be long remembered. What we do here can change the world.

不过,我们在这里所讲的话,人们不会长久地记住,但我们在这里所做的事却能改变世界。

20. This is the hour. This is the day for our two peoples to rise to the heights of greatness which can build a new and better world.

现在就是只争朝夕的时候了,是我们两国人民攀登那种可以缔造一个新的、更美好的世界的伟大境界的高峰的时候了。

例19,译文将两个短句合在一起。例20,译文将一短一长合成一句。并句之后,句子显得较为紧凑,语气也更为连贯。也许这正是译者并句的初衷吧。

Appendices

翻译重在实践[*]

庄绎传

我喜欢翻译,时常夜读,研究名家的译文。觉得仿佛在晴朗的天空下,在海滨漫步,到处是五光十色的贝壳,有时甚至能拾到珍珠。

两本书摆在我面前。一本是英文的,是英国作家高尔斯华绥写的 *The Forsyte Saga*,一本是周煦良教授的中译本《福尔赛世家》。掀开第一页,一句漂亮的英文展现在眼前:

Those privileged to be present at a family festival of the Forsytes have seen that charming and instructive sight—an upper middle-class family in full plumage.

译文是:碰到福尔赛家有喜庆的事情,那些有资格去参加的人都曾看见过那派中上层人家的兴盛气象,不但看了开心,也增长见识。

看了这样的译文,我感到兴奋,受到启发,比捡到珍珠还高兴。

名词前面的两个形容词 charming 和 instructive 放到后面去处理,多么精彩。一个译例也许说明不了什么问题。看得多了,同类的例子积得多了,便可悟出一条规律。研究译文诚然是会有收获的,但不是最重要的。

"翻译重在实践,"傅雷说。要想提高翻译能力,必须亲自动手。听说有些自学者学我编著的《英汉翻译教程》和《自学辅导》,只看我怎么译,自己并不动手,这可不行。学翻译犹如学游泳。只在岸边看别人游,或只听教练讲解,是学不会的。你说是不是这么个理儿?

---

* 此文载于《英语学习》2001 年第 4 期。

有一次，邓小平同志接见外宾，概述了我国怎样建设有中国特色的社会主义。最后他说:"如果说构想，这就是我们的构想。"译文是：Well, those are our plans. 这译文使我激动，使我惊异，世上竟有这样简洁、生动而又恰到好处的译文。well 一词，尽人皆知。为什么用不出来呢？缺乏实践。

译海无涯。赶快到水里来游一游吧。

我怎样学翻译

庄绎传

我很喜欢《英语世界》这个刊物,因为我喜欢翻译。每当我看到英汉两种语言并排印在一起,心里便感到一种说不出的乐趣。

我是怎样跟翻译结下这不解之缘的呢?在大学时代,打下了一点基础。当时有一门翻译课,学校甚至请到许孟雄教授来给我们讲课,批改作业。他上课的情景,至今仍历历在目。

回忆自己的成长过程,主要是靠实践。

六十年代初,我有幸参加了《毛泽东选集》的英译和译文的修订工作,以及一系列重要政论文章的英译工作。当时我觉得学英语,能做这样的翻译工作,可以说是最大的光荣。因此,我怀着无比的热情认真地完成交给我的每一项任务。

这段时间的实践是多方面的,包括译初稿、核对、参加讨论等。在这过程中,观察到翻译涉及的各方面的问题,积累了很多有趣的译例,得到了大量的感性认识。例如:

"吃一堑,长一智"(《毛选》1卷,283页)

"A fall into the pit, a gain in your wit"(p.297)

译文不但对称,而且押韵,很像谚语的样子。

"三个臭皮匠,合成一个诸葛亮"(《毛选》3卷,956页)

"Three cobblers with their wits combined equal Zhuge Liang the master mind."(p.158)

"不入虎穴,焉得虎子"(《毛选》1卷,287页)

"How can you catch tiger cubs without entering the tiger's lair?"(p.300)

---

* 此文载于《英语世界》2001年第10期。

这两个例子本可以在英语中找到相应的说法,如"Two heads are better than one","Nothing venture, nothing gain",但译者都舍弃不用,就是为了保留原文的形象。

夺取这个胜利,已经是不要很久的时间和不要花费很大的气力了;巩固这个胜利,则是需要很久的时间和要花费很大的气力的事情。(《毛选》4卷,1439页)

To win this victory will not require much more time and effort, but to consolidate it will. (p.373—374)

我第一次看到这个译文时,感到不胜惊喜。一个小小的 will 竟然替代了原文里很长的一段话,何等简洁。

40年过去了,这些例子仍然深深地印在我的脑海里。

"感性认识有待于发展到理性认识。"当时程镇球教授是负责人之一,他不但带头总结经验,而且鼓励我们一帮年轻人进行研究,选些小题目,写出文章,并为我们组织讨论会,联系在刊物上发表。

这样久而久之,自己也就养成了习惯,看书,学习,研究问题,发表文章。70年代学术刊物复刊后,我的文章陆续在《英语学习》和《外语教学与研究》上面发表。1980年出版了我的《汉英翻译五百例》,其中列了20个小题目,这便是我参加汉英翻译实践,观察研究的结果。

20世纪80年代初,我又有机会参加另一种类型的翻译实践——英汉翻译。

1980年,中国对外翻译出版公司创办双月刊《翻译通讯》(即《中国翻译》的前身)。吴运楠老先生找我负责一个栏目,名叫"翻译练习"。在他的指导下,我自己选材、翻译,并加解说。从1980到1982年,我一共提供了15篇稿件。后来承蒙公司领导的好意,将这15篇稿汇集成册,出了个单行本,这就是1984年出版的《英汉翻译练习集》。

在这过程中,我深深体会到读者对我的帮助。译文刊出后,便有读者来信指出问题。例如:"Einstein has created a new outlook, a new view of the universe."我的译文是:"爱因斯坦创造了一种新的观点,一种新的宇宙观。"一位读者建议将"创造"二字改为"创立"。

我接受了这个建议。在出单行本的时候,我并没有改变原译文,而是增加了一个脚注。单行本中,译文一律保持原样,凡是需要改进或改正的地方,我都以有特殊标记的脚注明确告诉读者这里原译有问题,需要修改。我觉得这样可能对读者帮助更大。

我为单行本《英汉翻译练习集》写了一篇前言,从自己的实践中归纳出了25点,这便是我对英译汉的体会。

有的看官看到这里,也许会想,既有这等小书,何不找来一看。不看也罢。一来事隔一二十年了,书也不见得好找。二来看别人的文章不会留下很深的印象。要想得到较深的印象唯有亲自参加实践、观察、研究,得出自己的结论。写文章的人才是最大的受益者。

也许有人会说,搞理论,写文章,可太难了。在翻译理论方面有所贡献诚然不是易事,但我以上所谈,20题也好,25点也好,都不是翻译理论,都只说明了英汉两种语言的特点。说真的,研究两种语言的特点并不难。把一篇好的译文和原文放在一起,那差异是再明显不过了。同类的例子积得多了,就可以看出一些规律,如果加以总结,就可以使你的知识系统化,即便不是为了发表,也可以使你对两种语言特点的认识深入一步,做起翻译来就会比较得心应手了。

最近看到这样一个例子:

The cold weather frosted up the track last night.

译文是:

昨晚寒冷的天气使跑道上结了霜。

这个译文和原文相比,虽然个别地方有些小的变化,但基本句型未变,仍是一个主语带一个谓语。我把它改译成:

昨晚天气寒冷,跑道上结了霜。

这样译文就成了两个主谓结构,也就是两个短句,中间也不用任何连词。我觉得这样译似乎更合乎汉语的说法。

理论也是可以谈的。我在"也谈中式英语"一文（载于《中国翻译》2000年第6期）末尾引了美国翻译理论家奈达的一句话：

To preserve the content of the meassage the form must be changed. 上面那个例子，从第一个译文改为第二个译文，不正是符合奈达提出的这条理论吗？所以翻译理论是有其自身的价值的，是可以指导实践的。

不过话又说回来了，理论也好，特点也好，都有一定的限度，而且要运用得当。作翻译，最重要的恐怕还是要把两种语言学好。语言学好了，可以运用自如，事情就好办了。你说是不是这样？

也谈中式英语*

庄绎传

摘 要：我国某些出版物中的英译文有使用"中式英语"的倾向。其原因有二：一是对原文理解不透，只顾字面上对应，二是对英语特点不熟，沿用汉语的搭配和结构。这样译文就显得过于机械，有时甚至产生语法错误。为避免中式英语，可在透彻理解原文的基础上，注意英语的三个特点：（1）替代；（2）主谓搭配；（3）主从关系。

关键词：中式英语 英语的特点

Abstract: Chinglish is often seen in English translations published in Chinese publications. There are two reasons for this phenomenon: 1.the translators try to give a word-for-word rendering for lack of a thorough understanding of the original; 2.they follow the Chinese collocation and sentence structure without paying enough attention to the features of the English language. To avoid Chinglish, it is suggested that, on the basis of a thorough understanding of the Chinese original, attention be paid to the following points: (1) substitution; (2) subject-predicate; and (3) subordination.

Key Words: Chinglish features of the English language

在'99年全国外事翻译研讨会上，王弄笙大使就中文式的英文作了一个发言[1]。曾在中央编译局工作的美国专家琼·平卡姆又于最近发表了她的新作《中式英语之鉴》（*The Translator's Guide to Chinglish*）。因此，我在这里也想谈一谈中式英语的

---

* 此文为作者在2000年全国中译外学术研讨会上的发言，载于《中国翻译》2000年第6期。

问题。

中国的译者不但要作英译汉的工作,而且要承担汉译英的任务。在汉译英方面,如果说有什么问题,最大的一个就是我们往往使用中式英语。

最近看到一本论文集,有中文版,也有英文版,介绍我国改革开放二十年的经验。这本书的内容非常重要,原文也十分流畅,译文虽也力求符合英语的说法,却未能避免中文的味道,请看几个例子。

例1:农业产业化 the industrialization of agriculture

例2:高新技术产业化 the industrialization of high and new technology

"产业化"一词在这两个短语里的含义是不同的,不能都译成 industrialization,这样会使读者产生误解。其实,这两个短语早有正式发表的译文,可以借鉴。前者是 industrial management of agriculture,[2] 后者是 application of high and new technology to production。[3]

例3:邓小平是中国改革开放和现代化建设的总设计师。

Deng Xiaoping is the chief architect of China's reform, opening-up and *modernization construction*.

例4:他还多次强调,要大胆吸收和借鉴人类社会创造的一切文明成果,包括资本主义发达国家的一切反映现代化社会生产规律的先进经营方式、管理方式。

He also emphasized time and again that we should boldly absorb and utilize all *civilization achievements* created by human society, including all advanced operation and management methods that reflect the law of socialized modern production in the developed capitalist countries.

例3将"现代化建设"译作 modernization construction,例4将"文明成果"译作 civilization achievements,都用很长的名词作定语,修饰另一个很长的名词,这样的搭配是不妥的。

其实,这两个短语也早有正式发表的译文。"现代化建设"可以只用 modernization 一个词,[4] 也可以译作 modernization drive.[5]

例4是根据邓小平"南巡讲话"中的一句话改写而成的。原话是:总之,社会主义要赢得与资本主义相比较的优势,就必须大胆吸收和借鉴人类社会创造的一切文明成果,吸收和借鉴当今世界各国包括资本主义发达国家的一切反映现代社会化生产规律的先进经营方式、管理方法。[6]

译文是:

In short, if we want socialism to achieve superiority over capitalism, we should not hesitate to draw on the *achievements of all cultures* and to learn from other countries, including the developed capitalist countries, all advanced methods of operation and techniques of management that reflect the laws governing modern socialized production.[7]

此处"一切文明成果"译作 the achievements of all cultures。将"文明"译作 culture,也是一种常见的译法。用作形容词时,尤其是这样。例如:

总起来说,就是要把中国建成富强民主文明的现代化国家。

In a word, it is to build China into a prosperous, strong, democratic and *culturally advanced* modern country.[8]

然而这并不意味着 civilization 一词不能用。将"文明"译作 civilization,也还是常见的,问题在于如何搭配。例如:

一切进步文明成果 all fruits of human progress and civilization[9]

世界一切先进的文明成果 fruits of advanced world civilization[10]

先进文明成果 advanced results of civilization[11]

从以上的例子可以看出。"文明"一词可译作 culture,也可译作 civilization,但没有一处将"文明成果"直译作 civilization achievements。

《中式英语之鉴》第 7 章 The Noun Plague 专门谈了这个问题。作者首先承认英语的确有名词修饰名词这种作法。但她接着指出：

This does not mean, however, that you should feel free to use any given noun to modify any other. Outside the circle of familiar combinations like the ones above, it is well to exercise caution. Most often the sentence will be clearer and flow more naturally if the noun is not made to serve as an adjective.[12]

古罗马政治家、雄辩家西塞罗说过这样一段话：

In doing this, I did not think it necessary to translate word for word, I preserved the general style and force of the language. For I did not believe it was my duty to count out words to the reader like coins, but rather to pay them out by weight as it were.[13]

可见逐词对译的办法是不可取的。

例 5：他指出，中国还处在社会主义初级阶段，社会主义的本质是解放生产力、发展生产力，途径是改革开放。

He pointed out that China has been at the primary stage of socialism; the essence of socialism is to liberate and develop the productive forces through reform and opening-up.

这段译文有两点是可取的。第一，"生产力"一词在原文里重复出现两次，而在译文里，the productive forces 只出现一次，作 liberate 和 develop 两个动词的宾语，从而避免了重复。第二，原文"途径是改革开放"是主谓结构，也可以说是一个短句，译文只用了一个介词引导的短语 through reform and opening-up，这是符合原文的意思和语气的。这两点都是合乎英语的行文习惯的。

译文的不足之处在于中间用了分号。原文"他指出"后面有两项内容，这两项内容之间虽然没有连词连接，却都是他指出的内容，这是毫无疑问的。译文在中间用了分号，这样用，在译法上是可以的,但意思就不清楚了。分号后面的话好像也是 He pointed out 的内容,但更像是作者自己的话。

王力在《中国语法理论》一书中提出了两个概念:"意合"与"形合"。他说:"中国语里多用意合法,联结成分并非必需;西方多用形合法,联结成分在大多数情形下是不可缺少的。"[14]由此看来,例5的译文如果把分号改为 and that,意思就清楚了。

例6:邓小平的经济思想给了中国改革开放以巨大的推动力,为中国改革开放作出了历史贡献。

Deng Xiaoping's economic thought has given huge impetus to China's reform and opening-up and made historical contribution in this regard.

这句话,原文里"邓小平的经济思想"是主语,后面跟了两个并列的谓语。仔细一看又可看出这两个谓语并不在一个层次上,前者较为具体,后者更加概括。在这种情况下,英语喜欢层次分明,多用主从结构。试改译作:

Deng Xiaoping's economic thought, giving (*or*: which has given) huge impetus to China's reform and opening-up, is a historical contribution in this regard.

这样译可能较好地突出了句子的重点,因为这是文中一节最后的一小段话,而这一节的标题是:邓小平经济思想对中国改革开放的巨大贡献。

例7:积极推进农业产业化,是实现农村两个根本转变,促进城乡经济一体发展的重要内容。

Actively *carry* forward the industrialization of agriculture *is* an important part in realizing the two basic transformations in the countryside and in promoting the development of urban and rural economies in a unified way.

例8:引导农民进入市场,把千家万户的农民与千变万化的市场紧密联系起来,推动农业产业化,这是发展社会主义市场经济的迫切需要,也是广大农民的强烈愿望。

Steer the peasants into the market; *get* them involved in the constantly changing market, and *promote* the industrialization of agriculture *are* the urgent needs of the development of a socialist market economy as well as the strong wishes of the broad masses of peasants.

用动词作主语，在汉语里是可以的，在英语里则不行，是违反语法的。书中连续出现这样的语法错误，就说明这不是偶然出现的印刷错误，而是译稿本身的问题了。

前些时候看到一篇文章，介绍山西的旅游业，刊登在我国对海外发行的一份中文报纸上。文章占了一版的篇幅，而且是英汉对照的，因此引起了我的注意。这篇文章和上面提到的论文集一样，从总体上看，译文还是不错的，但有些句子带浓厚的中文味道。

例 9：Shanxi is one of the birthplaces of the civilization of the Chinese nation, Shanxi is the miniature of the 5000 years civilization of China, Shanxi is also the root of all people of Chinese descent.

在这个句子里，Shanxi 一词重复出现三次，各分句之间也没有联系。这些问题在英语里都是要尽量避免的。

例 10：In recent years, Shanxi has been making effort to develop and construct its tourist resources, because of this, the tourist industries of Shanxi has been developed rapidly, both hardware and software environments has been greatly improved, the number of domestic and foreign visitors to Shanxi has been increasing year by year.

这样长的一句话，既分不出层次，也没有连词相连，这在英语里也是要尽量避免的。

怎样才能避免中式英语呢？换言之，在使用英语的时候，应注意英语的哪些特点呢？我认为可以考虑三个要点：（1）替代（Substitution）；（2）主语（Subject）；（3）主从（Subordination）。抓住了这"三 S 要点"，或许可以使中式英语大大减少。

关于替代。汉英两种语言有一个重大的差别,那就是"英语不喜欢重复,如果在一句话里或相连的几句话里需要重复某个词语,则用代词来代替,或以其他手段来避免重复。汉语不怕重复,连续使用某个词语是常见的事。汉语也用代词,但不如英语用得多。所以汉译英时要千方百计避免重复,多用代称;英译汉时则要少用代称,多用实词。"[15]关于这个问题,外国语言学家和语法学家都有详细的论述。[16]

例11:哈佛是最早接受中国留学生的美国大学之一。中国教育界、科学界、文化界一直同哈佛大学保持着学术交流。

Harvard is among the first American universities to accept Chinese students. The Chinese educational, scientific and cultural communities have all along maintained academic exchanges with this university.[17]

这个例子,原文"哈佛"出现两次,而译文中 Harvard 只出现一次,第二次使用了代称 this university。这样译,既避免了重复,又体现了两句之间的联系,译文也就显得流畅。而如果译者忽视了英语的这一特点,注意力过分集中在单个句子上,照样重复,译文便成了两个孤立的句子了。

关于主语。这里主要是指译文以什么作主语,也就是考虑主谓怎样搭配的问题。"英汉两种语言的主谓搭配,在大多数情况下是相通的。英语里一个主谓搭配,译成汉语后可以保持原来的搭配。但有时却不行,汉译英时也是一样。一般说来,汉语的主谓关系没有英语那么密切。英语对于主语能否做后面的动作考虑较多。因此,译文以什么作主语,怎样和谓语搭配,是一个经常需要斟酌的问题。"[18]

例12:鲁镇的酒店的格局,是和别处不同的:都是当街一个曲尺形的大柜台,柜里面预备着热水,可以随时温酒。[19]

译文1:The layout of Luzhen's taverns is unique. In each, facing you as you enter, is a bar in the shape of a carpenter's square where hot water is kept ready for warming rice wine.[20]

译文 2：The wine shops in Luchen are not like those in other parts of China. They all have a right-angled counter facing the street, where hot water is kept ready for warming wine.[21]

原文以"格局"为主语，译文 1 以 layout 为主语，与原文完全吻合，但一篇故事这样开始，英语显得颇为突然，远不如译文 2 以 wine shops 为主语，因为整篇故事就是围绕着酒店展开的。此外，译文 1 第 2 句不得不换用 bar 作主语，而英语一般是不喜欢不断更换主语的。译文 2 第 2 句则可以用 they 作主语，与第一句呼应，译文就显得流畅自然。

关于主从。英语大量使用定语从句、分词短语、介词短语等，汉语则没有这么多表达方式。"因此英语句子里主从关系很多，体现出不同的层次。这与汉语有很大的不同。汉语……多用并列动词或并列分句，因此汉语句子里并列关系居多，层次不甚明显"。[22]

例 13：海洋覆盖了地球表面的 71%，是全球生命支持系统的一个基本组成部分，也是资源的宝库，环境的重要调节器。

The ocean, which covers 71 per cent of the earth's surface, is a basic component of the global bio-support system. It is also a treasure house of resources and an important regulator of the environment.[23]

原文的第一个谓语，译文用一个 which 引导的从句来表述。"覆盖了地球表面的 71%"是对客观情况的描述，也可以说是表述了一个已知的事实，它不是句子的重点，但文章必须从这里作起，后面才是句子的重点。译文把次要的部分用从句处理，这就显出了层次，突出了句子的重点。

抓住以上三个要点，可能避免许多中式英语。中国人介绍中国的情况，写出来的英文有中文的味道也许是不可避免的。但我觉得至少应该做到两点：一是不要让外国读者产生误解，二是不要违反英语的词法句法，也就是不要把汉语的词法句法强加在英语身上。

美国翻译理论家奈达说过这样几句话：

Each language has its own genius...Rather than force the formal structure of one language upon another, the effective translator is quite prepared to make any and all formal changes necessary to reproduce the message in the distinctive structural forms of the receptor language.[24]

To preserve the content of the message the form must be changed.[25]

有些译者不喜欢翻译理论。我也一向偏重于实践，对理论没有研究。然而理论自有其存在的价值。我觉得以上奈达的两段话，对我们避免中式英语，提高译文质量，是大有好处的。

---

1. 这篇发言后来登在《中国翻译》2000年第2期。
2. 1999年政府工作报告，第3部分。
3. 2000年政府工作报告，第5部分。
4. 同上，第1部分。
5. 同上，末段。
6. 《邓小平文选》第3卷，第373页。
7. *Selected Works of Deng Xiaoping*, Vol. Ⅲ, pp.361—362.
8. 江泽民主席在美国哈佛大学的演讲。(1997)
9. 江泽民主席在东亚首脑非正式会晤时的讲话。(1997)
10. 江泽民主席在英国剑桥大学的演讲。(1997)
11. 江泽民主席在瑞士工商界人士集会上的讲话。(1999)
12. 琼·平卡姆，《中式英语之鉴》，外语教学与研究出版社，第179页。
13. Appendix to *The Craft and Context of Translation*.
14. 王力，《中国语法理论》下册，第310页。
15. 庄绎传，《英汉翻译教程》，外语教学与研究出版社，

1999，第 60 页。

16．参看 M.A.K. Halliday 等所著 *Cohesion in English*，和 R.Quirk 等所著 *A Grammar of Contemporary English*。

17．江泽民主席在美国哈佛大学的演讲。(1997)

18．庄绎传，《英汉翻译教程》，第 341 页。

19．《鲁迅全集》第 1 卷，人民文学出版社，1957，第 20 页。

20．杨宪益，戴乃迭译 *Lu Xun Selected Works*，1956，1980，第 52 页。

21．杨宪益，戴乃迭译 *Selected Stories of Lu Hsun*，1960，1972，第 19 页。

22．庄绎传，《英汉翻译教程》，第 92—93 页。

23．"中国海洋事业的发展"前言，《人民日报》1998 年 5 月 29 日第 5 版。译文载于《北京周报》1998 年第 24 期。

24．Eugene A. Nida and Charles R. Taber, *The Theory and Practice of Translation*, pp.3—4.

25．同上，第 5 页。

怎样培养外事翻译[*]
——两点体会与一点困惑

庄绎传

我很高兴来到西安,与这么多同行见面,共同讨论我国的外事翻译工作。

我在北京外国语大学高级翻译学院工作,所以想着重谈一下怎样培养外事翻译的问题。

一、高级翻译学院的前身——联合国译员训练部

七十年代初,我国恢复在联合国的合法席位以后,联合国日益感到中文翻译之不足,乃与我国政府商定,于 1979 年在北外设立联合国译员训练部。当时联合国在全世界只有两个这样的培训机构,一个设在莫斯科,一个设在内罗毕,在北京设立的是第三个。译训部成立后,面向全国单独招生,在北京、上海、广州设了三个考点。每年招生 25 人,其中 15 人学笔译,10 人学口译,后来招生人数有所减少。正式的学制是一年,但学生实际上接受两年的培训,因为一年的时间是不够的。每年夏天,联合国总部组织考试团到北京来主持毕业和录用考试。译训部先后办了十二期,培养口笔译译员 217 人,全部通过了考试,进入了联合国的录用名单。所以在联合国各机构工作的许多译员都是译训部培训出来的。后来联合国的职位有限,许多译员虽被录用但派不出去,有的进入机关,为国家领导人作翻译,有的就做教师了。在大量译员积压,联合国又经费紧张的情况下,双方商定从 1993 年开始暂停为联合国招生。虽然如此,牌子并没有摘,机构也没有解散。93 年我们就又招了一届学生,为国内培养高级

---

[*] 此文为作者在 2001 年全国外事翻译理论与实践研讨会上的发言。

翻译人才。直到 2000 年底和 2001 年初，联合国总部在国内招聘国际职员，还委托联合国译训部这个机构为它操作。

既然不再为联合国输送译员，而是为国内培养人才，我们就于 1994 年学院升格为大学之机，开始启用"高级翻译学院"这个名称了。

二、高级翻译学院

高级翻译学院与联合国译训部相比，最大的不同之处就是它是一个硕士学位课程。根据教育部最后确定的学科专业目录，属于外国语言学与应用语言学硕士学位。国务院学位办确认我们这个项目属于应用类研究生，以别与研究类研究生。

我们的培养目标是英汉同声传译和其他高级口笔译人才。面向全国招生，每年参加全国统一的研究生入学考试。学制二年，包括写论文和答辩。

关于课程设置，一年级是基础课。除政治和二外，设笔译（英译汉，汉译英），口译（交替传译英译汉和汉译英）、视译、翻译理论。此外还有用中文开的世界文学、国际经济等课程。二年级主要是同声传译课，也包括英译汉和汉译英。不适合学同声传译的学生继续学笔译。

关于教学内容与教学方法，我一直教汉译英笔译课，就着重说一说这门课的情况。

一部分教材是围绕我国改革开放这个主题的，主要是选自《邓小平文选》第三卷，再配以有关的领导人讲话。《邓选》第三卷里三分之二的文章是接见外宾的讲话，这种文章的译文最能体现英汉两种语言的差异。

另一部分教材是围绕我国对外关系和国际会议的，如中美关系、中俄关系、亚欧会议、亚太经合组织会议、联合国等。关于中美关系，三个公报和九七年联合声明（中英文）就是必读教材，然后配以最新的有关讲话。关于联合国，《联合国宪章》就是必读文件，再选用一点最新的讲话。

因此，有些固定的教材可以年年使用，临时搭配的教材则需年年更新。

至于教学方法，一半的时间用来研究译文，一半时间用来讲评作业，而且是先研究译文，也就是研究那些比较固定的教材，再让学生译一篇类似的材料作为练习，然后讲评。

我觉得这样做可以使学生学到有关的方针政策，提高翻译的能力，同时也扩大知识面，可以说是一举三得。

三、两点体会：

1. 要打好基本功。

七十年代初，周总理曾指出："外语教学有个基本功。……基本功包括三个方面：政治思想、语言本身和各种文化知识。"[1]这三条对在校的学生乃至在职的外事翻译干部都是适用的。但我今天只想着重谈一下语言基本功，或者说得更具体一点，也就是英语基本功。

所谓"英语基本功"，指的是什么？我觉得可以概括为两个字：平稳。具体说来，也就是：词语要合乎用法，句子要合乎语法。做到这两条，就可以算得上平稳了。外事翻译不是翻译文学作品，没有那些细腻的描写和生动的对话。因此，做到译文平稳就不错了。

然而，就连这样的要求，我们的学生也是不容易做到的。因为他们不是在国外长大的，他们从来没有出过国留过学，有的甚至是从农村来的，都是在国内学英语，而且学的时间并不长，因此基本功都不很好，有的好一些，有的很差。

严格说来，基本功方面的问题不是翻译问题，不在翻译探讨的范围之内，因为一个人如果不是作翻译，而是在用英文写作，他也需要有良好的基本功。可是我们要把一个学生培养成一个翻译干部，就不能不帮他解决这个问题。

基本功方面常见的问题很多。比如：

冠词用得不对。该用的时候不用，不该用时反而用了冠词。

可数名词既不用复数,也不加冠词。

及物动词和不及物动词不加区别,不及物动词后面出现宾语。

时态用得不对。在有过去时间状语的句子里用现在完成时。

介词用得不对,如 on the meeting.

连词用得不对。该用时不用,或以副词代连词,或以 because 引导一个句子。

我希望学生能把这些问题消灭在学校里,因此我就不厌其烦地讲,但还是消灭不了。这也不奇怪,处处照顾得周到,并不是一件容易的事,再加上学生不用心,反复犯同样的错误,并把错误带到后来的工作中去。因此,英语基本功必须常抓不懈。

2. 要研究两种语言的特点。

要想提高学生的翻译能力,最重要的是引导学生通过对比来研究两种语言的特点。有经验的翻译家精通两种语言,不用研究这些问题。但是我们的学生,母语就掌握得不好,外语更差,他们的汉语和英语都是分开学的,从来没有作过比较,以为汉语可以这样说,英语也可以这样说,而往往意识不到英语不一定能像汉语那样说,而有其特有的说法。要解决这个问题,最好的办法就是引导学生进行两种语言的对比。这也就是我在上面提到的用一半的时间研究译文时所做的事。

研究译文,进行两种语言的对比,注意些什么呢?

我在2000年全国中译外学术研讨会上作过一个发言,题目是:也谈中式英语[2]。我在发言中突出了"三 S 要点",即(1)替代(Substitution);(2)主语(Subject);(3)主从(Subordination)。为了突出重点,各强调了一个方面,举了一个例子。其实,每一点都包含很多内容。下面我就简单作一点补充说明。

关于替代。上次我只提到用代称来避免名词的重复。实际上动词、副词(状语)等也都有代称。英国一本权威性语法著作有一节题为 pro-forms,就是专门谈这个问题。书中举的例子有:

A:'He didn't *give her an apple*'   B:'Yes, he *did*'

They suspected that he had *given her an apple* and he had (done)³

Mary is *in London* and John is *there* too

Mary arrived *on Tuesday* and John arrived *then* too

John searched the big room very *carefully* and the small one less *so*⁴

下面举一个翻译的例子。

例1：就我们国家来讲，首先是要摆脱贫穷。要摆脱贫穷，就要找出一条比较快的发展道路。⁵

For China, the first thing is to throw off poverty. To do that we have to find a way to develop fairly rapidly.⁶

关于主语。上次我主要是突出了主语和谓语怎样搭配的问题，强调要在译文里找一个适当的词作主语。其实，有时候也不一定换主语，而是找一个适当的动词和它搭配。说起搭配，也不限于主谓搭配。动词和宾语也有搭配的问题。形容词和副词与被修饰语之间也有搭配问题。

例2：我感谢陆登庭校长的邀请，使我有机会在这美好的金秋时节，来到美国你们这座古老而又现代化的学府。⁷

译文1 I wish to thank Dr. Neil L. Rudenstine, President of Harvard University, for inviting me to this *ancient* yet modernized institution of the United States in this golden fall.⁸

译文2 I wish to thank President Rudenstine for inviting me to this *old* yet modern institution of the United States in this golden fall.⁹

纵然哈佛大学有367年的历史，此处用 old 也比用 ancient 作定语更为恰当。

关于主从。汉语多用并列结构，英语多用主从结构，主要是因为英语有各种手段使句中的意思分出层次，突出重点。这当然不限于使用定语从句。

例3：中国是一个发展中的沿海大国。中国高度重视海洋的开发和保护，把发展海洋事业作为国家发展战略。[10]

As a major developing country with a long coastline, China attaches great importance to marine development and protection, and takes it as the state's development strategy.[11]

这个例子，原文是两句话，不过第一句话说的是大家都很熟悉的一个情况。这样一句话，在英语里没有必要单独用一个句子来表述。译文妙就妙在连定语从句也没用，只用了一个介词引导的短语就解决问题了，实在精彩。

要说汉英两种语言的特点，也不限于这三点，但这三点所谈的都是翻译中经常遇到的问题。在课堂上研究译文的过程中也还会涉及其他一些问题。总之，凡是能帮助学生打好基本功的论点，凡是能够揭示汉英两种语言差异的论点，都值得谈，而且要不厌其烦地反复地谈才能加深印象。

四、一点困惑

几年来，一直有一个问题困扰着我，怎样提高学生的英语水平，或者说，怎样在他入学时英语水平的基础上再提高一步。看一看我们的课程，是以技能训练为主的，都是让他们把已掌握的语言知识用出来，用得熟练一些。当然，在翻译的过程中，他们在语言方面也有一定的收获，但是我们没有哪一门课是专门给他们输入一些东西，扎扎实实地提高他们的英语水平的。于是我就带着这个问题走到哪里问到哪里。

1997年我带着这个问题到复旦大学去讨教。他们对我说：英语各专业的研究生都上一门必修课：阅读与写作。后来我又带着这个问题到北京外交学院去请教。他们对我说：我们的文学课是用英文开的。他们的经验对我很有启发。

我开始把原作引入课堂。在有限的课堂时间里匀出一点时间阅读一点原文写的东西，如从 *The Economist* 和其他杂志上选的时文，或从书里摘出的选段，如 *The Glory and the Dream*，和 *the Rise and Fall of the Third Reich*。在课堂上把这些材料和学生一起过一过,指出一些值得注意的地方,总比只让学生自己读效果好一点,至少我自己心里踏实一点,因为总算在这方面为他们做了点事情。

我为什么要这样做?那是因为我深深感到:无论你的词法句法掌握得多么好,无论你对英汉两种语言的差异了解得多么清楚,最后决定译文质量的还是译者的英语水平。不断提高自己的英语水平,恐怕是一个译者时刻不能放松的。

杨宪益先生说"……要多读一些好的英美文学作品,逐步理解这种外国语言的内在规律"。[12]这是他的亲身经验,也是许多译界的前辈走过的共同的道路。后来者恐怕也只有沿着这条路走下去,才能在翻译方面取得成就。

---

1. 《周恩来选集》下卷,第469—470页。
2. 载于《中国翻译》2000年第6期。
3. R. Quirk 等所著 *A Grammar of Contemporary English*,第50页。
4. 同上,第49页。
5. 《邓小平文选》第三卷,第255页。
6. *Selected Works of Deng Xiaoping*, Vol. Ⅲ, p.250
7. 江泽民主席在美国哈佛大学的演讲。(1997)
8. *Beijing Review*, November 24—30, 1997, p.7
9. 《努力建立中美建设性的战略伙伴关系》,世界知识出版社,1998,第65页。
10. "中国海洋事业的发展"前言,《人民日报》1998年5月29日第5版。
11. *Beijing Review*, June 15—21, 1998, p.13
12. 杨宪益为单其昌所著《汉英翻译技巧》写的序言。

翻译中的创造性[*]
——学习《邓小平文选》英译本的一点体会

庄绎传

《邓小平文选》英译本出版以后,我对照原文学习了其中的若干篇文章,主要是接见外宾的谈话,感到很有收获。中共中央编译局翻译的《邓选》是当今政论文章最好的英译文。对学习翻译的人来说,它也是一本极好的教材,因为它最能体现汉英两种语言的不同特点。我体会最深的一点就是译文体现出来的创造性。

关于创造性,我国著名翻译家有过不少论述。

茅盾先生说:"这样的翻译的过程,是把译者和原作者合而为一,好象原作者用另外一国文字写自己的作品。这样的翻译既需要译者发挥工作上的创造性,而又要完全忠实于原作的意图,好象一个演员必须以自己的生活和艺术修养来创造剧中人物的形象,而创造出来的人物,又必须完全符合于剧本作家原来的意图一样。"[1]他还说:"这样的翻译既需要译者的创造性,而又要完全忠实原作的面貌,这是对文学翻译的最高的要求。"[2]

王佐良先生说:"文学翻译不是机械乏味的事,而是一种创造性的努力。"[3]他还说:"虽然困难不少,我却仍然喜欢译诗,也许是因为它毕竟是一种创造性的艺术活动,它的要求是严格的,而它的慰藉却又是甜蜜的。"[4]

是不是只有文学作品,小说、戏剧、诗歌,翻译时才需要有创造性呢?

杨宪益先生的夫人戴乃迭说过:"我们的灵活性太少了。有一位翻译家,我们非常钦佩,名叫大卫·霍克斯。他就比我们更

---

[*] 此文为作者在2001年全国中译外研讨会上的发言。

有创造性。我们太死板,读者不爱看,因为我们偏于直译。……应该更富有创造性。翻译家应大致做到这样。然而,我们长期以来一直受过去工作环境的限制,以致现在我们的翻译家比较拘泥于原文,译文平庸,还是深受过去老框框的影响。"[5] 她还说:"我觉得我们传统的翻译法是直译,过于死板的直译,以至使读者常常搞不懂我们说的是什么意思。政治性的社论尤其如此。"[6]

这最后一句说得再清楚不过了,说起翻译的创造性,政论文章也不例外。

然而,究竟什么是创造性,他们谁也没有展开论述。也许下面两段引文能给我们一点启发。

记者问:"杨先生,你觉得把中国的古典名著译成英语,困难吗?"杨宪益先生说:"我不认为这是一件容易的事;但是如果你在从事翻译工作,你就得竭尽全力去做,把原文的意思用另一种语言表达出来,但它又必须是确切的,尽可能使译出的意思接近原文。"[7]

傅雷先生说:"以甲国文字传达乙国文字所包涵的那些特点,必须象伯乐相马,要'得其精而忘其粗,在其内而忘其外'。而即使是最优秀的译文,其韵味较之原文仍不免过或不及。翻译时只能尽量缩短这个距离,过则求其勿太过,不及则求其勿过于不及。"[8]

从这两段引文可以看出,他们都认为译文是难以和原文完全吻合的,译者所追求的无非是尽量接近原文。这就给译者发挥创造性留下了很大的余地。译者越主动发挥创造性,他的译文就越接近原文。反之,译者若不注意发挥创造性,他的译文就可能离原文很远了。

《邓小平文选》的译者是怎样发挥了他们的创造性的呢?这可以从两方面来看。

一、选词。

例1:这是中国从几十年的建设中得出的经验。(《邓选》Ⅲ 290)

That is <u>what we have learned</u> from decades of development. (*Deng* Ⅲ 283)

例2：从我们自己这些年的<u>经验</u>来看，经济发展隔几年上一个台阶，是能够办得到的。(《邓选》Ⅲ 376)

Juding from <u>what we have accomplished</u> in recent years, it should be possible for our economy to reach a new stage every few years. (*Deng* Ⅲ 364)

例3：改革、开放是一个新事物，没有现成的<u>经验</u>可以照搬，一切都要根据我国的实际情况来进行。<u>实践</u>证明，步子放大些有利。(《邓选》Ⅲ 248)

Reform and opening up are new undertakings, so we have no <u>precedent</u> to go by; all we can do is to proceed in the light of the specific conditions in our country. Our <u>experience</u> indicates that it should be beneficial to go a little faster. (*Deng* Ⅲ 244)

例4：总之，几年的<u>实践</u>证明，我们搞改革、开放的路子是走对了。(《邓选》Ⅲ 240)

In short, our <u>achievements</u> in the last few years have proved the correctness of our policies of reform and of opening to the outside world. (*Deng* Ⅲ 237)

例5：当然，随着<u>实践</u>的发展，该完善的完善，该修补的修补，但总的要坚定不移。(《邓选》Ⅲ 371)

Of course, as <u>the reform</u> progresses, some of these policies should be improved or amended as necessary. But we should keep firmly to our general direction. (*Deng* Ⅲ 359)

例6：社会主义中国应该用<u>实践</u>向世界表明，中国反对霸权主义、强权政治，永不称霸。(《邓选》Ⅲ 383)

Socialist China should show the world through its <u>actions</u> that it is opposed to hegemonism and power politics and will never seek hegemony. (*Deng* Ⅲ 370)

"经验"和"实践"这两个词在汉语里用得比较多。我们一看见这两个词,往往首先就想到 experience 和 practice。如果每次都这样译,就显得很重复,而英语恰恰不喜欢重复。现在的译文根据上下文采用不同的译法,灵活多样,读起来比较顺。

例7:现在要进一步解决科技和经济结合的问题。所谓进一步,就是说,在方针问题、认识问题解决之后,还要解决体制问题。(《邓选》Ⅲ108)

We should go a step further to integrate science and technology with economic development. By this I mean that having established the principle of integrating them and come to <u>a correct understanding of the importance of doing so</u>, we should now tackle the system for managing science and technology. (Deng Ⅲ114)

例8:就我们国内来说,什么是中国最大的政治?四个现代化就是中国最大的政治。(《邓选》Ⅱ234)

What is the <u>most significant political task</u> for China? It is the achievement of the four modernizations. (Deng Ⅱ238)

"认识问题"和"最大的政治"都是汉语特有的说法。如果直译,谁也不明白是什么意思,因为英语里不允许这样搭配。现在的译文用了比较具体的词语,充分表达了原文的内在含义,文字通顺,意思也清楚了。

例9:外国有的评论家说,中国的现行政策是不可逆转的。我认为<u>这个看法</u>是正确的。(《邓选》Ⅲ114)

Some commentators abroad say that China's current policy is irreversible. I think <u>they</u> are right. (Deng Ⅲ120)

原文第二句的从句明明是以"这个看法"为主语,译文为什么以 they 为主语?这才是好的英语,既合乎英语的说法,又符合原文的含义。下面看几个动词的例子。

例10:基本路线要管一百年,动摇不得。(《邓选》Ⅲ371)

<u>We should adhere to</u> the basic line for a hundred years, with no vacillation. (Deng Ⅲ358—359)

例11:从一九五八年到一九七八年这二十年的经验告诉我

们：贫穷不是社会主义，社会主义要消灭贫穷。(《邓选》Ⅲ116)

Our experience in the 20 years from 1958 to 1978 teaches us that poverty is not socialism, that socialism means eliminating poverty. (Deng Ⅲ122)

例12：目标确定了，从何处着手呢？就要尊重社会经济发展规律，搞两个开放，一个对外开放，一个对内开放。(《邓选》Ⅲ117)

How are we to go about achieving these goals? We must observe the laws governing socio-economic development and follow an open policy both internationally and domestically. (Deng Ⅲ122—123)

这几个例子主要说明动词和主语或宾语搭配的问题。例10里的"管"字很不好译，译文若仍以 the basic line 作主语，很难找到一个合适的动词和它搭配。改用 we 作主语，问题就很好解决了。例11"经验"后面接"告诉"，但在英语里 experience 可以 teach，可以 show，可以 demonstrate，可以 indicate，若让它 tell，就显得勉强一点。例12原文是"尊重……规律"，译文与其说 respect，就不如说 observe 了。

例13：我国是社会主义国家，国民生产总值达到一万亿美元，日子就会比较好过。更重要的是，在这样一个基础上，再发展三十年到五十年，我们就可以接近发达国家的水平。(《邓选》Ⅲ57)

As China is a socialist country, $1 trillion will mean a higher standard of living for its people. More important, it will allow us to approach the standard of the developed countries in another 30 to 50 years' time. (Deng Ⅲ67)

例14：所以社会主义阶段的最根本任务就是发展生产力，社会主义的优越性归根到底要体现在它的生产力比资本主义发展得更快一些、更高一些，并且在发展生产力的基础上不断改善人民的物质文化生活。(《邓选》Ⅲ63)

Therefore, the fundamental task for the socialist stage is to develop the productive forces. The superiority of the socialist system is demonstrated, in the final analysis, by faster and greater development of those forces than under the capitalist system. <u>As they develop</u>, the people's material and cultural life will constantly improve. (*Deng* Ⅲ 73)

这两个例子都有"在……基础上",但译文都没有用 basis 一词,而是用了比较灵活的译法。

二、句子。

汉语句子结构比较松散,连词用得不多,但意思是连贯的,这就是王力先生所说的"意合"。9 英语句子结构比较紧凑,句子内部连接之处,一般都要用具体的词语来体现,也就是王力先生所说的"形合"10。这句子中间的连接往往就是需要译者发挥创造性的地方。

例15:七年前,也是三月份,开过一次科学大会,我讲过一篇话。主要讲了两个意思,两句话。(《邓选》Ⅲ 107)

Seven years ago, also in the month of March, we held another conference on science at which I spoke. I talked mainly about two points <u>that can be summarized in</u> two sentences. (*Deng* Ⅲ 113)

例16:说过去说过来,<u>就是</u>一句话,坚持这个路线、方针、政策不变。(《邓选》Ⅲ 371)

After all that's been said, I can <u>sum up our position</u> in one sentence: we shall keep to this line and these principles and policies. (*Deng* Ⅲ 359)

例17:中国的对外政策是一贯的,<u>有</u>三句话,第一句……。(《邓选》Ⅱ 415)

China's foreign policy is consistent and <u>can be summed up in</u> three sentences. First,... (*Deng* Ⅱ 407)

第15例"两个意思"后面紧接着就是"两句话"。例16用"就是"二字引出"一句话"。例17用一个"有"字引出"三句

333

话"。这些说法,在英语里都不能照办,因此译文用 summarize 或 sum up 来解决过渡的问题。

例18:他们自己总结经验,由内向型转为外向型,就是说能够变成工业基地,并能够打进国际市场。(《邓选》Ⅲ239)

The people in Shenzhen reviewed their experience and decided to shift the zone's economy from a domestic orientation to an external orientation, which meant that Shenzhen would become an industrial base and offer its products on the world market. (Deng Ⅲ237)

例19:我去过一次深圳,那里确实是一派兴旺气象。(《邓选》Ⅲ239)

I visited Shenzhen a couple of years ago and found the economy flourishing. (Deng Ⅲ236)

原文里的"总结经验"和"经济转型"是个什么关系?"去过深圳"和"兴旺气象"是个什么关系?原文都没有说,也不需要说,因为意思是清楚的。译文则需要有适当的词来过渡一下,因此用了 decided 和 found 两个动词。

例20:要提倡科学,靠科学才有希望。(《邓选》Ⅲ372—373)

We must promote science, for that is where our hopes lies. (Deng Ⅲ365)

例21:计划经济不等于社会主义,资本主义也有计划;市场经济不等于资本主义,社会主义也有市场。(《邓选》Ⅲ371)

A planned economy is not equivalent to socialism, because there is planning under capitalism too; a market economy is not capitalism, because there are markets under socialism too. (Deng Ⅲ361)

例22:抓住时机,发展自己,关键是发展经济。(《邓选》Ⅲ375)

If we are to seize opportunities to promote China's all-round development, it is crucial to expand the economy. (Deng Ⅲ363)

这三个例子很典型,说明汉语可以不用连词,而英语要用连词。译者必须揣摩原文的内在关系,在译文中选用适当的连词,所以译文分别加了 for, because 和 if。重要的是选词要适当,否则就会歪曲原意了。

另一个特点是汉语不怕重复,同一个词语可以连续使用。英语则不然,总是千方百计地换一个说法,以避免重复。

例 23:革命是解放生产力,改革也是解放生产力。(《邓选》Ⅲ 370)

Revolution means the emancipation of the productive forces, and so does reform. (Deng Ⅲ 358)

例 24:中国对外政策的目标是争取世界和平。在争取和平的前提下,一心一意搞现代化建设,发展自己的国家,建设具有中国特色的社会主义。(《邓选》Ⅲ 57)

The aim of our foreign policy is world peace. Always bearing that aim in mind, we are wholeheartedly devoting ourselves to the modernization programme to develop our country and to build socialism with Chinese characteristics. (Deng Ⅲ 67)

例 25:人们提出这样一个问题,如果中国不搞社会主义,而走资本主义道路,中国人民是不是也能站起来,中国是不是也能翻身?(《邓选》Ⅲ 62)

You may ask, what if the Chinese people had taken the capitalist road instead? Could they have liberated themselves, and could they have finally stood up? (Deng Ⅲ 72)

第 23 例为了避免重复"解放生产力",译文用了 and so does... 这一句型。例 24 为了避免重复"争取和平",译文换了一个说法,译作 always bearing that aim in mind,"前提"也就不译了。例 25 原文的词句并不重复,但意思重复。"走资本主义道路"就是"不搞社会主义"。汉语喜欢从这面说了,再从那面说一说。然而英语就连这种意思上的重复也是不喜欢的。因此译文省略了"不搞社会主义",只留了 had taken the capitalist road。这就体现了译者的创造性。这样译,是需要有一点勇气的,因为

335

弄不好会有漏译之嫌，但这样的译文的确是合乎英语说法的好译文。

译文好不好，理解是关键。有时若机械地按照字面的意思译，会违背原文的意思，甚至造成误解。这时译者就要开动脑筋，根据上下文来判断原文的意思究竟是什么，然后加以很好地处理。

例26：我曾经请人转告布什总统，中国如果不稳定就是个国际问题，后果难以想象。(《邓选》Ⅲ357)

I asked others to tell President Bush that if the political situation in China became unstable, the trouble would <u>spread to the rest of the world</u>, with consequences that would be hard to imagine. (Deng Ⅲ344)

例27：要注意解决好少数高级知识分子的待遇问题。……我们不论怎么困难，也要提高教师的待遇。这个事情，<u>在国际上都有影响</u>。我们的留学生有几万人……(《邓选》Ⅲ275)

We must try to increase the material benefits for the few top intellectuals... No matter how many difficulties we have, we must try to improve the treatment of teachers. If we do that, it will <u>affect our intellectuals in other countries</u> too. We have tens of thousands of students studying abroad... (Deng Ⅲ270)

例28：当时我们决定先搞深圳经济特区，除了深圳以外，还有珠海、汕头、厦门。一共四个经济特区，广东省占了三个，福建省占了一个。(《邓选》Ⅲ239)

We decided to set up three more special zones in addition to Shenzhen: Zhuhai and Shantou, both also in Guangdong Province, and Xiamen in Fujian. (Deng Ⅲ236)

这三个例子，译者都是费了脑筋的。例26"国际问题"没有机械地译作 international issue，如果这样译，各国就可以采取行动，而这显然不是作者的本意。例27"在国际上有影响"也没有译作 have international influence，而是根据上下文判断，理解为会对我们在国外的留学人员产生影响。例28 为了让读者明白哪个城市在哪一省,译者把句子重新作了安排,这一点很重要,因为只有读者能得到清楚的理解,翻译才算是真正达到了目的。

例29:即使没有新的主意也可以,就是不要变,不要使人们感到政策变了。<u>有了这一条</u>,中国就大有希望。(《邓选》Ⅲ 371)

It doesn't matter much whether we can come up with new ideas. What matters is that we should not change our policies and should not make people feel that we are changing them. <u>Then</u>, the prospects for China will be excellent.(*Deng* Ⅲ 360)

例30:<u>如果说构想</u>,这就是我们的构想。(《邓选》Ⅲ 65)
<u>Well</u>, those are our plans.(Deng Ⅲ 75)

在一段话或一篇谈话结束的时候,会有一些概括性的话,这种话往往很不好译。如果机械地照字面来译,不是费解,就是很啰嗦。这时候,多考虑一下说话人的语气,可能得到一些启发。例29"有了这一条"译作 then,例30"如果说构想"译作 well,既简洁,又传神,而且避免了重复,实在精彩。

从以上这些例子可以看出《邓小平文选》的译者怎样发挥了创造性。所谓创造性,我认为就是摆脱原文的束缚,在译文里使用最好的表达方式。

发挥创造性,要有三个条件:

第一,理解要深。对原文的理解越深越透,发挥创造性的自由度就越大。

第二,英语要好。知道在什么场合话怎么说最好,而且多掌握一些说法,以供选择。

第三,精益求精。好的译文往往不是一下子就能轻易想出来的,有时需要冥思苦想,花很长时间。因此,必须有孜孜不倦、精益求精的精神。只要功夫下到了,是会创造出好的译文的。

1．罗新璋《翻译论集》，商务印书馆，1984，第511页。

2．同上，第519页。

3．王佐良《翻译：思考与试笔》，外语教学与研究出版社，1989，第74页。

4．王佐良《英国诗文选译集》，外语教学与研究出版社，1980，第2页。

5．同3，第84页。

6．同3，第88页。

7．同3，第83页。

8．同1，第559页。

9．王力《中国语法理论》下册，中华书局，1954，第310页。

10．同上。

北外英语翻译资格证书考试简介
Certificate of English Translation and Interpreting
(CETI)

概况:

北京外国语大学推出的英语翻译资格证书考试是目前国内惟一面向全国的翻译资格认证考试。其目的是对考生的英汉翻译能力做出认定。

北外是我国创办最早的外国语大学,是我国培养外语人才的主要基地。多年来,北外为我国政府机关等单位培养了一大批高级译员,我国几代领导人的翻译均出自北外。北外的毕业生具有优秀的外语口笔头表达能力,一直受到用人单位的青睐和英语国家教育界的好评。考取北外英语翻译资格证书不仅是自身语言运用能力的最佳证明,更是求职就业的理想途径。

考试等级:

北外英语翻译资格证书考试分笔译和口译两种,各分三个等级,共六种资格认证考试。

• 初级英语翻译资格证书(笔译):通过该级证书考试的考生能够就一般难度的非正式材料进行英汉互译。

• 初级英语翻译资格证书(口译):通过该级证书考试的考生能够承担一般非正式会谈或外宾日常生活的口译工作。

• 中级英语翻译资格证书(笔译):通过该级证书考试的考生能够就普通英汉原文材料进行互译,能够胜任专职翻译工作。

• 中级英语翻译资格证书(口译):通过该级证书考试的考生能够胜任一般性正式会谈以及外事活动的口译工作。

• 高级英语翻译资格证书(笔译):通过该级证书考试的考生能够担任各种国际会议文件及专业性文件的翻译或审定工作,

能够承担政府部门高级笔译工作。

• 高级英语翻译资格证书（口译）：通过该级证书考试的考生能够担任国际会议的交替传译或同声传译工作，能够承担政府部门的高级口译工作。

考试形式及适用对象：

• 初级（笔译3小时，口译约30分钟）：

笔译部分包括：英译汉（要求考生将两篇各250词左右的英文译成中文）；汉译英（要求考生将两篇各为250字左右的中文译成英文）。

口译部分包括：对话（要求考生将一篇400词左右的对话分别译成英文或中文）；交替传译1（英译汉，要求考生将一篇250词左右的英文发言译成中文）；交替传译2（汉译英，要求考生将一篇250字左右的中文发言译成英文）。

对象为英语专业大专毕业及本科二年级以上学生，非英语专业通过大学英语六级考试者；具有同等水平的各类英语学习者、工作者。

• 中级（笔译4小时，口译约30分钟）：

笔译部分包括：英译汉（要求考生将两篇各300词左右的英文译成中文）；汉译英（要求考生将两篇各为300字左右的中文译成英文）。

口译部分包括：交替传译1（英译汉，要求考生将一篇500词左右的英文发言译成中文）；交替传译2（汉译英，要求考生将一篇700字左右的中文发言译成英文）。

对象为英语专业本科毕业生或研究生；具有同等水平的各类英语学习者、工作者。

• 高级（笔译6小时，口译约30分钟）：

笔译部分包括：英译汉（要求考生将三篇各400词左右的英文译成中文）；汉译英（要求考生将三篇各为400字左右的中文译成英文）。

口译部分包括：交替传译 1（英译汉，要求考生将一篇 600 词左右的英文发言译成中文）；交替传译 2（汉译英，要求考生将一篇 800 字左右的中文发言译成英文）；同传（通过第一、二部分者参加面试）。

对象为英语专业优秀本科毕业生或研究生；具有同等水平的，有一定翻译实践经验的各类英语学习者、工作者。